BRITAIN THEN & NOW

PHILIP ZIEGLER

THE FRANCIS FRITH COLLECTION

BRITAIN THEN & NOW

SEVEN DIALS

Contents

4

PART TWO : THE BRITISH
AT WORK AND PLAY 132

3

PART ONE : BRITAIN 22

The Friths

I

WHEN FRANCIS FRITH WAS BORN in Chesterfield in 1822 there was no such thing as photography. It was to be another five years before the French physicist, Joseph Niepce, made the first known photograph. If Frith's father had been asked what his hopes and plans were for his son's career he would probably have said that the boy should be apprenticed in some trade or industry where hard work and talent would be rewarded. For his part, Frith's father saw it as his duty to give his son the sort of education that would enable Francis to better himself in life. He himself had been a cooper, though operating on a grander scale and much better read than that description might suggest. He was also a devout Quaker, and when he wanted his son to better himself he would have felt it more important that his son should do good by others and serve his God diligently than that he should achieve more worldly success.

At the age of twelve Francis Frith was sent to a Quaker boarding school in Birmingham. He hated it; boarding school, he later wrote, was 'the most insipid and mechanical portion of existence'. In spite of this, he emerged with a fair grasp of mathematics, a deep interest in metaphysics, and boundless enthusiasm for the English poets, to whose output he was to contribute extensively, though with little distinction, throughout his life. He would have liked to continue his studies at university but his parents would have found difficulty in paying for it and anyway felt that further education smacked of self-indulgence if not frivolity.

Instead, he was apprenticed to a cutler in Sheffield. He learned to apply himself to his task, he claimed, but the work itself proved uncongenial. He abandoned it as soon as possible. Probably the training served him better than he supposed; a photographer, especially a photographer at a time when the craft was in its infancy, had to be part scientist, part aesthete, and though the cutler had to be more of a technician than an artist, his flair and taste mattered too. But the extraordinary energy and resilience — both physical and psychological — that marked his later life, was lacking at this point in his career. After five years in Sheffield he suffered what seems to have been some kind of nervous breakdown and fell back on his family for a period of rest and recuperation.

The chronology of the next few years is hard to chart. In partnership with a young man of the same sort of age and background he set up a wholesale grocery business in Liverpool. It prospered, and Frith made enough money to finance a start in something closer to his heart. Probably in about 1850 – though Frith himself suggested a later date – he opened a small printing company. This too proved a success; by 1856 the turnover had reached £200,000 a year[*], at which point he sold out and renewed life as a man of independent means.

[*] See the Table of Comparative Values in p. 424.

THE STILL FLEDGLING ART OF PHOTOGRAPHY

When it was that he turned his attention to the fledgling art of photography is still harder to establish. Bill Jay, the leading authority on the subject, believes that Frith was already a respected amateur photographer before he took his first trip abroad in 1856. Probably for his earlier work he used the wet-plate collodion process invented by Frederick Scott Archer a few years before. Only one photograph of the British Isles is dated earlier than 1856 (plate 434) and there is some doubt whether that dating is correct.

His fame as a photographer, however, was established by the trips he made between 1856 and 1859 up the Nile and in the Holy Land. Even if he had not been saddled with the enormously heavy and cumbersome equipment required by his new pursuit, his expeditions would still have been extravagantly ambitious. He preferred to travel on untrodden routes, time and again was set upon and robbed, was captured by brigands and had to bargain for his release, battled with fever, and subsisted for weeks on whatever he could manage to shoot, including fried, boiled or curried crocodile chops – 'a toughish white meat rather like veal with a flavour of musk', he noted. A decade before Stanley and Livingstone had their celebrated meeting, he ventured fifteen hundred miles south of the Nile Delta, well beyond the Sixth Cataract, to a point which hardly any European had reached before and few were to reach in the next fifty years.

Two photographs taken by Francis Frith on the Nile, probably during his first visit in 1856. The plate LEFT (2) was of his camp near Alexandria; the small black tent in the centre contained his dark room. The plate OPPOSITE (3) featured the yacht which was used to transport him and his equipment up the Nile.

Throughout these peregrinations he carried with him crates of enormously heavy and fragile glass plates – some of them 16 x 20 inches in size, a cornucopia of elaborate chemicals and dark-room equipment, the dark room itself, and three cameras, one of them a vast mahogany instrument for use with the largest glass plates. Given the difficulties, it was something of a miracle that he achieved any results at all, let alone the sophisticated and sensitive prints which he finally produced (plates 2, 3). His photographs, *The Times* maintained, 'carry us far beyond anything that is in the power of the most accomplished artist to transfer to his canvas' – a comment which suggests some confusion about the role of the artist as landscape painter, but also attests to the reverence with which the astonishingly skilful work of the early photographers was rightly greeted.

Photographer to a nation

In 1859 Frith married Mary Anne Rosling, fifteen years younger than him and from a prominent Quaker family in Reigate. With his reputation as a photographer firmly established he decided to settle down and devote himself to what was to be the predominant, almost the obsessive crusade of the rest of his life – to capture on camera every city, town and village, every river and canal, every beach and cliff, every church, park and stately home, throughout the British Isles. Unsurprisingly, he failed to achieve one hundred percent success; but by the time he died he had accumulated a photographic archive which was spectacular both in its range and in its quality.

He knew exactly the sort of image he wanted to attain. The great strength of photography, he argued, was its 'essential truthfulness'; this could not be valued too highly and must never be compromised. But this strength was also an incipient weakness; the trouble about photography, Frith saw, was that it could be 'too truthful. It insists on giving us the truth, the whole truth, and nothing but the truth. Now we want, in Art, the first and last of these conditions but we can dispense very well with the middle term . . . very rarely indeed does a landscape arrange itself upon [the photograph's] focusing glass as well, as effectively, as he would arrange it if he could.' The photographs must abide by these limitations – Frith deplored those of his colleagues who would wilfully blur or distort a subject in the name of art. But he was also a painter, for the most part in oils, of considerable competence if little inspiration. He approached his photography with an artist's eye and would have felt his work a failure if it failed to satisfy an artist's sensibilities. Photographs could be, indeed should be, both beautiful *and* truthful.

Francis Frith and Co

Soon after Frith's marriage he established a photographic firm in his wife's home town of Reigate. At first most of the income was derived from the photographs taken on his travels in the Middle East, but increasingly his swelling treasure-house of British photographs provided the mainstay of his business. He quickly realized that book illustration or the sale of prints could not provide enough turnover to support his growing family. Picture postcards were his eventual answer; though he had to wait until the Post Office agreed to carry cards which they had not originated. They were printed for him in enormous quantities by a firm in Saxony and sold through more than two thousand tobacconists, newsagents and other outlets throughout the British Isles (plate 117). Over the next decades millions of such cards were produced; even today if one encounters a faded sepia view of the high street of Much Binding in the Marsh in 1890 the chances are that it will bear the signature of Frith scrawled proudly on the bottom right-hand corner.

Frith's horse and trap travelled far and wide across the British Isles in his quest to record every view of interest. In the plate ABOVE *(4) he was crossing the Kirkstone Pass in Cumberland in 1865, and the plate* OPPOSITE *(5) shows him penetrating the Cheddar Gorge in 1873 or thereabouts.*

It soon became clear that no one man could produce work on the scale which the potential market demanded. Like some Renaissance court painter, he began to employ assistants who would work under the supervision and in the style of the master. Frith and his team would descend on a country town, hire a horse and trap, and systematically record every view of interest in the town or the surrounding countryside (plates 4, 5). The scale of the enterprise meant that the results were sometimes no better than workmanlike, but the coverage was remarkably comprehensive and the overall standard high. His collection provides a record of what Britain looked like in the 1860s, 1870s and 1880s which is probably unequalled in any other country.

The next generation takes over

Photographs show Francis Frith as the archetype of the successful Victorian businessman, though the eyes indicate a disposition more visionary than his formal dress and watch chain would suggest. He looks quite as much at home, romantically bearded in the Egyptian clothes which he affected on his travels (plate 1). The Friths had settled in Reigate in a large but unpretentious house called Brightland. There they had eight children, seven of who survived to maturity (plate 6). As he got older he continued to work at his photography and his painting but progressively handed over the running of the company to his sons Eustace and Cyril. By the time that he died in Cannes at the age of seventy-six, Francis Frith and Co existed almost entirely independently of its founder.

It did not prove a change for the better. Eustace decided that it was a waste of time and money to have the postcards produced in Germany and set up a printing works in Gloucestershire. The experiment was an expensive failure: the works were slackly run and technically ill equipped for collotype printing. By the outbreak of the First World War the family had accepted failure and the

The Frith family at home in Reigate in the mid-1870s ABOVE (6). *Mary Anne was in the centre and Francis on the right. The children, from left to right, were: Alice, Edgar, Mabel, Julius, Cyril and Ernestine. Eustace, who with his brother Cyril was to take charge of the firm on Francis's retirement, was away at boarding school.*

Francis Frith OPPOSITE (7) *in Reigate at the age of about forty assuming a classic Victorian pose.*

works had been sold for a nominal amount to a group of its employees. It was not till after the war, when Francis Frith's grandson, Francis E Frith, joined the rump of the printing firm, that it regained momentum and succeeded in taking on not just the printing of postcards for the parent company but for all the other major British postcard publishers as well. By this time it called itself the Cotswold Collotype Company and had installed itself in Wootton-under-Edge, some fifteen miles north-east of Bristol.

THE FIRM LANGUISHES AND DIES

Meanwhile Francis Frith and Co drastically reduced its stock, sold its Reigate building to a jam-making firm, and moved into Cravenhurst, a substantial mansion on the Raglan Road. Competition was by now fierce and, as the pace of physical change quickened in the towns and villages, retailers began to insist that new views should feature in each year's crop of postcards. The antiquarian interest in what things had once looked like was still something of a rarity in the 1930s and in the years directly following the Second World War; for thirty years or more the treasure-house of the Frith archive was suffered to languish almost unseen.

With the death of Eustace Frith direct family involvement in Francis Frith & Co largely ceased. Under different management it survived, flourished for a time, then fell on hard times and in 1971 ceased to trade. The photographic archive, long neglected, was threatened with destruction. By the time Bill Jay and other like-minded enthusiasts rediscovered it much had already been lost, including many of the glass plates which Frith had used on his travels in the Middle East. The damage was tragic; the miracle is that so much survived. Some sixty thousand original glass plates and 250,000 prints remain. Some of the prints had been bought in over the years from other photographers but the great majority bear the hall-mark of both the Friths and their immediate entourage.

Today the collection, in apple-pie order and meticulously catalogued, is installed in the little Wiltshire village of Teffont, not far from Salisbury. It is difficult to exaggerate its importance. No other photographic archive provides so comprehensive, so wide-ranging and so technically accomplished a portrait of the physical evolution of the British Isles since the 1860s. To study it is to understand something of what has happened to this country in this momentous period. But photographs pose as many questions as they answer. Few people could look at them without finding themselves possessed by the liveliest curiosity as to why things evolved as they did and what the changes have meant for the men and women who lived in those houses, walked those streets, ploughed those fields, served in those shops, prayed in those churches, lived their lives over the last 140 years. If this book provides some sort of answer to even a few of these questions it will have served a useful purpose.

A Photographer's View

John Cleare's photograph of North Hallsands on Start Bay in Devonshire OPPOSITE. *Comparison with the same view taken in 1924 (page 128) shows how the sea has chipped away at the cliff face; less than a mile away at South Hallsands it had drowned the village altogether.*

MY TASK HAS BEEN TO LOCATE, where possible, the scenes of those Frith photographs selected by Philip Ziegler and then to re-shoot them as nearly as practicable from the same position. It has not always been easy, sometimes it has been frustrating and occasionally even disappointing, but always it has been a fascinating task. As a photographer I am a professional observer concerned essentially with things visual rather than with sociology. I thought I knew the British Isles rather well after photographing our landscapes for nearly forty years but this assignment has led me to places new and corners odd that I would never otherwise have visited. I have covered well over seven thousand miles doing it. What then are my perceptions of Britain at the end of this Century of Change?

Three particular observations stands out. The first is surprising – the countryside is overgrown. Time and again I have located the exact spot on which Francis Frith or his photographer stood, only to find my view obscured by vegetation. Hedges have become woods, saplings bushy trees, while sizeable copses or even forestry plantations have sprung up where there were none before. Discussing this with farmers I have concluded that the few farmer workers of today have better things to do than tidy the landscape. There were more spare hands a century ago with less pressure on their time.

The second is predictable – the ruinous visual impact of the ubiquitous motor vehicle on every built-up area. In small towns and villages this is a fairly recent phenomenon, although in Frith's day the cities were clogged with horse-drawn vehicles. Attractive streets which I was able to photograph in pristine condition in the early 1960s have today become elongated car parks. It would have been suicide for me to photograph from many of the exact positions in city, town or village in which Frith's photographers stood as recently as the 1950s. The proliferation of street furniture and road markings, sited with little aesthetic consideration, has transformed scenes of erstwhile charm into clutterscapes of unnecessary ugliness.

My third observation concerns the British people themselves. In my travels from Aberdeen to Land's End I have encountered hundreds of friendly, helpful and courteous folk. When asking directions I have always been given every assistance. When asking permission to photograph it has almost invariably been granted and refreshment has frequently been offered to go with it. Once the old Frith picture has been shown and my task explained, people everywhere have gone out of their way to smooth my path, search their memories and tell me all they know. While in several cases there was official bureaucracy to overcome, it was sometimes circumvented, with an understanding wink, by the man actually on the ground.

Overall I have not been discouraged by what I have seen. Once away from the Home Counties or a mile or two out from the motorway corridors there are still wide regions of rural tranquillity where little has changed visually in the past century. People today seem more aware of their heritage

than they were and less keen to destroy it in favour of new developments. Certainly we are more vigilant about conservation – indeed we need to be. But rest assured that, though I am not complacent, during the photography for this book I found Britain still to be a green and very pleasant land.

JOHN CLEARE

The changing face of Britain

IF RIP VAN WINKLE — or Van Smith, or Jones, or Frith — had laid down to sleep one summer's afternoon in 1860 in the shade of a tree a mile or so west of the little hamlet of Harlington and had woken in 1999, he would have found himself perilously close to the runway at Heathrow Airport. Everything he saw would have been not merely strange but incomprehensible. Enormous stretches of the fields around him had been macadamized; a process with which he would have been familiar but only as a rare and expensive treatment reserved for the more favoured highways. On this surface huge metal constructions — several hundred times larger than any coach that he had ever seen — descended from the heavens at a speed and with a clamour that were terrifying to witness. After this the car that picked him up, though equally inexplicable in its apparent independence of any sort of pulling power, would have seemed relatively unthreatening. The people inside, though oddly dressed and speaking a language that was hard to follow but still some form of English, were recognizably human. So this was earth, and not some other planet.

But as the car drove him towards London he would have seen virtually nothing to remind him of the Britain that he had gone to sleep in 140 years before. Huge swathes of tarmac; innumerable horseless carriages, some of startling size, rushing at inconceivable speeds from here to there; high poles which at night carried glaring lights; above all, a blanket of new buildings everywhere, built of strange materials and for uncertain use, obliterating the largely pastoral Middlesex that he had known. If he remained alert he would have identified occasional landmarks to tell him that this was indeed familiar territory. The fourteenth-century tower of the Church of St Peter and St Paul at Harlington was still reassuringly visible and another mile or so on, though the mansion itself had disappeared, the red-brick stables of Cranford House were visible through the trees. Then those woods on the right must be part of the park at Osterley ... but they soon gave way to fields where people appeared to be playing the newly fashionable game of golf, and they in their turn gave way to further wastes of building. Only when he got to Central London and saw the great monuments of the past rearing triumphant — Kensington Palace still in its garden, Westminster Abbey, Barry's recently completed Houses of Parliament — would he have felt confident that this was indeed the London in which he had once felt at home.

SO MUCH HAS GONE, BUT SO MUCH STILL REMAINS

If, on the other hand, Rip Van Frith had gone to sleep a little to the west of Bonar Bridge in the Scottish Highlands and had progressed along what is laughingly described as the A837 towards Ullapool, he would have had no doubt at all as to where he was. He would have been surprised

2

that so remote a road had been macadamized to what would have seemed to him luxurious standards; he would have seen many inexplicable posts and poles, signs and wires; the vehicles that passed, though few and far between, would have been startlingly strange; but essentially the countryside and its occasional buildings would have been familiar. The intervening 140 years had left only the most superficial mark.

If he had taken to the air – in a balloon, perhaps, as being a not wholly unheard-of means of transport – he would have had the same confused impressions. Along the main roads of the South of England in particular he would have seen ribbons of development, villas, bungalows, garages stretching far outside the towns or villages from which they emanated; yet a hundred yards into the hinterland there might be copses, fields, streams, substantially unchanged. On the outskirts of the compact little villages he had once known he would have observed a formidable rash of new and often strident houses, yet in the centre, around the green and church, a surprisingly high proportion of the original buildings often survived. A very great deal had changed but much was still the same; a not particularly surprising conclusion which would have brought Van Frith some consolation and should do the same for us.

How best to illustrate this haphazard and inchoate evolution? By photographs, of course; best of all, photographs taken by a dynasty with common standards and – sometimes literally – a common point of view. But photographs require arrangement and some explanation. The system adopted here – first, the geographical, cities, towns, villages; then, the thematic, farming, fishing, playing – is far from satisfactory. There are inevitably grey areas between the various sectors: much of what happened in London happened also in Manchester or Glasgow; the factors that affected farming affected also the villages and the countryside. There are problems of delimitation; should the demise of the village shop, for instance, be considered under villages or shopping? I have taken the line that such questions do not matter much; provided a subject is covered and the Index tells the reader where to find it, the title of the chapter is relatively unimportant. There could be a dozen or more different ways of organizing this material but I have not found one which offered less pitfalls and disadvantages.

THE EVER-GATHERING PACE OF CHANGE

The Britain of 1860 had changed more in the previous hundred years than in the hundred before that. The Industrial Revolution had taken place, all the major cities had asserted themselves as conurbations, the railway network was substantially in place. Nobody could have predicted what was going to happen over the next 140 years, but it did not require much prescience to see that whatever it might be was likely to be dramatic, that the pace of change was growing and there was no good reason to expect it to slow down. Francis Frith's great-grandfather would have predicted the future with some confidence and have made it look very like the world he knew himself; Francis himself might have been more hesitant but at least would have realized that the future would be unpredictable. He would have been stunned, exhilarated, appalled by the world of 1999; but he would have expected to find something pretty odd and the shock probably would not have been overwhelming.

Two factors above all others both inspired and made possible the changes Frith would have encountered: electricity and the internal combustion engine. Unless he was very much in the scientific *avant garde*, steam would probably have seemed to Frith the force of the future as it had been of the immediate past; it had moved mountains and still had great feats to achieve, but once Faraday had devised a workable electric generator the reign of steam as the main source of power was bound to end. Together, electricity and the internal combustion engine have transformed communications and fuelled the revolution which has transformed not only the physical aspect of Britain but the assumptions and patterns of thought that for so long ruled the minds of humanity. 'The England of the past,' wrote C F G Masterman in 1901, 'has been an England of reserved, silent men, dispersed in small towns, villages and country homes. The England of the future is an England packed tightly in such gigantic aggregations of population as the world has never seen before.' Substitute Britain for England, pack the aggregations yet more tightly, accept that many parts of the world have now overtaken Britain, in ways both good and bad: and Masterman's prognosis still seems valid.

SET-BACKS ALONG THE PATH OF PROGRESS

The pace of progress – a dangerous word, and one used here as indicating forward motion without passing judgment on the merits of the destination – was not invariable, and there were set-backs along the way. The first Industrial Revolution had peaked by the time Frith was taking his earliest photographs; the 1870s and 1880s were a period of depression – the word 'unemployment' first appeared in *The Oxford English Dictionary* in 1882. By then, though, the textile and clothing industries were taking up the slack, mining was booming, growth continued vigorously till after the effects of the First World War wore off. Recession in the late 1920s and 1930s ran its course and all seemed set relatively fair when recovery was again distorted by world war. A decade of economic growth after the war gave way to rampant inflation and then successive waves of competition as new manufacturing countries picked off and destroyed the traditional staples on which British prosperity was founded. Textiles, ship-building, steel-making, mining: one by one the pillars of the Victorian economy crumbled, leaving impoverished cities, deserted factories, populations deprived of the occupations that had given them their livelihood. New industries, like the manufacture of motor vehicles, rose and fell. Agriculture seemed to be perpetually on the defensive, shattered by the imports of wheat from the United States and meat from Australia and New Zealand, revived each time war made it necessary, left to its fate once the emergency was over, dealt what some fear to be the *coup de grâce* by entry into Europe. In 1890 British productivity per worker had been the highest in the world. By 1913 the United States had taken the lead, but we were still far ahead of the rest of Europe. France, Germany, Sweden in turn surpassed us. Then came Japan and the tiger economies of the East. Down and down the scale slipped the United Kingdom. It was a sombre picture. And yet by some legerdemain which the man in the street hardly began to understand, the country seemed to grow richer and richer, against all the odds, the standard of living of the average Briton rose year by year.

Visually, there can hardly be room for doubt that Britain is an uglier place than it was in 1860. There have been some fine new buildings, some noble bridges and inspiring monuments, certain blots on the landscape have been cleared away, woods have grown up, vistas have opened, but on the whole the pressure of an increasing population and the demands of our affluent and materialist society have led to the obliteration of much that was beautiful and dignified. Today, at least temporarily, the growth of population seems to have been checked but the demand has not: each generation expects more and better housing, roads to take them to it, cars to drive upon those roads, a mesh of wires and cables to bring the new toys of an electronic age into its homes. It has sometimes been an effort to prevent an atmosphere of elegiac gloom permeating every chapter of this book, so that it becomes the wail of a sad old man, deploring the fact that things were done much better in his youth, and far, far better when his grandfather was a child. Only the knowledge that the author himself relishes those electronic toys, uses and appreciates those roads, rejoices in many of the good things that have happened over the last 140 years, will, with luck, save him from appearing a cantankerous old prophet — and a minor one at that — crying woe upon an evil and adulterous generation.

THERE IS MUCH TO REJOICE AT

For the average Briton of today is far better housed, fed and dressed than his mid-Victorian ancestor. Woman must rejoice at the transformation of her lot from that of second-class citizen, labouring under every kind of social and economic disability, to something which is recognizably close to parity with man. Every man, except perhaps for the descendants of the still small elite entitled to vote in 1860, must feel satisfaction at his acceptance into the body politic. The tiny proportion of children who were given the chance of higher education has grown dramatically; one may properly lament the failure of the educational system to eliminate illiteracy and give every boy and girl a chance to realize their full potential, but how much better things are than they used to be, and the structure is there within which they can become better still. People are far healthier than they used to be; we may from time to time invent a new disease to stop the complacency becoming intolerable but far less infants die during or shortly after childbirth, the expectation of life grows from generation to generation, the traditional killer diseases are mastered one by one. This has its dark side – the prolongation of life beyond the possibility of pleasure is a threat that faces us all, the demands on the Health Service and the ever diminishing proportion of the population which is of working age becomes more vexatious with the years – but are not such problems better than the shame of the stunted, disease-ridden ill-nourished workers who were rejected in their tens of thousands at the time of the Boer War because they were not deemed fit enough to fight?

A range of electronic gadgets – kettles, vacuum cleaners, washing machines – becoming cheaper by the year in terms of average earnings, have transformed the life of the housewife and have left immeasurably more time free for the pursuit of pleasure or self-education. New possibilities – cinema, radio, television, video, the computer – have become available for those who wish to join in those pursuits. Much of what such devices purvey may be cheap and nasty but the potential is there – an immense range of intellectual stimuli is now open to those who have the inclination to employ them.

BUT THERE IS A PRICE TO PAY

There has been a price to pay. The Britons of whom Masterman wrote may have been 'reserved and silent' but they were part of a far more cohesive and interdependent society than is found today. The destruction of the slums, in itself admirable, has involved the disintegration of long-standing and proud communities which have not grown again in the tower blocks or bleak estates that have been built instead; the decay of the traditional village has ended a way of life that might sometimes be narrow and claustrophobic but involved a high degree of sharing and communication; the fact that so much entertainment can be had at home has weakened the pub or whatever other community centre might exist, where people pursued their pleasures in each other's company. The structure of the family is changing: it would be premature to say that family values are being sacrificed as a result but at the very least it is plain to see that they are under strain.

Immigration has changed the face of Britain. In some ways it has enriched national life, certainly it has provided a welcome boost to a labour force increasingly reluctant to undertake menial tasks, but it has also introduced new tensions and generated animosities that from time to time flare into violence. The Sikh, Hindu and Pakistani communities may in themselves be closely knit, but by their very existence they fragment still further the unity of the British people.

There is a physical price to pay too for the delights of materialism. The motor car, by its very success, threatens to destroy the value that it was invented to promote, the freedom of individuals to range far and wide in pursuit of whatever it is that they wish to find. The streets of the towns are clogged, the highways congested, the life of those who live beside the roads is made hideous, the atmosphere is polluted. Smog hangs thick over the urban areas while from the skies above global warming seems to pose a long-term threat to the survival of mankind. Such problems are far from peculiar to Britain, in many ways we have so far suffered little compared with other areas of the world, but as a small and over-populated island entirely dependent on imports and earning much of our income from the trade and industry of others, we do seem to be more vulnerable than most others.

Can 'progress' go on progressing? Should it, if it can? Could one get off the merry-go-round even if one wanted to? Robert Skidelsky has written recently of 'growth fatigue' which is beginning to be experienced in Western Europe. 'There is increasing scepticism about whether growth of GDP is in any way an accurate measure of the growth of welfare, especially if it involves congestion, pollution, the destruction of natural beauty, the break-up of communities, the continued postponement of leisure and consumption – all in the name of faster growth!' Is it possible that society will one day cry 'Hold, enough!' and be blessed rather than damned for its reluctance to accept the further challenge? One would hesitate to predict with any confidence for the next ten years, let alone the 140 that lay ahead when Francis Frith began to photograph the British Isles. But if some future dynasty of photographers is now setting out to record what happens visually to these islands over the *next* 140 years, it does not seem too extravagant to suggest that the pace of progress may cease to grow ever more headlong, may even dwindle into a more tranquil amble. Either that, or there may be no British Isles to record.

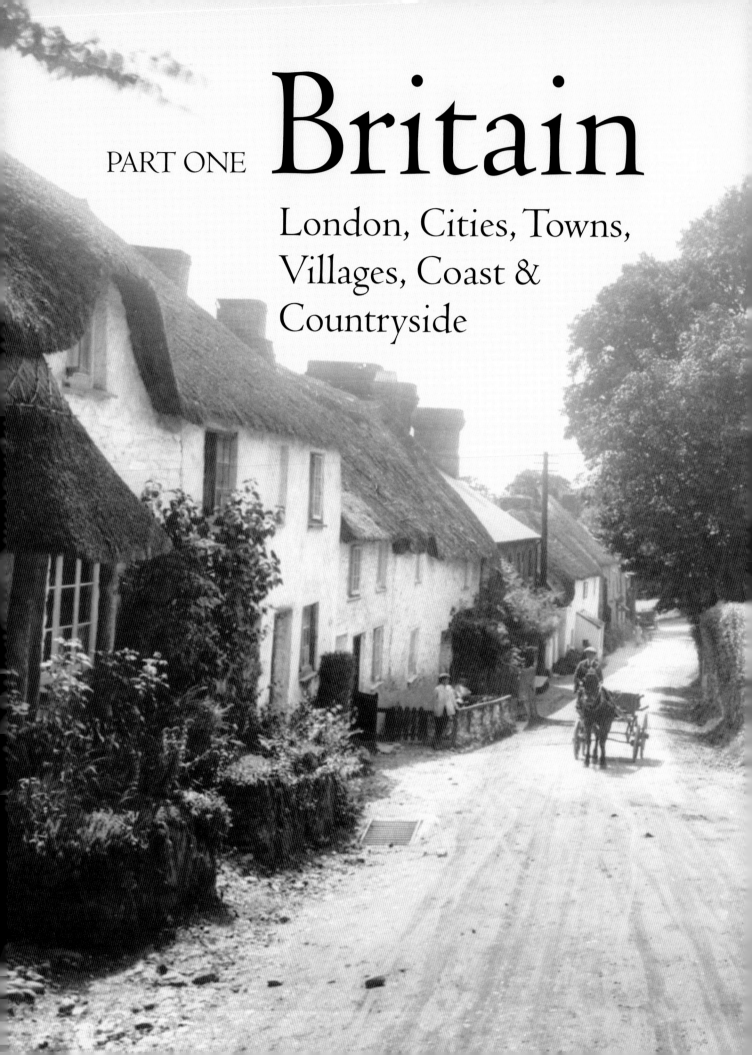

PART ONE Britain

London, Cities, Towns, Villages, Coast & Countryside

London

W HEN FRANCIS FRITH FIRST BEGAN to take his photographs of the British Isles London looked as if it had recently endured a protracted and devastating aerial bombardment. It was the railway engineers who were the most evidently responsible, gouging great trenches through the approaches to central London, erupting when they reached their destination with almost nuclear ferocity. By the late 1860s most of the mainline termini – Euston, Waterloo, King's Cross, Paddington, Victoria, St Pancras – were in place. But if Londoners hoped that they could now enjoy a little peace, they were quickly disillusioned. The railways each day brought multitudes to the termini, now something had to be done about getting them to their homes or offices. It was already obvious that the existing roads were proving inadequate, the answer seemed to be to burrow under the soil. A fresh series of convulsions racked London as first the Metropolitan Railway, then a network of new underground lines, pushed their way laboriously from point to point. Nor did the mainline stations survive unscathed for long: within a few decades Charing Cross had fallen down and been rebuilt in a plainer style; Waterloo had been reconstructed and enlarged, 'no finer or better ordered terminal station is to be found in any other city in Europe', announced a historian of London proudly; Victoria too was being extended. There seemed no end to the encroachments of the transport system on London's land space.

In fact this was only a symptom of London's problem rather than the problem itself. In the course of the nineteenth century London had become the largest, richest and most important city in the world. It was Britain's greatest port; its chief manufacturing centre; the legislative, judicial, executive and Royal capital of the most extensive empire that had ever been seen on earth. Each year it generated a larger proportion of the nation's wealth and absorbed a larger proportion of the nation's population. By 1870 about three million people lived in Greater London – nearly ten percent of the British population; by 1900 the figure was more like 6.5 million and the proportion of the national total seventeen percent. With the benefit of hindsight one can see that already by the latter date national power had passed its zenith but at the time it seemed that Britain, led by London, could only go from strength to strength. Queen Victoria's Diamond Jubilee in 1887, celebrated in a London festooned with flags and decorations (plate 9) provided the apotheosis of national glory and self-esteem.

London in 1897 was preparing for Queen Victoria's Diamond Jubilee BELOW (9). *Whitehall was festooned with flags and bunting and a stand had been erected next to the Banqueting House from which the procession could be watched.*

Fleet Street in 1897 OPPOSITE (10). *The railway that brought so many of these people into town crossed overhead at the foot of Ludgate Hill.*

Thurlstone in South Yorkshire (1918) PREVIOUS PAGES (8).

LONDON HAD GROWN
TOO BIG FOR ITS BUILDINGS

Some felt that London had grown too big for its boots; certainly it had for its buildings. It was small wonder that the last decades of the nineteenth century and the first of the twentieth were marked by frenetic growth. The most dramatic development of all took place around Aldwych and along the Strand. If communications were to be kept open between East and West, the old London and the new, the Strand had to be widened; with a thoroughness inconceivable today and which even the man who demolished so much of Paris, Baron Haussmann, might have respected, the entire north side of the road was swept away. Meanwhile in Aldwych and Kingsway six thousand houses were knocked down and an area the size of Hyde Park redeveloped. When the old Gaiety Theatre tumbled the swarm of rats dislodged in the process invaded a nearby restaurant and forced its closure. It was the most formidable rebuilding operation that

London had ever seen, and though posterity has not judged it as being of great architectural distinction, it served its purpose well enough. It did not involve the sacrifice of anything of supreme importance; indeed, the new Law Courts, an energetic though not particularly ingratiating building completed in 1882, rose on the site of some of the most squalid slums.

The characters to be seen in London's streets often seemed to date from an earlier period than the streets themselves. The bear-leader OPPOSITE BELOW (12), the 'Italian' street musicians (who probably hailed from Stepney) LEFT (13), the organ-grinder BELOW (14) — any one of them might have been met with up to the outbreak of the First World War, though they became increasingly rare as the century wore on. In appearance, though, they seemed almost Dickensian.

Inigo Jones's noble piazza in Covent Garden was already moth-eaten by the time that Francis Frith first saw it. Long before then, the Duke of Bedford had decided to increase his profits as landlord by adapting the square as a market for fruit and vegetables. The results were picturesque enough and the hurly-burly in which Bernard Shaw's Eliza Doolittle passed her days was to persist until recent times (even though plans to relocate the market were put forward as early as 1920). The Covent Garden porters (plate 11) were photographed in 1900 but they would not have looked so very different if it had been thirty years earlier or later. It is one of the more curious features of London that its buildings often change more rapidly than the people who mill around them. The street musicians, the organ grinder and the performing bear (plates 12-14) — all photographed in London's streets towards the end of the nineteenth century — seemed almost Dickensian in appearance, to belong to an earlier age.

The idea of conservation was remote from the minds of most Victorians. Nothing must stand in the way of progress — which by definition meant increased economic activity. Northumberland House, probably the finest seventeenth-century great house left in London, was swept away at the behest of the Board of Works who wanted to put

Northumberland Avenue in its place; the owners of Devonshire House, a still grander palace in Piccadilly, had not even the excuse of yielding to the irresistible force of government but sold their house to a jobbing builder for redevelopment. The stone lions from Northumberland House moved to the suburbs to grace the Northumberland family's house at Syon; the grand gates of Devonshire House were moved across Piccadilly to Green Park; otherwise not a wrack remains. The speed of change seemed to accelerate with every decade. The architecturally dotty Westminster Aquarium was only opened in 1876, yet in 1902 down it came to make way for the grandiose Methodist Central Hall.

The belief in 'progress' did not go out with the Victorians. As late as 1927 a self-styled architectural historian, Mr Harold Clunn, extolled the wonders of the new London. Every recently erected block was 'splendid' and 'noteworthy' – the 'magnificent new buildings

of Swan and Edgar'; every victim of the developer turned out to have been 'mean' and 'cramped'. Of the ignoble gallimaufry that replaced John Nash's splendid crescent, Clunn writes: 'Nobody requires any knowledge of the architectural profession to see at a glance that the new Regent Street is in every way a worthy successor to the old' (plate 15).

The impulse to destroy did not go unchecked

But the impulse to destroy did not go entirely unchecked. William Morris founded the Society for the Protection of Ancient Buildings in 1877, and though initially most people thought him a tiresome crank, the idea that ancient buildings were worth protecting gradually gathered force. The fifteenth-century Crosby Hall blocked the development of Bishopsgate, but instead of being destroyed it was painstakingly dismantled and re-erected in Chelsea. John Rennie's handsome Waterloo

Part of Nash's Quadrant in Regent Street in 1890 LEFT (15), a vital element in his great design to link the Prince Regent's home, Carlton House, with Regent's Park. Almost every building shown would have been demolished by the mid-1920s so as to make room for development.

Bridge was condemned by the planners in the 1880s but did not finally succumb until 1934 and was then replaced by a worthy successor — a 'burning shame', Clunn considered the delay, to have postponed it further would have been to surrender to 'the clamour of a noisy minority'. Clunn would undoubtedly have applauded the new Tower Bridge (plates 16, 17). Here posterity has approved his views, the bridge became an ancient monument overnight and to remove it today would seem almost as sacrilegious as to demolish the Tower itself.

It was a noisy *majority* which defended the parks against the depredations of the planners and the developers. When James Forsyte, in high summer, walked across Hyde Park from Bayswater to Knightsbridge he saw 'a pasture of short, burnt grass, dotted with blackened sheep, strewn with seated couples'. That was

Tower Bridge under construction in 1890 ABOVE (**16**) *and in 1965* BELOW (**17**). *The bridge became an ancient monument overnight; to remove it today would seem* almost as sacrilegious as to demolish the Tower itself. *The Pool of London was a far less busy place by 1965 and the cranes that then lined its banks would soon have lost their purpose.*

how it had been in living memory and that was how Londoners wanted it to stay – not prettified, not tamed, above all not chopped up to make way for new roads and buildings – or, for that matter, memorial gardens. A few corners were trimmed here and there to accommodate the demands of traffic, but on the whole the parks survived inviolate, as they have done to the present day.

THE FOETID SLUMS THAT DISGRACED THE CITY

To preserve the beautiful or the historic is one thing, to preserve the marginally picturesque at the expense of health and happiness is another. Large tracts of London in the 1870s deserved to be razed to the ground and the sooner the better (plate 18). The foetid riverside slums that Dickens described in *Bleak House* or *Our Mutual Friend* were very much the same ten or twenty years later. Inland, in Islington and Stepney, pressure of population drove out the affluent, or even the modestly well-to-do; into their crumbling homes crowded a multitude of the under-privileged, the under-employed, the uneducated. In 1911 a little over eight percent of the national population lived two or more to a room; in London as a whole the figure was twice as bad; in Shoreditch the average was thirty-six percent. Congestion, malnutrition and almost non-existent sanitation inevitably led to disease; more than half the children in the East End died before they reached the age of five. Jack London, the American novelist and pioneer sociologist, explored the slums in 1903. He went into one house in Spitalfields and climbed three flights of rickety stairs, each landing heaped with filth and refuse.

'In six of the rooms, twenty-odd people, of both sexes and all ages, cooked, ate, slept and worked … The seventh room

we entered. It was the den in which five men "sweated". It was seven feet wide by eight feet long, and the table at which the work was performed took up the major portion of the space. On this table were five lasts, and there was barely room for the men to stand to their work, for the rest of the space was heaped with cardboard, leather, bundles of shoe uppers and a miscellaneous assortment of materials used in attaching the uppers of shoes to their soles.'

The waterfront of Lambeth in 1880 LEFT (18): the sort of picturesque dereliction whose disappearance the sentimentalist might deplore and which certainly had more character than the dour office blocks which line the new embankment – but the foetid source, too, of much squalid misery.

Such patches of horror persisted deep into the twentieth century. When redevelopment came it was sometimes done intelligently, with space left for humanity to breathe and enjoy itself (plates 19, 20).

More often, however, when the authorities eventually addressed themselves to the problem, it was by way of massive demolition followed by the erection of housing estates which offered accommodation in material terms infinitely superior to what had existed before but in their bleak uniformity did little to raise the morale of the inhabitants. Such estates provided what might be called a spiritual slum, a term indeed which could be applied to whole tracts of London far removed from the degradation of the East End.

It was the world which Richard Church had in mind when – describing the London of 1900 – he wrote of 'the sinister labyrinth of Pimlico where row after row, through street after street, of mid-Victorian houses with pillared porticoes still stand flaking away gradually into a squalor that is not even brutal.

A kind of lethal greyness, like the scurf of leprosy on doomed human skins, covers the whole district.'

ELECTRICITY AND THE FINAL OVERTHROW OF THE HORSE

But a new London was fast emerging. Two factors, discrete but linked, above all shaped its growth: the first electricity, the second transport. London till the late nineteenth century was a city lit by gas. As early as 1879 Colonel Haywood, the borough engineer, had experimented by placing sixteen electric lamps on either side of the Holborn Viaduct. The cost proved to be unacceptably high and it was another twenty years before electric lighting began to be generally adopted. But in the field

London in 1890 was the city of the horse. On Rotten Row in Hyde Park LEFT (21) they could be seen in their glory: fashionable London parading the splendour of its equipages, the elegance of its dresses, and providing rich fodder for the gossips who loved to note who was talking to whom and who was in whose carriage.

The warehouses and shipyards which in 1890 rubbed shoulders with Barry's brand new Houses of Parliament ABOVE (19). Soon they would be swept away to make place for wooded banks and sedate gardens over which Rodin's 'Burghers of Calais' now preside LEFT (20).

of transport electricity made its mark far earlier. London in the 1870s was still a city of horses; for the rider, for private carriages, for horse-drawn carts and buses and, increasingly, for horse-drawn trams. Anyone who imagined that this implied a city of tranquil streets, disturbed only by the gentle clip-clop of horses' hooves, need only study the hurly-burly to be encountered in Fleet Street at rush hour (plate 10). But horse-drawn traffic was slow as well as noisy, and incompatible with regular commuting from the outer suburbs. An outing to Richmond in the 1880s was the equivalent of an expedition to Brighton thirty years later. The cost of additional surface railway lines within London was becoming inconceivable. The answer was to burrow underground.

Though the underground railway vastly increased the mobility of London's population, it was confined to a rigid framework and left large hinterlands still inaccessible. To meet this need came the electric tram. London lagged behind the provincial cities in having recourse to this new technology; by the end of the nineteenth century more than six hundred million passengers were being carried every year by horse-drawn omnibus or tram but it was not till 1905 that the first electric trams began to appear. They were never generally loved: the rails were a menace to the cyclist and the pedestrian, the tram itself as fearsome a threat to cars or carriages as a pike gliding among minnows. Nor, in central London, was it notably effective; a horse-drawn omnibus usually took half an hour to get from Victoria to Mansion House, an electric tram might manage the journey in twenty minutes. Around Hyde Park Corner or Charing Cross it played no part at all (plates 22-24). But when it came to expeditions to those parts of central London not served by the tube it was for many years unchallenged; not till 1910 did the motor omnibus become a serious rival to the electric tram; it was not till 1952 that the last electric tram clattered into retirement.

The underground and the tram transformed London. Until their advent only the well-to-do could live more than walking distance from their daily work; with improved transport huge new tracts of territory were opened up where the rapidly growing multitude of office workers could base themselves. Until then Hyde Park Corner had been a frontier post; there were pockets of habitation further west, some substantial settlements, but for most Londoners Chelsea and Kensington, let alone Hammersmith and Chiswick, were uncharted country. It was the first Great Exhibition of 1851, when the horse was still the only effective means of transport outside the

1900 APSLEY HOUSE

1908 APSLEY HOUSE

The Strand and Charing Cross in 1910 LEFT (**24**), *conspicuously free of trams — which were never widely accepted in Central London — but with the motor-bus rapidly becoming the predominant means of transport for most.*

The traffic in front of Decimus Burton's screen and Apsley House bears witness to the gradual supercession of the horse. In 1900 TOP (**22**) *not a car is to be seen. By 1908* ABOVE (**23**) *the proportions were roughly fifty-fifty, though there were still few private cars on the road.*

mainline railway, which provided the impetus for the development of South Kensington as a centre for cultural and academic life; its successor in 1862 set the great building boom in action. Until then the Cromwell Road had been a muddy track, and Knightsbridge a prosperous but still isolated village. Within a few decades the great museums, the Albert Hall, the Imperial Institute, were all in place, row upon row of substantial dwellings for the *bourgeoisie* clustered around them. In 1881 the path of the future was illuminated when Albert Hall Mansions, the first custom-built block of flats in London, opened opposite Kensington Gardens. There were, of course, curious gaps, inexplicable delays. Two new buildings in Knightsbridge – then towering above their neighbours – stood empty for so long that they were nicknamed Malta and Gibraltar, by-words for places that would never be taken. Today they are the French Embassy and the Thames Yacht Club; but though there were periods of retrenchment and occasional blunders, in general the tide was irresistible.

THE OUTER LONDON OF MR POOTER

These were the inner suburbs, today hardly considered to be suburbs at all by their inhabitants and even then beyond the purse of most office workers. Outside them came the great belt of suburbia proper: Chiswick and Hammersmith, Clapham and Balham, Ealing and Southall. Battersea Town Hall, of 1892, robustly asserted the self-confidence of these new communities (plate 25). Charles Pooter, a senior clerk in a city firm, lived in the 1890s in 'The Laurels', Brickfield Terrace, Holloway – 'a nice six-roomed residence, not counting

Battersea Town Hall, completed in 1892 and photographed seven years later ABOVE (**25**), *displayed the self-confidence and slightly bombastic complacency which was to be the hall-mark of the Edwardian Age. It was the work of Edward Mountford, whose many other public buildings in London included the Old Bailey.*

basement, with a front breakfast parlour' and a 'nice little back garden which runs down to the railway'. Pooter's was the diary of a Nobody, yet he was also Everybody. Thirty years before there would have been no nice residence, no terrace, no 8.45 bus to take him to his office; now the great army of Pooters had inherited the earth. 'You know how these streets fester all over the inner-outer suburbs,' wrote George Orwell of Ellesmere Road, West Bletchley. 'Always the same. Long, long rows of little semi-detached houses … as much alike as council houses and generally uglier. The stucco front, the creosoted gate, the privet hedge, the green front door. The Laurels, the Myrtles, the Hawthorns, Mon Abri, Mon Repos, Belle Vue. At perhaps one house in fifty some anti-social type who'll probably end in the workhouse has painted his front door blue instead of green.'

As the tide of suburbia washed over London's environs, small nuggets of the past survived (plates 26, 27). Literally hundreds of villages were overrun but usually the church, with luck the green and a cluster of older houses, resisted extinction. In the more fortunate or far-sighted suburbs the gardens of the old manor house would be preserved as an open space for the enjoyment of the inhabitants. Village life as such did not, could not survive; but not all sense of continuity with the past was lost. The members of the Ancient Order of Foresters who paraded so proudly through the streets of Upper Norwood (plate 28) would have been dismayed if thrust back into the forests which they were honouring; but they were paying a conscious – if perhaps rather self-conscious – tribute to Norwood's distant but still honoured sylvan history.

The windmill at Hornchurch was in good trim in 1909 ABOVE (26) *and, judging by the van beside it, it was still working. But it was already something of an anachronism. In the end it burnt down; the site itself is still clear but development clusters all around.*

Highbury, Edgware, Croydon, out and out flowed the diaspora. Sometimes a suburb was directly linked to a great industrial concern, Dagenham owed much of its prosperity to the presence of the Ford car factories. Sometimes it was conjured into life by a single road or rail link; Hendon hardly existed before the Hampstead line was continued beyond Golders Green. Sometimes a suburb remained an affluent and thinly populated enclave, like Virginia Water with its golf course and expensive houses occupied by celebrities or rich City folk. It was the world much loved by John Betjeman and which he frequently memorialized in verse:

> 'Return, return to Ealing
> Worn poet of the farm!
> Regain your boyhood feeling
> Of uninvaded calm!
> When smoothly glides the bicycle
> And softly flows the Brent
> And a gentle gale from Perivale
> Sends up the hayfield scent.'

CAN THE GREEN BELT HOLD?

But the scent of the hayfield became increasingly hard to find. In 1900 young Jolyon Forsyte surveyed the countryside around his home, Robin Hill, a prospect of unbroken woods and fields, and wondered whether it would hold its own or soon 'the giant London would have lapped it round and made it into an asylum in the midst of a Gerry-built wilderness'. When Galsworthy wrote this passage in 1920 he must have suspected that Robin Hill was doomed, twenty years later he

Hampstead, photographed in 1898 ABOVE **(27)**, *managed to preserve much more of its individuality than most of the outlying towns or villages swamped by the metropolis. The Ancient Order of Foresters, in 1900* BELOW **(28)**, *paraded proudly through the streets of Upper Norwood. The worthy citizens would have been dismayed if they had found themselves thrust back into the forest they were honouring, but they were still paying a conscious tribute to Norwood's past.*

might have been more optimistic. The concept of the Green Belt, a girdle of undeveloped land to be preserved inviolate around the great urban centres, was not an invention of the 1930s, but it was in those years that the authorities became seriously concerned about the damage that was being done by unchecked development. Not merely was much valuable farming land being lost but Londoners were being deprived of easy access to country air and open spaces. Merely to limit or prohibit new building, however, would exacerbate the problems posed by the ever-growing demands of, first, London's factories and, progressively, of London's service industries, for more and yet more labour. 'Greater London,' considered the London County Council in 1941, was 'already larger than is desirable on proper planning principles.' The Abercrombie Plan of 1944 was intended to enunciate those proper principles, to impose an organic order on the capital itself and to export a million Londoners to new towns outside the Green Belt. Like all such master plans for the improvement of London it was greeted with respectful acclaim; like all such plans it was soon tidied away and largely forgotten. When in the 1960s further attempts were made to shift population from the inner boroughs to the outer, the attempt foundered, in part at least because the inflow of immigrants from the Commonwealth more than made up for any reduction in population that might temporarily be achieved.

LONDON REACHES FOR THE SKIES

By and large the Green Belt held. But every year saw an increase in the number of people whose work required their presence in central London and who did not want to live intolerably far from their shop or office. The obvious solution, both for the office and for the habitation, seemed to be to build upwards. In the City the

process had already begun. The four or five storeys of the Victorians had given way to seven or eight of the Edwardians. 'The palatial new Gresham House,' wrote an awe-struck Harold Clunn in 1927 '… is eight storeys in height. It is no exaggeration to say that, as recently as twenty years ago, the City Fathers would have been shocked at the very suggestion of permitting such tall buildings.' Thirty years on again and the City Fathers would have been shocked at so mean-spirited an enterprise. In the early 1950s the development of London as the financial centre of the world, as well as the need to accommodate an ever swelling bureaucracy, led to the abandonment of controls and a virtual free-for-all in office building. With Richard Seifert spear-heading the operation, a rash of stark up-turned glass and concrete boxes erupted all over London, to the great detriment of the skyline (plate 29). Castrol House, built in 1958 in the Marylebone Road, was among the first of a new movement which led on to four-hundred-foot monsters like the Shell Centre and the Vickers' Tower, then to the NatWest tower,

inally to the overwhelming development of Canary Wharf, which changed the skyline of Eastern London from every direction. Only now are those responsible beginning to wonder whether they were premature. As office space has grown, so automation and new communication systems have made the need for office workers less pressing. To prophesy would be foolhardy but it is at least possible that there will be a lot of under-occupied skyscrapers in London over the next twenty years.

The rush to build high-rise residential units now appears still more misjudged. At the time it seemed a splendid idea; to replace sprawling slums by one clean-cut tower block which would offer the residents fine views and fresh air as well as ample space around for gardens, car parks and children's playgrounds. Four hundred such blocks existed in London by the late 1960s. Unfortunately the lifts rarely worked, the children could not be sent out to play because they were too far from their mothers, neighbourhood life was destroyed and a surprising number of apparently well-balanced Londoners developed symptoms of

advanced acrophobia. The clincher came in 1968 when a section of Ronan Point, a brand new tower block in Newham, collapsed like an ill-made house of cards, killing four people in the process. No formal change of policy was announced but the day of the tower block was over. One by one they have been coming down, giving more pleasure in their spectacular destruction than ever they did in their heyday.

A CITY IN RETREAT

The number of people who wanted to live in them was coming down as well. Though any given office might need less staff to do the same amount of work, the number of offices continued to multiply as London became ever more international. The government and some of the larger businesses made sporadic efforts to move their headquarters to provincial towns, but still the population of office workers did not shrink greatly. But other traditional sources of employment were more seriously affected. London had long ceased to be a centre of ship-building (plate 30) but in the mid-1950s the Port of London was still handling seventy

In 1910 the Thames was still an important centre for ship-building ABOVE **(30)**. *Soon it was all to disappear, to be followed in the 1970s and 1980s by the Port of London itself.*

million tons of goods a year and employing thirty thousand dockers, stevedores, carters and the like. The end of Commonwealth preference and increased competition from continental and other British ports, dealt a fatal blow to their activities; Tate and Lyle, the biggest sugar refiners in the world, closed their giant refinery at Plaistow Wharf; within thirty years the Port of London was dead. The sensational Docklands development gave rise to much building work but at the end of the day it meant more room for offices, more flats and houses in which the office workers could live, but no consolation for the dockers whose territory this for so long had been.

The factories closed too. London had always been a great industrial centre but between the two World Wars there had been vast expansion. The suburbs of West London, in particular, saw the arrival of major multinational companies, clustered around the Great West Road and the North Circular, Hoover and

Firestone, Osram and Gillette. At Dagenham Ford manufactured 250,000 cars a year; the conflux of factories that eventually became Leyland produced more buses and trucks than the rest of the British Isles put together. Then, in the 1970s and 1980s, all this withered, traffic congestion and increasing costs caused companies to move, competition from abroad accounted for many others. Within ten years London's industries lost 150,000 jobs.

Meanwhile, in the East End, the clothing industry which had employed 150,000 people in 1945, was shattered by competition from countries like India which previously had been its market. The pay had often been derisory, the working conditions appalling – traces of the city discovered by Jack London in 1903 were still to be encountered in 1960. The industry's demise was not an unmitigated tragedy. But it still meant that many jobs had been lost; one significant element of London's life-force had been extinguished.

Though the tourist industry has expanded dramatically since the Second World War, people have always wanted to see the sights of London. In 1900 a paddle steamer was taking aboard trippers from the jetty outside Lambeth Palace ABOVE *(31). The difference between such a scene then and now is that in 1900 the crowd would have been almost entirely British; the majority of today's visitors come from abroad.*

As the factory worker vanished, so the tourist took his place. Sight-seeing was nothing new to London; a photograph of 1900 shows a boatload of trippers at the pier outside Lambeth (plate 31); Christopher Robin and Alice were not the only people to watch the Changing of the Guard at Buckingham Palace. But most of these were British; it was not till the 1960s and 1970s that the Americans and Europeans began to arrive *en masse*, not till the 1980s that the Japanese and Arabs joined the invasion. Today half the twenty million or so overseas visitors to Britain each year spend all or a large part of their time in London, tourism accounts for five percent of the Gross Domestic Product, one job in ten is connected with the industry, a plethora of hotels and restaurants have opened to cater to the new demands. Near Buckingham Palace, Kensington Palace, Trafalgar Square, it is possible to walk for hundreds of yards through thick crowds without encountering a single man or woman who seems an obvious Londoner.

If Francis Frith were to revisit London today he would be flabbergasted by the buildings and the traffic, by the immense scale of the new constructions, whether Canary Wharf (plate 359) or the Millennium Dome (plate 32). But it would be the people who most astonished him. It is not just the tourist, of course. Immigration has produced dramatic change; nearly half the population of Brent comes from ethnic groups within the Commonwealth, a third of the inhabitants of Newham, Tower Hamlets and Hackney are West Indian or Asian in origin. Hundreds of thousands of Americans, Germans, French, are working in London, often for years at a time. The phenomenon is universal, but London must be the most cosmopolitan great city in the world.

Whether this is a matter for rejoicing or regret, whether it is invigorating and exciting, or dangerous and disruptive, must be a matter for individual judgment. What is certain is that the Londoner of today is very far removed from the Londoner of Francis Frith.

It is the immense scale of modern developments that would particularly surprise Francis Frith if he were to revisit London today. Even the first man to photograph the pyramids would blanch when confronted by the Millennium Dome BELOW *(32) near Docklands.*

Cities

WHAT IS A CITY? For the purposes of this book, at least, it is not what it is sometimes deemed to be – any urban area that boasts its own cathedral. Salisbury, for instance, owns one of the finest cathedrals in the country, yet in spirit it remains a swollen market town. (The same might be said of Winchester, but that, after all, was once the capital of England and so retains the status of city by inheritance if not by size.) In some cases there is no room for doubt; by any definition Manchester, Cardiff, Glasgow, must be cities; Montgomery, King's Lynn, Kilmarnock are equally obviously towns. There is a grey area in between, however. Whitaker, in his invaluable *Almanack*, lists the thirty-seven 'principal cities' of the British Isles, and that will do as well as any other definition. In the last resort it matters little. To be an inhabitant of a city is as much a state of mind as a matter of wealth or population. If you believe that you live in a city you probably do. Certainly no one will be in a position to contradict you.

The very word is enough to stir up violent emotions. John Ruskin hated cities; 'spots of dreadful mildew,' he called them, 'spreading by patches and blotches over the country they consume'. He wrote at a time when the cities were growing with explosive violence. In 1860 half Britain's population still lived in villages or the countryside; forty years later when Ruskin died the proportion had dropped to twenty percent, yet at the same time the national population had swollen dramatically. It was not just that the great cities had grown; it was they who generated most of the wealth that fuelled Britain's expansion and they whose insatiable demands for labour sucked in the unemployed or under-employed from throughout the British Isles. After the potato famine in Ireland in the mid-nineteenth century the influx of cheap labour from that unfortunate island was a boon to Britain's industrialists but a nightmare for anyone with a social conscience: often diseased, almost always badly nourished, the new arrivals added to the already horrifying problems of the industrial cities and turned the unpalatable into the intolerable.

Not all Victorian cities grew at the same pace. Manchester and Birmingham almost rivalled London in the rate of their growth though never competing with the capital in wealth or

The Exchange in Liverpool
in 1887 LEFT (33). At the
heart of what was then the
second most prosperous city
in the British Isles, it each
day handled transactions
which bore comparison with
most European capitals.

Ever innovative, Liverpool
in 1893 opened what was
claimed to be the first
overhead railway in the
world. It was photographed
two years later RIGHT
(34) and survived until
after the Second World War,
but it became increasingly
expensive to maintain and
obstructive to traffic and
was closed and largely
demolished in 1956.

population. Glasgow made a slower start, though it came through fast at the end of the century; its population doubled between 1871 and 1921. But it was Liverpool which epitomized most vividly the dynamic materialism of the Victorian age; it generated wealth on a scale which few if any British city outside London could come near (plates 33, 34). The Rev. Francis Kilvert visited the port in 1872. 'Nothing,' he wrote, 'gives one so vivid an idea of the vast commerce of the country as these docks, quays and immense warehouses, piled and cumbered with hides, cotton, tallow, corn, oilcake, wood and wine, oranges and other fruit and merchandise of all kinds from all corners of the earth.' They travelled the last mile in one of the large horse-drawn omnibuses that trundled up and down Liverpool's main streets and visited Layard's,

then the largest ship-building yard in the world, employing four thousand men. The engineer in charge, Kilvert noted in mingled admiration and dismay; 'had to be there at 4 am and did not leave till 9 pm'.

The Victorians devastated and rebuilt with equal zest

Some of these cities preserved their old medieval or eighteenth-century core. As late as 1933 J B Priestley found in the heart of Coventry much that was 'genuinely old and picturesque,' with rows of half-timbered and gabled houses that 'would do for the second half of the *Meistersinger*'. Some streets, however, had been swept away to make room for two 'new and enormous bank offices, very massive and Corinthian'. Coventry was fortunate that so far only a few streets had been thus

Birmingham New Street ABOVE (35). *The bicyclist to the front of the picture must have been something of a rarity in 1890. The building he is passing has now been demolished, and the statue beyond it removed in the interest of freer traffic flow, but otherwise the street looks much the same. The pillared Town Hall at the end was modelled on the temple of Castor and Pollux in Rome and designed by Joseph Hansom — of the hansom cab.*

George Square, Glasgow, in 1897 LEFT (36). The centre of Glasgow was substantially rebuilt in the nineteenth century, making it one of Britain's finest Victorian cities. The monument to Walter Scott in the centre of George Square was erected in 1837 and the tower on the Merchant's House — now the Glasgow Chamber of Commerce — in 1874. In 1998 BELOW (37) it was substantially unchanged.

demolished. On the whole the Victorians devastated their city centres with ruthless abandon and rebuilt with equal zest (plates 35-39, 43). They had some excuse for their excesses. Not merely was every kind of business expanding but the authorities had to build offices from which they could undertake a whole range of new functions undreamt of by their grandparents.

The city corporation in the mid-nineteenth century would have needed to levy a rate, to accept responsibility for the police and possibly a fire service, to employ a town clerk and a borough surveyor, to staff the meetings of the mayor and councillors, but on the whole people were left to muddle along with whatever degree of neighbourhood co-operation seemed practicable or desirable. Half a century later expectations and demands had altered considerably, and that same corporation had to cater for schools and libraries, museums and art galleries, gas, electricity, water, sewers, health, parks and a vastly more elaborate machinery for raising and spending funds. No wonder that ever bigger buildings were called for to meet the demands of the new services.

But though the Victorians could legitimately claim that they needed more space, the municipal buildings erected in the second half of the nineteenth century reflected not only a genuine requirement but also a vainglorious statement of pomp and splendour. The city fathers, conscious of the vast new wealth

Union Street, Aberdeen (1890) RIGHT (38). *The splendidly craggy Town House contrasted with the bland classicism of the rest of the street. The city was well to the fore with its electric trams; London would not install them for a few years yet. The building at the end of the street belonged to the Salvation Army, who modelled it on Balmoral. Today* RIGHT BELOW (39) *the trams and the hats have gone, but little else has changed.*

1890 UNION STREET ABERDEEN

1998 UNION STREET ABERDEEN

which was every day accruing and jealously surveying the achievements of rival cities around the country, determined to proclaim their own greatness and the greatness of the people whom they represented, by raising palaces of civic might, richly decorated, majestically fanciful, sprouting great domes and towers and pinnacles. They were no doubt functional enough so far as office space was concerned, but the cavernous great halls and rich decorations were intended to impress and over-awe (plate 40). But though the town halls

might have been among the most dramatic of the new buildings, there were plenty of other ways by which a corporation, or rich individuals, could glorify themselves as well as their city. In the mid-nineteenth century a philanthropist called James Donaldson left the bulk of his enormous fortune for the building of an orphanage for the indigent young of Edinburgh. Eschewing both Grecian and Gothic, the architect created a Tudor palace (plate 41), modelled on Burghley, the Cecils' sixteenth-century home in Lincolnshire. It was

like a baronial hall fit to receive Henry VIII, Anna Bullin and Wolsey,' he wrote proudly to a friend. Certainly Henry VIII would have felt more at home there than the orphans; indeed, within a few years of its opening it was clear that it was wholly unsuited for its purpose. Eventually it became a school. No such fate awaited the Birmingham Art Gallery or the Walker Art Gallery in Liverpool, which survived to house what were to become two of the finest collections in the country.

Art galleries and museums, were intended for the edification of the citizens as a whole but only a small minority made use of them.

Probably the average Mancunian was more gratified when their cricket club was expelled from its ground in the district of Old Trafford and re-opened on a site a mile or so away in a grand and custom-built pavilion with 'an excellent wine cellar' thrown in for good measure (plate 42). The parks were another amenity which were prized by the poorer inhabitants of the cities. On the whole the authorities were conscientious in preserving the open spaces which they had inherited in the centre of the city but did little about planning new ones in the vast areas that were being developed around the fringes. Such new parks as did come about were usually the gardens and immediate surrounds of some large house which had been swamped by the tide of building but had been fortunate enough to escape more or less unscathed.

THE ABYSMAL LIVING CONDITIONS OF THE URBAN POOR

The trouble was that, though the lord mayor and corporation were eager to pursue grandiose schemes which would redound to their credit, they were less energetic when it came to bettering the living conditions of the lower classes. The last thirty years of the nineteenth century were marked by economic stagnation if not recession. Agriculture was hit worse than industry, but the irresistible economic growth that had impelled Britain's cities into such turbulent expansion was faltering markedly. Immigration, however, continued; indeed, the hard days that were being endured by the farmers meant that ever more countrymen decided that their future must be brighter in the cities. A rapidly growing population seeking the same number of or still less jobs could only lead to gross over-crowding of the anyway cramped and decayed accommodation and exert still further pressure on the usually inadequate services which was grudgingly provided by the city authorities.

The result was slums. Throughout the British Isles at the end of the nineteenth century the urban poor were living in conditions of abject sordidness. 'The streets were filled with a new and different race of people, short of stature, and of wretched or beer-sodden appearance,' wrote Jack London in 1902. 'We rolled through miles of brick and squalor, and from each cross street and alley flashed long vistas of brick and misery.' He was describing the capital, but it might as well have been Liverpool or Manchester or Glasgow. Health suffered. Seebohm Rowntree in 1901 calculated that nearly a third of the population of York was living below the level necessary for physical efficiency.

Rising prices and falling wages in the years before the First World War exacerbated an already horrifying situation. Birmingham's civic motto was 'Forward,' but it seemed to be 'Forward' for profits and 'Backward' for the working classes. In 1911, of the 525,000

Old Trafford, Manchester (1897) LEFT **(42)**. *The purpose-built pavilion and cricket ground in fact stand a mile or so from the district of Old Trafford, from which site the club was expelled by developers in 1856.*

inhabitants, ten percent lived two or more to a room. In some areas thirty people were dependent for water on a single tap, which any way was only turned on at certain hours of the day. Forty thousand houses were cramped together back to back, a fashion of building which was deemed anti-social but was still common in Halifax and Bradford until well into the twentieth century. Housing conditions had in fact generally improved in the years before 1900; the next two decades saw the gains wiped out as more houses were needed, few were provided, and the old stock decayed.

One can over-stress the horror of human existence in cities before the First World War. Many people lived contentedly in back-to-backs, finding them warm and quite sufficiently

Piccadilly, Manchester LEFT **(43)**. *Frith seems to have taken his photograph from the Queen's Hotel. The year was probably 1887, if the placard advertising the Royal Jubilee Exhibition is anything to go by.*

airy. Indeed in Leeds, where the building of back-to-backs was banned in 1900, the practice was resumed in 1980. It was possible to achieve a fulfilled existence, even in the poorest areas. Neville Cardus, the incomparable critic of music and cricket, was brought up in one of the bleakest districts of Manchester. There were back-to-back tenements within a hundred yards, but 'there was a Free Library round the corner, and also there were fields or, let us say, an "open space" not yet built upon and utilized for the disposal of rubbish'. It was also utilized for impromptu games of cricket. 'Given a library and a cricket pitch, both free of charge, I was obviously blessed with good luck.' There were improvements, though they were slow in coming. When Cardus was born, less than a quarter of the houses in Manchester enjoyed piped water and a water closet. By the time he left the city just before 1914, it was rare indeed not to enjoy that amenity. But for those with less intellectual resources, less energy and less

ambition than Neville Cardus, the prospects were dire enough. When Winston Churchill visited suburban Manchester he looked around him with dismay. 'Fancy living in one of these streets,' he exclaimed, 'never seeing anything beautiful, never eating anything savoury, never saying anything clever!'

After a slow start, house building between the two World Wars speeded up. The price of materials fell, the cost of labour remained steady, a series of governments provided subsidies which turned healthy growth into a rampant boom. Tenement blocks became a commonplace, often built by one of the great charitable foundations of which Peabody was the prime exemplar. These were cheap, and certainly more comfortable than the slums they replaced, but they were rarely regarded with much affection by the inhabitants. Then came the council house. In fact there had been fleeting manifestations of these in the nineteenth century – in Liverpool, for instance,

Newcastle's famous swing bridge, built in 1876, photographed in 1890 ABOVE **(44)**, *and still at work today.*

Between 1896 RIGHT (45) *and 1998* RIGHT BELOW (46) *the river front of Newcastle changed remarkably little; except, of course for the Tyne Road Bridge of 1926, from which the later photograph was taken. Inland, however, there has been much development; the view of the cathedral is now partly obscured and a drear black slab of offices has intruded offensively on the right.*

1896 NEWCASTLE

1998 NEWCASTLE

in the 1880s – but it was another forty years before the idea really took off. Council estates provided small and monotonous but decently built houses, usually with a patch of garden and endowed with far better facilities than anything the inhabitants had been used to in the past. They were vastly and rightly popular.

THE FLIGHT FROM THE INNER CITY GATHERS PACE

The idea of 'industrial zones', of a segregation between residential areas and the place of work, had been largely alien to the Victorians. Most manufacturing took place in small workshops in the centre of the city, with the workers living either on the premises or nearby. If the city was a port, the docks and warehouses bustled right up into the heart of civic life; not until the end of the Victorian era was Liverpool's George's Dock filled in to make way for some of the city's grandest Edwardian buildings. Markets continued to be held in the centre of many

cities until well into the twentieth century (plates 47, 48). Whether or not people wanted to move out, the demands of work made it impossible for them to do so.

But by the end of the nineteenth century all this had begun to change. It was the suburban railway that did most to transform the situation; while the horse remained the only effective means of transport not even the well-to-do could manage a decent day's work and still get home to the country when the office

Until the end of the nineteenth century, and sometimes far later, markets were held where they had always been, in the heart of the city. The cattle market at Norwich in 1901 LEFT (47) took place beneath the castle walls; the market at Nottingham BELOW (48) was just as much a part of city life.

closed. When Frith took his first photographs the main line rail network was largely in place but when the train reached the termini the railwayman called it a day. Between 1870 and 1914, however, many more miles of line were added, making possible the opening up of new suburbs and, incidentally, destroying much working-class housing in the process.

In South Manchester, for instance, the suburbs at Heaton, Mersey, Didsbury, Withington and Chorlton were fitted into a mesh of link lines which provided a fast and cheap means of access to the centre. An army of skilled artisans, bank clerks, shop assistants, discovered that they could enjoy at least a simulation of rural life and yet work every day in their accustomed place.

Even the suburban train, however, was still inflexible, leaving large areas undeveloped and apparently inaccessible. The electric tram provided a solution. Bristol pioneered the new device; by 1895 it had imported American equipment and set up a network which already served a large part of the city. The idea caught on; before the outbreak of the Second World War similar systems operated in every city and many large towns. Meanwhile the motorbus was also beginning to figure on the transport scene. At first it was considered more unreliable than its electric rival but gradually public confidence grew. By 1914, for every three people who travelled by tram one used the motorbus, and the gap was closing every day. Out-matched by both, in cost, in speed and in convenience, the horse was beginning its long retreat from the British urban scene.

And so the great middle-class exodus began. On the whole, the richer one was, the further one went. The outer suburbs, where there was easier access to the countryside, space for shrubberies and tennis courts, a neighbouring golf course, were kept for the rich, increasingly

for those who enjoyed the use of a motor car and could thus carry the children to school or the bread-winner to the rail-head without serious inconvenience. It was a temporary development; within thirty or forty years, as gardeners and domestic servants became harder to find and taxation rose, many of the mini-stately homes of outer suburbia were broken up into flats and their gardens turned into building plots. But the 1920s and 1930s were a golden age for the upper middle classes.

For every mansion standing proudly in its own grounds, however, there were forty nearer to the centre; street upon street, district upon district, of neat little semi-detached boxes, each with its strip of garden in the front, coloured glass, leaded panes, mock-Tudor timbering, or whatever eccentricity was possible in an age of mass production. Inexorably the tide swept out, first ribbon-developing along the roads, then filling in the gaps left in the hinterland. The development was in bad taste perhaps, unimaginative certainly, but it still provided for millions a measure of privacy and a comfortable house at an affordable price within easy reach of a place of work. It is easy to sneer at the suburbs, but it is still important to remember how much satisfaction they gave to their inhabitants.

THE DEATH OF THE INNER CITY

But this satisfaction was bought at a high price. The rich and relatively rich, with their

The opening of the Mersey Tunnel ABOVE (49) *in the 1920s gave the prosperous a chance to escape from the heart of Liverpool into the new suburbs and left the city's centre to shops, offices and the poor.*

purchasing power and their social expectations, abandoned the inner cities to shops, offices, factories and the poor. Central Liverpool at the end of the First World War was still a prosperous and vibrant community until in the 1920s the opening of the Mersey Tunnel (plate 49) provided an easy escape route for those who felt a spuriously country home life would be better for their children and their reputations. It was as if a plug had been pulled from a basin of water; within a few years the large houses in the centre had been converted into offices, the gardens bull-dozed into car parks. Entertainment by night continued to be provided but no longer as the natural expression of a coherent and self-aware community. The concert hall in Bradford where J B Priestley had listened to Richter and Nikisch when he was a boy became a cinema; the theatre suffered a similar fate, then closed altogether. Priestley in the 1930s took a 3ᵈ tram ride from Birmingham city centre and during half an hour 'saw nothing, not one tiny single thing that could possibly raise a man's spirits. Possibly what I was seeing was not Birmingham but our urban and industrial civilisation. The fact remains that it was beastly.' Neville Cardus felt much the same when he left central Manchester through 'rows and rows of dismal houses with backyards full of old cans and bedsteads and torn oilcloth; long vistas of streets with lamp-posts and corner shops'. It was possible to be happy and fulfilled in such an environment – Cardus himself had proved it – but the odds seemed increasingly to be stacked against those seeking to achieve it.

Most of the new suburbs grew up in a more or less haphazard way, as the whim of the developer or the private purchaser dictated. Sometimes, however, a conscious effort was made to produce something more carefully

1956 BURSLEM

planned and congenial to the inhabitants. Manchester's Victoria Park was a case in point. More often such developments took place on a grander scale and on a virgin site, related to but not part of an existing city. Ebenezer Howard founded the Garden City Association in 1899, dedicating his life to the creation of small, self-sufficient communities, with enough light industry to make them economically viable yet enjoying easy access to the surrounding countryside. Letchworth and Welwyn are the towns by which he is best remembered. More ambitious still were the creations of the great industrialists who decided to transport their factories and work-forces to a new and more spacious site. William Lever led the way at the end of 1880s. He invented, or at least exploited, Sunlight Soap, a product based largely on vegetable oils and so immensely successful that he soon found his works in Liverpool inadequate. Boldly he crossed the Mersey and at Port Sunlight created a new town with its own churches, schools, clubs, parks and Art Gallery (plate 52). The Cadburys followed suit a few years later, establishing their new settlement at Bournville, outside Birmingham. No house, it

was decreed, was to occupy more than a tenth of its site, factories were not to take up more than a fifteenth of any developed area, one tenth of the whole must be reserved for parks and recreation areas. In the seven years before 1931 child mortality in Bournville was just over half the national average.

THE DECLINE OF INDUSTRY

The development of suburbs, let alone garden cities, assumes a thriving economic base. In the 1870s it seemed inconceivable that this should not endure perpetually. The twentieth century demonstrated the fragility of such optimism. The three basic industries — coal, ship-building and textiles — never recovered fully from the economic malaise that afflicted the industrial world at the end of the 1920s. Their sickness, if not yet demise, struck a fierce blow at the prosperity of several of Britain's proudest cities. In the 1970s and 1980s the process was still more fiercely renewed: the virtual extinction of ship-building was a cataclysmic blow to Liverpool and Clydeside; the port of Liverpool was hit even harder by the loss of a great part of its transatlantic trade; Bradford, whose huge wool industry had already suffered

from Asian competition before the war, now saw its almost total collapse as the world demanded cheaper fabrics. One-industry cities, whose one industry went out of fashion, were particularly vulnerable: Stoke-on-Trent — the conglomerate formed from Arnold Bennett's 'Five Towns' in the potteries — found that the demand for its products was dramatically reduced. Its extraordinary city-scape of chimneys and narrow-necked pottery kilns and ovens — a mis-shapen San Gimignano of the industrial world (plates 50, 51) — was rendered an anachronism fit only for demolition or preservation as an ancient monument.

The Lady Lever Art Gallery at Port Sunlight (1960) BELOW (52). The gallery was built by Lord Leverhulme to house part of his huge art collection and embellish the town he had created around his enormously successful soap-works.

1896 WINCHESTER HIGH STREET

1955 WINCHESTER HIGH STREET

Winchester High Street changed little between 1896 ABOVE **(53)** *and 1955* RIGHT **(54)**, *having escaped the attentions of Hitler's bombers and the property developer (though the road surface in the earlier picture left some room for improvement).*

Today, Britain's cities are a mess

As J B Priestley had found in Coventry, most British cities in 1939 preserved at their centre much which survived from the nineteenth, eighteenth or even earlier centuries. Some, mainly the smaller and more old-fashioned which did not attract the attentions of Hitler's bombers or the still more destructive developer, have changed remarkably little even today. Winchester High Street for instance, though boasting little of architectural distinction, looks much as it did in 1896 (plates 53, 54). Nearby Southampton, on the other hand, suffered severely in the war and bears the marks of its tribulations. Others, like Edinburgh (plates 56-58) also largely escaped bombing and were so patently of architectural and historical importance that many of the most important elements have been preserved. Winchester and Edinburgh, however, are the exceptions; too often the *Luftwaffe*, well-intentioned and enthusiastic post-war planners along with greedy property developers have combined in a lethal partnership to destroy much of the remaining character of many British cities.

The post-war period was the golden age of the grand design; the planners conceived a brave new world of broad avenues, spacious gardens, convenient and salubrious subways conveying the citizen from pedestrian precinct to pedestrian precinct, airy tower blocks, a Le Corbusier cityscape in which men and car would be neatly separated and everyone would live happily ever after. All but domestic traffic would be siphoned off on to vast ring roads that would strike boldly through the inner suburbs and sometimes the very heart of the city itself. Grandiose shopping centres would eliminate the need for those messy and unhygienic corner shops — a fortunate circumstance since most of those shops would

The chief complaint about the Bull Ring in Birmingham LEFT (55) *is that it ripped the heart out of a living city and substituted development on an inhuman scale. It seems that it has already outlived its popularity and is under sentence of death.*

anyway perish in the great clearances needed to make room for the glass and steel palaces of the future (plate 55).

It would never have worked, of course; even if the planners had been sufficiently bold and resolute; even if their projects had not constantly been derailed by one economic crisis after another. The plans may have been immaculate in their conception but they ignored both the people and the climate; the British did not want to live in tower blocks, plunge into what usually turned out to be dark and damp tunnels when they crossed the road, battle against wind and rain in the heroic plazas that the planners had imposed upon them. Some slums were too far gone and had to be eliminated, others were crying out for loving restoration. The mass destruction of the Gorbals in Glasgow and its replacement by residential tower blocks without any proper infrastructure of shops, pubs and schools, was an example of superficially logical but disastrously ill-conceived city planning. Inevitably the new blocks were rapidly to became slums themselves, but they were slums

1998 EDINBURGH

The view of Edinburgh from Calton Hill in 1897 LEFT (56) *is in essentials much the same as in 1998* LEFT BELOW (57), *though most of the old Calton Jail in the left foreground of the former has been pulled down. A hotel — once the North British, now the Balmoral — blocks the view of the Scott Memorial. The prominent obelisk in the Old Calton Burial Ground, however, still dominates the scene.*

Nothing could diminish this spectacular view of Edinburgh Castle from the Grassmarket, taken in 1897 RIGHT (58). *In fact the setting is remarkably much the same. The Black Bull survives today, though sadly no longer offering lodgings for 'Travellers and Working Men'.*

without the sense of community and the generous turbulence that had marked their predecessors.

Today, Britain's cities are a mess. It is hardly surprising that, except where special circumstances prevail as in Cardiff or Belfast, the net exodus continues. The approach of the planners today is more modest and restrained than thirty years ago but the problems seem even greater as the Victorian infrastructure crumbles and the funds to replace it grow ever less adequate. One thing one can predict with some confidence is that, for reasons that are both economic and technological, the next few decades will show less dramatic physical changes than the same period in the past. Whether the cities will be any pleasanter to live in as a result is another matter.

Towns

THERE WERE MANY REASONS for a town to exist in the 1860s. It might be an inland spa, like Bath or Harrogate, already well established in the eighteenth century, sedate, prosperous, perhaps growing a little seedy. It might be a seaside resort – though this was still something of a rarity. Francis Frith might have visited Brighton as a child, but if he had been to Bournemouth he would have found only a scattering of houses and a deserted beach. By 1900 it was a rapidly growing but still unpretentious seaside town. Within twenty years the central square had been refashioned and replaced by something grander; another thirty and the same had happened again. It might be a port like Ipswich, or a town like Grimsby which lived above all by its fishing fleet (plate 60). Towns grew up in mining areas, particularly in those parts of the country where rich fields of coal were being exploited; in 1900 half of the towns with more than fifty thousand inhabitants owed their prosperity to coal. There were naval towns like Portsmouth; towns like St Helens that specialized in making glass and chemicals; and towns like Burton-on-Trent, that were famous for their beers.

But the quintessential British town grew up to serve the countryside around it, and the heart of that town, the principal instrument by which it performed its function, was the market. Indeed, for many people the definition of a town was that it *had* a market. Anyone in the nearby villages and countryside who had business to transact or who hankered for a wider social life would journey to the local town on market day. Around the market grew up a host of ancillary services, providing specialized equipment or labour that no ordinary village could afford. Any village worthy of the name would have a blacksmith's forge and perhaps a wheelwright, but few could offer a range of farm equipment for sale or tackle complicated repairs. The shops in Thomas Hardy's Casterbridge offered not only scythes and hoes but sheep-shears, bee-hives, butter-firkins, field-flagons, carts and wheelbarrows, horse embrocations and hedging-gloves. As Jonathan Brown has pointed out in his excellent study of the market town, in many ways the shops became more important than the market to which they owed their being. The corn market which was opened in Droitwich was in

A typical shopping street in Droitwich in 1904 LEFT *(59), with the tower of St Andrew's presiding in the background. But the facilities were not good enough to satisfy the farmers' wives, who had grown used to shopping in Worcester or Bromsgrove, and the new Corn Market in Droitwich foundered as a result. By 1998 the church had followed the Corn Exchange and lost the greater part of its tower.*

The docks at Grimsby in 1893 RIGHT *(60). Grimsby owed its existence to its port, though most similar towns subsequently developed other roles as manufacturing or market towns. The noble tower owed its inspiration to the Torre di Mangia in Siena, but was used more prosaically to store water for the control of the lock gates.*

Skipton High Street in 1900 LEFT (61), 1955 LEFT BELOW (62) and 1998 OPPOSITE (63). Though Mr Wm Mattock gave way to Mr Clayton and then to the Edinburgh Woollen Mill, and the wholesale bakery was replaced by remedies for poultry and cagebirds and then by scarves and jerseys, the buildings are little different. The atmosphere in the street, however, is that of another world. In 1900 it was taken for granted that cattle should be brought into the centre of town for market; by 1955, though the market still existed, the cattle had been banished.

1955 SKIPTON HIGH STEET

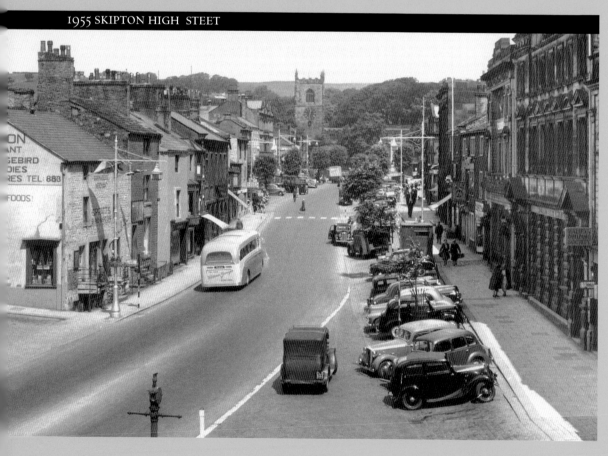

no way inferior to its established rivals in Worcester or Bromsgrove but it closed within twelve months because the farmers' wives of the vicinity had formed the habit of shopping in the latter towns and saw no good reason to change their ways (plate 59).

THE MARKETS MOVE OUT OF TOWN

Most markets were in the centre of town, in a square or wide street, close to or sometimes adjoining the church (plates 61-69). As the pressure of traffic built up in the twentieth century, the street market gradually receded. Sometimes the deserted lots were filled in by new buildings, more often the wide streets were preserved but now used as car parks to accommodate the shoppers who still poured in on market or any other day. But the farmers and traders, who had used the sites as a market for centuries, were not easily displaced. Often a compromise was reached; part of the street was surrendered to the ever-growing traffic, the rest was reserved for its ancient purposes. For six days of the week, however, a litter of cars covered the vacant territory, and where, as was often the case, there was too little room for manoeuvre, the market in the end lost the battle and either closed or retreated to the outskirts of town. Most large towns would also boast a covered market, often flamboyant and substantial (plate 475). But as the shops became better established and handled an ever wider and more sophisticated range of goods, market stalls found it harder to compete. No stall-holder could stock the range of books or kitchen equipment that a properly equipped shop could supply. Increasingly the markets confined themselves to fresh foods, where they could hope that their lower overheads would allow them to undercut their rivals, secondhand goods, or tat of the cheapest and most meretricious kind.

A surprisingly large number of markets survive in one form or another. But they are only a shadow of their former glory: as that intrepid traveller Bill Bryson discovered, 'In French markets you pick among wicker baskets of glossy olives and cherries and little wheels of goat's cheese, all neatly arrayed. In Britain you buy tea towels and ironing board covers from plastic beer crates. British markets never fail to put me in a gloomy and critical frame of mind.'

Though hygiene was rarely an important consideration in the British town before the mid-nineteenth century, an army of cattle milling around the central square seemed undesirable on many grounds. It took time to evict them, however. When George Orwell described Lower Binfield in 1900 or thereabouts, he wrote that: 'Thursday was market day. Chaps with round red faces like pumpkins and dirty smocks and huge boots covered with dry cow-dung, carrying long hazel switches, used to drive their brutes into the market place early in the morning.' But the noise, the dirt, the congestion, the bulls in china shops (or, in one recorded case, in Banbury, a bullock rampaging around a sweet shop) finally became too much. By the time of

1998 SKIPTON HIGH STEET

the Second World War almost every cattle market had been moved to the outskirts of town, usually near the railway station. The existence of the railway cattle truck meant that the farmer could pick and choose among the markets in the neighbourhood. If an additional ten or twenty miles by rail meant that he was likely to get a higher price or buy a better quality of beast, then the extra fare would be well worth paying. The larger and more efficient market prospered, the weaker failed. In the course of the nineteenth century the number of cattle markets dropped dramatically and though the decline slackened after 1900, the total still slips year by year.

The corn exchange was first cousin to the cattle market but a rarer, more ephemeral arrival on the scene. The need for a separate hall, where dealers in corn could set up their stands and exhibit their offerings, does not seem to have occurred to anybody much before 1840 and the impulse to build died quickly after 1870 when the flood of cheap corn from North America dealt a crippling blow to the local industry. Before the end of the nineteenth century many of the exchanges had closed, those that survived traded precariously and often at a loss. In their heyday, however, they were numbered with the church, the town hall and, ever increasingly, the leading banks, as the most monumental buildings of the town (plates 70, 71).

ALL THE FUN OF THE FAIR

The country came to town for the market, it flocked there for the fair. Like the cattle markets these tended to be held increasingly on the outskirts of town, though more because they required extra space than to avoid the noise and dirt. Sometimes, however, a centuries' old tradition was maintained; Nottingham's Goose Fair was held in the centre of town

Market Drayton in 1911 RIGHT (66) *and 1921* FAR RIGHT (67). *The earlier scene was taken on market day, and though the street had lost its cobbles ten years later the market still took place — and still takes place today — on the same site.*

Richmond market place in 1893 FAR LEFT (64) *and* 1965 LEFT (65). *Between those dates the buildings around the church have been demolished, thus making way for an intrusive bus, but the structure of the square otherwise remained remarkably unchanged.*

1921 MARKET DRAYTON

1908 HAWES

1924 HAWES

Market day in Hawes in 1908 above (68) and 1924 right (69). Except for the substitution of motor cars and vans for carts and gigs all was as it used to be. In the autumn, in either year, the market at Hawes would have been a sea of Swaledale sheep.

while in King's Lynn the February fair in the market place became the focal event of a provincial social season. On the whole, the further from London and the newer the town, the more rumbustious the entertainment. Wakes Week, in Arnold Bennett's Bursley, in 1870 or so, was 'an orgiastic carnival, gross in all its manifestations of joy'. There was a menagerie in a vast, oblong tent, with elephants and lions to delight the inhabitants of the Five Towns, and hundreds of booths offering excitements to titillate any palate: 'You could see the atrocities of the French Revolution, and the Fiji islands, and the ravages of unspeakable diseases, and the living flesh of a near nude female human guaranteed to turn the scale at twenty-two stone, and the skeletons of the mysterious phautoscope, and the bloody

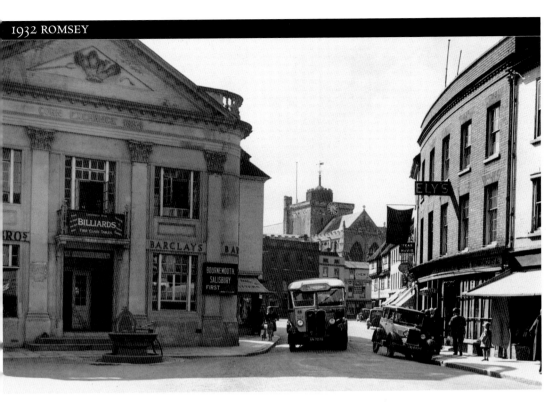

1932 ROMSEY

The Corn Exchange in Romsey in 1932 LEFT **(70)**. *It was built in 1864, in characteristically dignified style with the traditional sheaves of corn, sickle and pitchfork on its pediment, but it fell on hard times and sold out to Barclay's Bank. Still more of a come-down, a billiards saloon was installed on the piano nobile. At least by 1998* BELOW **(71)** *this indignity had been removed.*

contests of champions naked to the waist.'

Bursley would have been only a village a hundred years earlier. So would a large number of Britain's most rapidly expanding towns. It was the Industrial Revolution that had disturbed the balance. At the beginning of the eighteenth century the normal market town, even those close to London or another great city, had been largely self-sufficient. The local shoe-maker would make shoes for the whole population, except perhaps for a pretentious or discriminating handful who would look further afield. The local breweries would supply the beer. Carpenters would satisfy the needs of the citizens and also of any villagers from ten miles around who wanted something more elaborate than their own community could produce. With the advent of mass production and the railway, all these industries were threatened. How could the local shoe-maker compete with a great factory that was able to manufacture shoes at half the cost and in a far greater variety of patterns? Most market towns languished as

1998 ROMSEY

the traditional craftsmen and cottage-scale enterprises lost their customers and the wealth they had generated flowed out of the area to enrich the new industrialists. Others benefited greatly, because of the luck of geography, proximity to raw materials, or the energy and skills of some entrepreneurial inhabitant: Middlesbrough grew rich on iron-ore, Burton on brewing, Peterborough on bricks.

IT WAS THE RAILWAYS THAT TRANSFORMED THE NINETEENTH-CENTURY TOWN

The railway, more than any other factor, transformed the nineteenth-century town. The first victim was the coaching inn (plates 72-74). In fact, in the long run, most of them survived, though they lost the overnight travellers who would once have broken their journey at the inn but now thundered through the mainline station as they hastened towards their final destination.

They had to adapt themselves, however; an army of ostlers and stable boys was put out of work, and though some of these may have found employment in ferrying guests and their luggage to and from the station the net loss of work must have been serious. But the results were still more damaging when the railway missed a town altogether. Such cases arose partly from tricks of geography, more often when some local magnate made life so difficult for the railway company involved that they decided to take the path of least resistance and choose another route.

This could be catastrophic for the economy of the town involved. In the Dorset town of Beaminster, when the railway passed five miles to the north, the population fell by over forty percent between 1851 and 1901. Over the same period Dorchester, only fifteen miles away, grew by a third. An even more extreme example was Basingstoke and nearby Odiham. When the railway came to the first but not to the second, Basingstoke was about twice the size of its Hampshire neighbour. Within fifty years it was five times as big. The result for ports specializing in coastal trade was equally calamitous. It was quicker and surer to transport from point to point by train than by boat; ports which had enjoyed a comfortable existence for centuries brutally lost their business in the course of a few months.

GRANTHAM 1893

The Salutation Hotel in Haverfordwest in 1906 RIGHT (**74**). *It was to renew life as the County Hotel, lose its balcony and gain a flagpole, but its staid and dowdy sobriety was not affected.*

GRANTHAM 1955

The Angel Hotel in Grantham changed little between 1893 FAR LEFT (72) *and 1955* LEFT (73), *though the ivy was stripped off, it gained a 'Royal' in its title, unsightly signs protruded, and a hideous swan-necked street lamp was substituted for its dignified predecessor.*

A railway station, especially if it was on a branch line, was not in itself enough to ensure the economic prosperity of a town. On the whole, the train tended to emphasize existing trends, to reinforce the success of the stronger and most go-ahead and weaken further those which were already falling behind in the race for growth. Out of six towns manufacturing bricks, one might prove the most successful because of the quality of the raw materials, the dedication of the work-force, the skills of the management. The railway played no part in this competition, but it ensured that the best and cheapest product was readily available in the five less successful towns. Soon the weaker brickworks went out of business. The survivor grew ever larger and could compete with rivals a hundred or two hundred miles away. Thanks to a group of energetic and innovative entrepreneurs Reading ceased to be a placid market town and grew to be a principal supplier of beer, bricks and biscuits to the South of England; in the case of biscuits, to large parts of the world. Without the railway it could never have achieved this.

Sometimes the railway was the decisive factor in the development of a town. Rugby possessed one of the leading cattle markets of the Midlands but it would never have become a major industrial town if its status as a railway junction had not made it an ideal site for development. Swindon was still more a railway town, being divided sharply into the residential and shrinking 'old town' and the thrustingly energetic 'new town'. The latter was created almost entirely to accommodate the works of the Great Western Railway, one of the largest and best producers of locomotives in the world. Not that such success necessarily made for a particularly attractive or congenial town:

Bent's brewery in Stone, Staffordshire (1900) BELOW **(75)**. *The bigger breweries would dominate the skylines of the towns they served, like medieval castles from which the brewer baron would emerge to do battle with his enemies.*

1895 BURY

In 1895 the Textile Hall in Bury LEFT **(76)** *stood in solitary splendour with only some mean mill buildings by its side; seven years later the mill had been swept away and a spectacular new art gallery* BELOW **(77)** *with rich reliefs in stone had risen in its place.*

B Priestley spent an evening in Swindon in 1930 and found the experience disagreeable: 'no light, company, cheerful noise, gaiety', just a pub or two, mere little boxes of smoke and the smell of stale beer'.

Breweries were another of the staple industries which were radically changed by the railway. Of all the industries which contributed to the traditional country town, none seemed more soundly based. In the mid-nineteenth century almost every town had its own brewery, often two or three. These might also serve the surrounding countryside. A big brewery would dominate the skyline of the town it served, rearing above it like a medieval castle from which the brewer baron might at any moment sally forth to do battle with his enemies (plate 75). The canals made possible limited competition between the brewers of different towns, but the testing time did not properly come until the railway age. Then, one by one, the smaller, less efficient breweries perished to leave only a solitary champion in each town — five breweries in Grantham in the 1850s became one a half century later. The next stage

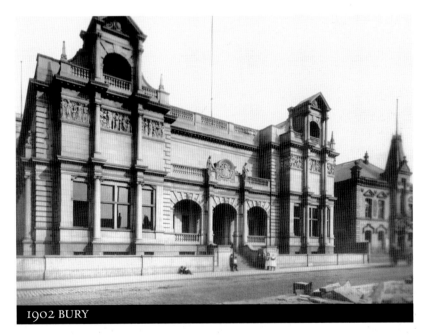

1902 BURY

was that breweries in the smaller towns succumbed to larger rivals from fifty or a hundred miles away. Finally vast national chains came to dominate the market. The smaller independent brewer has survived on the basis of a superior — or at least different — product, but he is constantly under threat; like Alice in *Through the Looking Glass*, it takes all the running that he can do just to keep in the same place.

THE PACE OF GROWTH SLACKENS

For many if not most market towns the period between the 1860s and the First World War was one of dramatically slowed growth. Sometimes there was no growth at all. Sometimes, if the railway passed it by and industry saw no reason to move in, the town would slip in all but name to the status of village. The agricultural depression at the end of the nineteenth century made its lot still more difficult. Northleach in Gloucestershire had been a small but prosperous market town in the mid-nineteenth century, with some fourteen hundred inhabitants. If it had grown in proportion with the national population it would have been several thousand strong by the turn of the century. Instead it shrank to a mere

968. Meanwhile the population of Leicester had grown twenty-fold and seemed if anything to be gathering speed in its advance. Within a few decades it had unequivocally become a city.

The towns that grew, of course, were those which attracted industry. In the case of Leicester it was largely, though by no means exclusively, shoes and hosiery which fuelled the dramatic expansion; in Swindon it had been railway locomotives; in Stoke-on-Trent pottery. Leicester did not entirely lose its links with the countryside; on the contrary, the superior facilities that it enjoyed made it in some ways still more attractive to the Leicestershire farmer, but the almost symbiotic relationship between town and country that still existed in the smaller market towns was lost for ever. It had

Eastgate, Chester in 1903 ABOVE **(78)**. *The town council had decided to embellish the street, and the old gate that had barred entrance to it since Roman times, by crowning it with a clock to commemorate Victoria's Diamond Jubilee of 1897.*

never existed to the same extent in the mill towns, where the mill had come first and the town grown up around it to meet its appetite for labour. Their rise had been as rapid as that of Leicester, their downfall sharper as the demand for their products dwindled and their great towers were one by one demolished. This had its redeeming side. The results of this were not all bad. When Priestley visited Blackburn in 1930 he noticed that there was far less smoke and the buildings were appreciably cleaner. He concluded that the town must be a healthier and happier place to live in; then stopped to calculate the price that had been paid in poverty and unemployment. In fact when smoke and pollution had proved particularly offensive, some efforts were made to improve matters in the late nineteenth and early twentieth centuries. Arnold Bennett's Sophie returned to Bursley after a long absence abroad. Little seemed to her to have altered. "Same smoke!" said Sophie. "Same smoke," Constance agreed. "It's even worse," said Sophie. "Do you think so?" Constance was slightly piqued. "But they're doing something now for smoke abatement." "I must have

Rochdale's Gothic Revival Town Hall (1892) ABOVE **(79)** *was particularly esteemed by the inhabitants because it had cost them more than the corresponding building in Leeds. The campanile of the Municipal Buildings in Greenock (1897)* RIGHT **(80)**, *245 feet high, would not have disgraced any city in Europe, let alone neighbouring Glasgow.*

forgotten how dirty it was!" said Sophie.' But the 'something' that was done for smoke abatement was rarely whole-hearted enough to put things right again – it was to take the collapse of the industry concerned to restore the, by then impoverished, town to cleanliness.

The trouble about the new industrial towns, at first at least, was that they had all the dirt and ugliness of the cities without the corresponding amenities. D H Lawrence inveighed against the blackened brick and mud of Tevershall. 'It was as if dismalness had soaked through and through everything. The utter negation of natural beauty, the utter negation of the gladness of life … the utter death of the human intuitive factor was appalling.' Tevershall was a town founded on coal, but then even Flora Thompson's agricultural Candleford had its own slum – 'a narrow lane of poor houses with ragged washing slung on lines, which was between windows and children sitting on doorsteps'.

THE TOWN COUNCILLORS SHOW OFF

As the towns grew and generated wealth, however, the councillors perceived the need for a wider range of public buildings and relished the opportunity to exhibit their town's wealth and importance (plates 76-80). A plethora of new public buildings sprang up in an extraordinary variety of shapes and styles; the architect who enjoyed this sort of commission can never have had a more rewarding time. There was not a 'public bath, nor a free library, not a municipal park, nor a telephone, nor yet a board school,' wrote Bennett of the Five Towns in 1865 or so. Within a few years the first Free Library was opened and the other amenities will not have been far behind. Parks could not be conjured out of nothing, but most old towns had a field on their perimeters which had traditionally been assigned for public use, and most new towns were able to dedicate part of a neighbouring farm or the garden of a big house to the same purpose

Darlington's South Park in 1911 ABOVE (81). Parks were not often a main priority in nineteenth-century towns, but most councils in the older towns had a field available which had traditionally been designated for public use, and in the new towns there was often the garden of a large house which could be set aside for the same purpose. The authorities had been quick off the mark in providing a floral portrait of the King on the bank of the lake – he had only acceded the year before.

plate 81). H G Wells's Mr Polly was taken by is cousins on a walk 'to the Stainton wreckery-tion ground – that at least was what they alled it – with its handsome custodian's ottage, its Jubilee drinking fountain, its clump f wallflowers and daffodils, its charmingly rtistic notice-boards with green borders and art" lettering, and so to the new cemetery and istant view of the Surrey hills'.

Grandiose new building was not left entirely o public enterprise. Many of the theatres which had adorned country towns in the late ighteenth century had gone out of business by 860 but they now came back into fashion, and or any of those towns which had prospered conomically and wished to register its cultural retensions, a theatre seemed almost as mportant a symbol of success as a grandiose own hall.

Banks too dwindled in numbers and liversity but grew in splendour. In the 1860s rancis Kilvert used to man the Savings Bank n Hay on Thursday afternoons. Twenty years ater such amateurishness would never have been tolerated. By then the majority of small private banks, often family owned and with capital quite inadequate for the new needs of industry, had been taken over by a handful of large joint stock banks.

There were regional variations – the Royal Bank of Scotland maintained a decent showing in its own territory – but four or five names recurred again and again in Britain's high streets. Sometimes, as in Romsey or Ulverston (plates 70, 82) a suitably prestigious building was available to be taken over, more often an imposing local headquarters was constructed. The new banks had to inspire confidence in savers and to exude sobriety and dignity, so nothing too fanciful could be tolerated. Heavy classical, possibly with baroque trimmings, was the generally favoured style. Gothic was an acceptable alternative – though it perhaps seemed somewhat too rugged to win general favour among the bankers. Shopping arcades could afford more frivolity; the Leyland Arcade in Southport (plate 83) looks like the grandson of the Crystal Palace.

The bank in Ulverston, Cumbria (1912) RIGHT 82) looked as if it had aken over some existing mansion for its business, but t could hardly have found a more dominant position.

The Leyland Arcade in
Southport in 1899 RIGHT
(83) — at different periods
known as the Cambridge
Arcade and Burton's
Arcade. It looked like the
grandson of the Crystal
Palace and was the genteel
shopping centre for a genteel
town. A band used to play
to shoppers in need of a
cultural break, hence the
array of chairs.

1965 GUILDFORD HIGH STREET

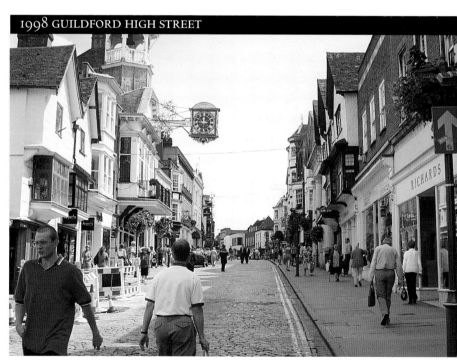

Guildford High Street in 1903 OPPOSITE ABOVE **(84)**, *1923* ABOVE **(85)**, *1965* OPPOSITE BELOW **(86)** *and 1998* RIGHT **(87)**. *The shop fronts grew brasher, the incursions of cars became more relentless, but the structure remained. Then in 1998 came rescue from the traffic with pedestrianisation of the high street. The Bull's Head has become a goldsmith's, but otherwise all is for the better.*

1928 ARUNDEL

The centre (more or less) holds,

The outskirts grow bloated

The explosion of development in town centres came in the second half of the nineteenth century. The heart of most country towns remained reasonably constant over the next sixty years or so, though too often they were then ripped apart in a rash of new development. Sequence after sequence of photographs show that the buildings remain much the same, only the coming of the motor car has changed the character of the town (plates 84-90). Encouragingly, though, contemporary photographs sometimes show the motor car banished from the scene and a more seemly appearance thereby restored.

It is on the outskirts that the fundamental change has taken place. The hero of George Orwell's *Coming Up For Air* revisited in 1939 the market town of Lower Binfield which he had last seen forty years before. From the hill outside the town he paused to look for the familiar landmarks. 'All I could see was an enormous river of brand-new houses which flowed along the valley in both directions and half-way up the hills on either

1998 ARUNDEL

1939 ARUNDEL

A compulsive urge to tidy up seemed to have afflicted the authorities in Arundel between 1928 ABOVE LEFT (88) and 1939 ABOVE RIGHT (89). The handsome balustrade on the bridge was removed and buildings that evidently incorporated old ruins had been demolished. By 1998 LEFT (90) the telegraph pole had been removed as well, to the improvement of the view.

Beacon Terrace, perched above the harbour at Torquay, was pretty much unchanged between 1888 ABOVE (91) and 1998 RIGHT (92). For nearly a century the slopes above the Terrace were also more or less inviolate, but recently the insatiable demand for tourist accommodation has led to some significant — aesthetically at least — painful development. The presence of the crane suggests worse to come.

1998 TORQUAY

side. Over to the right there were what looked like several acres of bright red roofs, all exactly alike. A big council housing estate, by the look of it. But where was Lower Binfield? Where was the town I used to know? All I knew was that it was buried somewhere in the middle of that sea of bricks.' In the distance he saw 'two enormous factories,' which he supposed accounted for the growth of population. No doubt they did, but even where enormous factories were lacking there was almost certainly an outlying industrial estate to fuel the demand for housing. In some of the larger towns, like Rochdale (plate 93), a go-ahead or deluded council supplied the need by tower blocks; more often, there was street upon street, block upon block, of neat little semi-detached boxes. Architecturally these were hardly distinguished but they were economical, well appointed, and provided room to breathe. Often they were laid out in a series of linked enclaves which gave the inhabitants a chance to create the sort of community life that was so significantly denied them in the grander tower blocks.

If there is one charge above any other that can justifiably be levelled against the British town it is that of uniformity. In the modern suburbs a degree of sameness is only to be expected but in the centre of town, too, a common culture has been imposed. Again and again the same elements recur. It seems every high street has its NatWest and its Barclay's, its bookmaker, its Woolworths and its W H Smith, its Chinese take-away, its Thresher's or Oddbins. Behind and above the familiar façades the bones of the old town are still to be found, but they often take some looking for. Montgomery and Kirriemuir, Alnwick and Truro, have a long way to go before they lose their individuality, but the pressure towards bland conformity is always there. May it long be resisted.

The Memorial Gardens in Rochdale LEFT (93). *Behind stretch the tower blocks which, when they were built, seemed to the planners to provide the answer for accommodation in the nation's overcrowded towns and cities.*

Villages

1893 ST NEOT

EVERYBODY HAS HIS OR HER VISION of the ideal village (plates 94, 95). Everybody agrees that the village is not what it used to be. It has become too large or it has become too small. It has lost its heart, it has lost its soul, it has lost its *raison d'être*, it is no longer the nucleus of English rural life, let alone provincial life. Much of this is no doubt true, but one must just decide what the village was supposed to be before it fell into such dereliction. At one end of the spectrum a village may be a tiny, architecturally homogeneous group of buildings clustered around the gates of some big house and formerly, if not today, belonging to its owner. At the other it could be a mining village of six thousand inhabitants or more; the sort of conglomeration which D H Lawrence knew so well and described in *Lady Chatterley's Lover* as 'a village which … trailed in utter hopeless ugliness for a long and gruesome mile: houses, rows of wretched, small begrimed, brick houses, with black slate roofs for lids, sharp angles and wilful, blank dreariness'. Can one generalize to any good purpose about something so infinitely varied?

There were certain minimum qualifications for a village to be so styled in the 1860s. It had to have a church, which was almost always the most prominent of its buildings (plate 96). Flora Thompson's Lark Rise had a meagre thirty cottages and its only shop was an appendage of the inn, but it might still just have passed muster if the inhabitants had not had to walk to nearby Fordlow for Sunday service. Even more decisive; the children took the same path every day to school. Fordlow was in population smaller than Lark Rise, but it had the church, the school, the rectory. Fordlow was a village, Lark Rise a mere hamlet.

THE REASON WHY IT'S THERE

As well as church and school, the pub was another invariable feature of the nineteenth-century village. So too, of course, was the shop. A photograph of Yately in Hampshire (plate 98) shows

The Cornish village of
St Neot LEFT (94), at the
very end of the nineteenth
century, was the
quintessence of what the
traditional village was
supposed to be: compact,
prosperous, picturesque,
clustered around its church
and with a fine new school
— the whole set amidst
rolling farmland. Today
BELOW (95) the view is
strikingly unchanged. The
school is now pleasantly
mellowed, the layout of the
fields and hedges appear
almost exactly as a hundred
years ago.

1998 ST NEOT

Most villages were dominated by their church. The extravagantly tall and thin tower at Quethiock in Cornwall (1908) ABOVE (96) made midgets of the children in the lane below; and left the villagers in no doubt what was the most important building.

Sometimes it was a bridge or
ford that gave a village its
origin and perhaps its name
as well. The bridge of the
Devonshire village of
Sidford (1906) LEFT (97)
is said to date from the
eleventh century; the pram is
clearly contemporary with
the picture.

More often than not the
green provided the focal
point for the village. Here at
Yately, in Hampshire
(1906) LEFT (98), the
fifteenth-century timber-
framed church, pub, shop
and bakery are all grouped
cosily around the green.

1911 RUAN MINOR

1998 RUAN MINOR

Sometimes, as in Ruan Minor in Cornwall LEFT (99), a crossroads provided the reason for the village's existence and was the point at which such activity as occurred took place (though in 1911 the cat provided the only sign of animation). In 1998 LEFT BELOW (100) the scene was almost equally as tranquil; the forge on the left had become 'The Old Forge' and a village home, but the school on the right unusually still survived in its proper role.

Most compact and homogeneous of villages were those built by — usually — benevolent employers to accommodate their work-force. Richard Arkwright's Stanley Village, near Perth (1900) ABOVE (101) was a prime example, built as an appendage to his new cotton mill. Lower Row, in Cark, on the Cartmel peninsula in Cumbria (1897) LEFT (102) was less in the style of 'model village' but was clearly there to service the mill that loomed in the distance.

nn and church and shop clustered together ound the village green. Most often it was the green which provided the nucleus of the community. Sometimes a crossroads was both he reason for the village's existence and its centre, sometimes a bridge played the same role (plates 97-100).

Other villages straggled disconsolately along a road, the church no more than the largest of the buildings, jostling for its place among its humbler brethren. A few did not even enjoy hat degree of cohesion. George Sturt described Bourne, near Farnham: 'all about the steep slopes the little, mean dwelling-places are scattered in disorder … wanting in restfulness to the eyes.' Generally the 'closed' estate villages, belonging to or at least dependent on the big house, were the more compact and better organized; the 'open' villages, either belonging to ancient freeholders or new developments of the nineteenth century, were able to enjoy their independence, but paid for the absence of a powerful patron by a measure of economic insecurity. Most compact of all were the villages built by a — usually — benevolent proprietor to house his work-force, as in Richard Arkwright's Stanley Village or at Cark in Cumbria (plates 101, 102).

The decay of the landed gentry, their wealth eroded by recurrent agricultural depressions

and taxation, their will to survive sapped by the
loss of so many sons and heirs in successive
wars, was to be a significant factor in the
disappearance of the traditional village. There
were good landlords and bad landlords, and it
is arguable that the whole system of large-scale
land-owning was regrettable in the past and
indefensible in the present, but it is hard to
deny that the existence over several centuries of
a dominant family in the big house lent
cohesion and purpose to a village.

Remove that family, substitute an Arab sheik
or a successful commodities broker, let the
house fall down or be broken up into flats, and
the focal point had gone. It might be replaced,
even improved, but things would never be the
same again.

Until the twentieth century the roads that meandered through British villages served only riders and pedestrians, farmers' carts and the occasional carriage. For most of the time they were little more than an extension of the poultry yard and a place where the children could sit and play. Axmouth in Devon (1898) LEFT **(103)**, *Wadebridge* LEFT BELOW **(104)**, *and Cadgwith in Cornwall (both 1911)* BELOW **(105)**, *were ill-prepared for the heavy demands of modern traffic.*

IT WAS THE BICYCLES AND CARS THAT CAUSED THE TROUBLE

But it was what happened on the roads that provided the greatest stimulus to change. The lanes that meandered through the nineteenth-century villages served little but riders and pedestrians, farmers' carts and an occasional carriage. For most of the time the dusty track served as an extension of the cottage poultry yard or a place where the children could safely play (plates 103-105).

In the late nineteenth century villagers walked, as a matter of course, distances that today would seem remarkable. The children of Lark Rise took it for granted that they would walk three miles a day to school at Fordlow; labourers would often have to travel five miles or more before they even reached the field or quarry where they were to work all day; if a visit to the nearest market town was necessary and there were cattle to be driven or no other means of transport was available, then a walk of eight or ten miles would be nothing out of the ordinary (plates 107, 108). Those whose

Many itinerant craftsmen or pedlars spent most of their lives on the road. This knife-grinder at Eversley in Hampshire (1906) RIGHT **(106)** *would probably have been on his way to the next village within an hour or two (for the pub's sake one must hope that an itinerant sign painter would be next to arrive).*

occupation required that they should move from village to village – the pedlar, skilled artisans like the knife-grinder or clock-mender who could not find enough business in a single locality, and the travelling entertainers: organ-grinders, ballad-mongers, animal trainers with a performing bear – might if they were prosperous enough have a pony or donkey to bear the heaviest load, but almost always they would walk beside it (plate 106).

The bicycle was the first device to breach the pattern of life established over the centuries. At first it was a plaything for the rich, but by the 1890s mass production was bringing down the price to a level that villagers could afford. With the help of a bicycle a labourer could save hours a day going to and from his place of work; he could thus increase his earnings or have more time available for his own pursuits. And those pursuits need not now be confined to the village. Until then the market town had been just that; the town to which the villagers went to market or the occasional fair. Now it became a centre of entertainment to which they could bicycle on a Saturday evening or even, if they had the energy, in the middle of the week.

Then came the motor car. The physical impact on the village of its arrival was, of course, strikingly apparent. The typical village high street was a tranquil backwater, used mainly by pedestrians, riders or carts with the very occasional coach or carriage. It was first invaded by the bicycle. Cars were a rarity before the First World War and the surface was unlikely to have been tarred until well on into the 1930s. By 1939 cars were a commonplace but the necessary infrastructure of white lines, parking bays and the other delights of a motorized society were not generally evident until the 1950s.

Until well into the twentieth century most people walked if they had to get from A to B. This Norfolk shepherd in 1929 LEFT (107) may well have had seven or eight miles to cover before he got his sheep to market; the Somerset labourer with the hay rake photographed the same year BELOW (108), could still have been far from his place of work.

1908 LYNDHURST

1934 LYNDHURST

1892 LYNDHURST

Twenty years later again if the village had the bad luck to be on the main road from A to B, the high street would have become a car-clogged hell spot. It might have been saved by a by-pass, at the cost of the neighbouring countryside, but even then it would probably still be unpleasantly crowded with the cars of residents and shoppers. More and more it seemed that Britain was being adapted to serve the car, instead of the car to serve Britain (plates 109-116).

But though the physical impact of the internal combustion engine on the village was considerable, the economic and psychological effects were far more deeply felt. The car and bus simultaneously weakened the village by making it possible for the villagers to look elsewhere for their entertainment and their supplies, and changed its nature by bringing in new classes of settlers more demanding and with wider horizons than their predecessors.

The physical impact of the motor car on the village is striking. The High Street of Lyndhurst in 1892 LEFT *(109) showed only a scattering of pedestrians. By 1908* OPPOSITE ABOVE LEFT *(110) the distinction between road and pavement became more marked with bicycles in evidence. By 1934* OPPOSITE ABOVE RIGHT *(111) cars were more conspicuous, though the street was still hardly adapted for its new users. In 1955* ABOVE LEFT *(112) there were parking bays and white lines. In 1998* ABOVE RIGHT *(113), the caravan makes its baleful mark.*

THE VILLAGE SHOP GOES TO THE WALL

One of the most obvious victims of this process was the village shop. The first half of the nineteenth century had seen an enormous increase in the number of shops to be found in British villages. By the 1870s even the tiniest village was likely to have its general store, offering a basic line of groceries as well as an assortment of draperies and perhaps a stock of ironmongery as well. The smallest of these might be run on a part-time, almost amateur basis by a housewife seeking to eke out her husband's income as a farrier or farm labourer, but these increasingly became the exception; most village general stores were serious businesses supplying all but the most *recherché* needs of the locals who patronized them. A large village, or one serving a rich farming area around it, might well boast two or three general stores of this nature, as well as a butcher, a baker, and perhaps a specialist ironmonger, usually attached to the blacksmith's forge. The squire, the doctor, the parson, might buy a few luxuries from the market town or even London, but it was taken for granted that the bulk of their wants would be met by the local shops. It would never have occurred to the villager to look elsewhere for his needs.

*Grassington in 1900
OPPOSITE (114) the square
is a pleasantly uncluttered
place in which the villagers
could congregate to gossip, or
do their business. By 1926
RIGHT (115) the trees had
grown up and seats were
provided, but motor cars
were ominously making an
appearance. In the mid-
1960s BELOW (116) the
square was clearly on the
way to becoming a car park.*

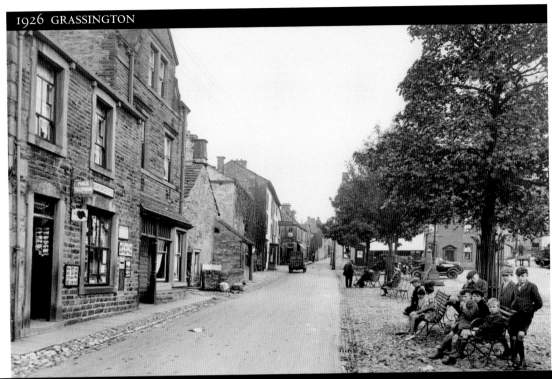

1926 GRASSINGTON

C. 1960 GRASSINGTON

The last decades of the nineteenth and the first of the twentieth were the golden age of the village shop. Windows were re-fashioned, a large range of manufactured and pre-packaged goods became available, advertisments began to appear for the better-known brands of food and drink. The bicycle and the earliest buses and motor cars seemed to open up new opportunities; people began to move about the countryside more freely and to discover the village as a place of pilgrimage where the picturesque could be worshipped and the inhabitants observed as quaint fauna in their natural habitat. Frith's postcards were just one of the wares which the village shopkeeper displayed to interest this new and potentially profitable clientele. 'Broadway is at Ye Olde game,' wrote J B Priestley indignantly when he visited the Cotswolds in the 1930s. 'The morning we passed through it was loud with bright young people who had just arrived from town … I noticed that one of Ye Olde Shoppes proudly announced that it had been established in the Nineties' (plates 117-119).

But if people were now able to look in, so were the inhabitants able to look out. As the

The village shop in Hawkshead, Cumbria, in 1912 RIGHT (117), *had new-style windows and clearly catered for the tourist trade — witness the fine display of Frith postcards.*

1873 CHEDDAR

range of manufactured goods became more extensive than the village shop could handle, the car and the bus made the journey to the market town less of an undertaking, villagers began to desert their local shops. First they went outside the village only for branded goods which they had seen in their neighbours' houses or advertised in the press and which were not to be had in the village; then they discovered that the basic commodities also were fresher and more varied in the market town. The town shops carried the battle to the villages; first occasionally by horse van, then more frequently by motor, they began to supply goods to rural customers. Mail order too weakened the dependence of the villager on his local store. With the abolition of retail price maintenance in the 1960s, advantages of scale meant that the larger shops in the market towns could undercut their village rivals. The proliferation of supermarkets made the differential still more marked. Today, it is said, five village shopkeepers are closing every day, unable to cope with the competition and unwilling to work the grossly unsocial hours which might have retained the loyalty of certain customers.

THE STRUCTURE OF THE VILLAGE BEGINS TO CRUMBLE

From the middle of the nineteenth century small branch post offices had provided a useful side-line for the local shop. At first these bobbed up everywhere – as an appendage to a blacksmith's forge, even in the back room of some village farmhouse – but increasingly they became a wing of the general store. They helped boost turnover and drew people into the shop, who took advantage of their visit to stock up with other goods. But this diversification,

The cult of the picturesque, popularized by the motor car, enriched but also endangered the British village. Cheddar, on the fringe of the awesome gorge in the Mendip Hills, was already celebrated in 1873 ABOVE (118); *by 1998* BELOW (119) *it had become a beauty spot.*

1998 CHEDDAR

too, has come increasingly under threat. Automation and the proliferation of bank accounts have meant that an increasing number of transactions by-pass the post office; the telephone, fax and E-mail have all greatly reduced the flow of letters. More and more sub-postmasters have found that their dwindling profits do not begin to justify the bureaucratic hassle, and have accordingly either resigned their roles or have been unable to find a replacement on their retirement.

The village shop was more than just a retail unit, it was a meeting-place and the centre of a network of gossip and information. Its disappearance is a blow to the very cohesion of the community.

So too is the loss of the village schools. These also reached their apogee towards the end of the nineteenth century. The reasons for their decline were partly economic, partly academic. The smaller the school, the greater the cost per pupil and the difficulty of catering for the increased range of subjects which even the primary school was supposed to cover. If there had been no alternative, the authorities would have been bound to keep open the local schools, however few the pupils or inadequate the teaching. Since the Education Act of 1944, however, transport must be provided for all pupils who live a certain distance from their school. The school bus has become a regular, and on the whole welcome, feature of the countryside. It soon proved to be far cheaper to close an ailing school and transport its pupils to the neighbouring market town than to keep it going and to build up its perhaps meagre numbers.

The population likely to support the local school anyway dwindled drastically throughout the twentieth century. Agriculture had once been at the heart of most village economies, but long before the era of set-aside,

mechanisation was reducing the number of labourers whom the farmer needed to employ. Between 1930 and 1950 alone the number of men working on British farms dropped by nearly a quarter; it is estimated today that there are more hairdressers in Britain than

agricultural labourers. The newcomers who took the farmhands' place in the village had no loyalty to village institutions and they were more ready to look elsewhere for the education of their children as well as for both their entertainment and their shopping.

Some village crafts survived. The descendants of the blacksmith at work in 1909 near Lyme Regis ABOVE *(120) could still be plying their trade today, but it is more likely that they turned their skills to motor cars or that they even abandoned the struggle altogether.*

THE VANISHING CRAFTSMEN

The fate of a mining village after the mine has closed is only the most striking example of a national phenomenon. Village economies have been wrecked over the last hundred and thirty years by the disappearance of innumerable trades in the face of competition from centralized mass production.

In 1874 the Inspector of Factories reported thriving cottage industries in the fields of lace-making, lace-clipping, chair-making, straw-plait-making, book and shoe making, winding for hosiery, knitting, gloving, button-making and slopwork. Within fifty years nearly all of these were dead except for occasional corners where the exponents of arts and crafts continued to produce their wares at high prices and for a tiny market. Basket-makers lasted a little longer than this, but by the end of the 1930s their numbers too were shrinking under the pressure of competition from abroad. Clay brick-making had been a village occupation in many areas, but before the twentieth century was far advanced mass production in the brickworks of towns like Bedford and Peterborough was driving rural rivals from the field.

These were relatively specialized pursuits, but the more general trades formerly practised in almost every village suffered also. As early as the 1890s Flora Thompson was mourning the death of the last of a family of carpenters in Candleford Green: 'Then the carpenter's shop was demolished to make way for a builder's show room with baths and tiled fireplaces and water closet pans in the window, and only the organ in the church and pieces of good woodwork in houses remained to remind those who had known them of the three Williams.' Most carpenters lasted longer than that, but the millers were in full retreat by the end of the nineteenth century. Large mills, using imported corn, produced flour at prices which the small local producer could not match, and all over the country windmills and watermills crumbled into ruin or, as the demand for housing grew, were adapted as residences for middle-class arrivals from the cities.

Some trades are still practised, though they have grown rarer and have had to modify their style to suit new needs (plates 121, 122). The thatcher has survived. He now very rarely undertakes the thatching of ricks of corn which was once a staple of his work – plastic heeting became the norm from the end of the Second World War – but houses and cottages continue to require his services. It is an expensive business today, however, and the insurance companies do not make the future of the trade any more secure by their reluctance to insure thatched properties. Blacksmiths still figure prominently in many counties, and though the banning of fox hunting, if it comes about, will deal the craft a blow, it will not perish so long as the pony club continues to hold its position in the hearts of British school-girls. But there is only a tiny number of blacksmiths working now compared with the army which existed when the horse was undisputed master of the road. Many converted their forges into garages so as to cater for the new demand, but only the larger villages can support their own motor workshops and over the years the village garage has itself become a rarity.

CHURCHES, PUBS AND VILLAGE HALLS

The church and the pub, those two stalwart institutions at the heart of the traditional village, have suffered too, though not as severely as the shop and the school. The churches are nearly all still open and many of them are in better trim – if not better frequented – than a century ago. But the rectory, often a grandiose eighteenth-century or Victorian mansion, is now the Old Rectory and occupied by some prosperous new arrival. The rector, if there is one, lives in a cramped modern bungalow – very possibly he will not be found in the village at all, for few country clergymen are today responsible for less than three or four parishes and it is anyone's guess which one will have the distinction of accommodating him. There are still fifty thousand pubs in Britain, but there were twenty thousand more in 1956 and twice as many when Francis Frith took his first photographs. The figures include urban pubs

but a high proportion of the casualties are in the villages, where a dwindling clientele has led to two pubs becoming one and then perhaps closing altogether. Ambridge is not the only village to find that potential users want more than the tepid beer and smoke-filled atmosphere that used to be the norm.

The village hall, on the other hand, has multiplied since the 1870s. Before the First World War it was a rarity; usually the gift of some rich land-owner who wished to demonstrate his benevolence towards his tenants. From 1918 onwards, however, it has become a common feature: sometimes taking the form of a tawdry ex-army hut re-erected to provide some sort of shelter, more often a bleak but adequate modern building offering facilities for games and concerts as well as meetings (plate 123). The village hall is often down-at-heels, inadequately heated, shoddily decorated, badly lit, but it still exists and offers some hope at least to those who wish to see the village survive as a living community.

EMIGRATION AND IMMIGRATION

The numbers and nature of those people differ from place to place, and the most benighted village can rapidly be transformed by a handful of enthusiasts with a gift for inducing people to work and play together. They are swimming against the tide, however. Shortage of jobs, the wish of the young to better themselves, impatience at the lack of entertainment, together mean depopulation. Towards the end of the nineteenth century the authorities seemed positively to abet this process. Between 1851 and 1901 the population of Puddletown (then, as it should be now, Piddletown) fell from 1,334 to 934. Throughout much of this period the *Dorset County Chronicle* was advertising free, or at least assisted, passages to Australia and New

Zealand. Where this emigration from the villages was matched by immigration the nature of the village changed. As the farm workers and the craftsmen deserted their cottages, so a new kind of would-be villager moved in from the towns and cities to fill their places.

The car was the most important single factor in bringing about this new migration, but it was by no means the only one. Improved conditions were another. The urban dweller demanded comforts which were not readily available in the pre-1914 village. In those days, even in the largest houses, a tolerable standard of living was only maintained by the activities of an army of domestic servants; in smaller houses and cottages there was no running water, gas or electric light, no indoor sanitation, no sort of heating except an open fire which probably smoked and was anyway inadequate at a range of more than a few feet. Except in high summer, when a picnic existence might seem tolerable for a few weeks, people from the city looked askance at rural life. Even when the car became relatively common, making fleeting visits a possibility, the state of the country roads deterred all but the most intrepid. E M Forster's Charles Wilcox, in 1910, left a cloud of dust behind him as he drove from the station at Hilton to Howard's End. 'Some of it had percolated through the open window, some had whitened the roses and gooseberries of the wayside gardens, while a certain proportion had entered the lungs of the villagers. "I wonder when they'll learn wisdom and tar the roads," was his comment.'

Gradually they learnt wisdom, or what the Wilcoxes thought was wisdom at least. Tar came to the villages. So did running water, electricity, mains drainage. So, later, did telephones and central heating. Deep freezes meant that the delights of urban cuisine could be available in a rural setting. First the wireless,

hen television, ensured that a wider range of entertainment was also to be had. For the first time it was becoming possible to experience the pleasures of country living without enduring the corresponding rigours. When the first wave of emigrants deserted their cottages they too often abandoned them to dereliction. One house in Lark Rise was left empty early in the twentieth century. By 1914 'the roof had fallen in, the yew hedges had run wild and the flowers were gone, excepting one pink rose which was shedding its petals over the ruin'. On another fifteen years and all had gone: 'only the limy whiteness of the soil in a corner of a ploughed field is left to show that a cottage once stood there'. Decay had become irreversible by the time rescue was at hand; but if the cottagers had not fled their nest until the 1920s or even the 1930s, it would most probably have been snapped up quickly and modernized for the use

of someone from the city (plates 124, 125).

Some of these new settlers became more deeply embedded than others. Most inconspicuous were those who acquired a cottage for their summer holidays – in Devon, perhaps, or the Lake District, or the Welsh hills. They would occupy their second home for a few weeks in August and perhaps at Christmas, might lend it out to friends or relations or let it for other fleeting periods; otherwise the house would stand empty, contributing nothing to the community, a natural target for schoolboy vandals or more politically activated extremists. Then, in the more accessible parts, there were the weekenders, usually coming from a city within a hundred miles or so of their chosen place of relaxation. They would arrive in a flurry late on Friday evening, spend Saturday trying to restore order in the garden, pack up on Sunday and be

The Cochrane Hall at Alva, near Stirling, in about 1960 ABOVE (123), *was an example of what a village hall could be if a benefactor and a lot of enthusiasts worked together. It was very unlike the bleak and austerely functional hut that most villages have to offer.*

on the way again. Such semi-detached residents might provide a little custom for the village shop and patronize the local pub, but for the most part they brought their supplies with them to the village and might as well not have been there for the impact that they made on local life and the countryside.

But there were also those who thought that they would spend their declining years in the country. These occupants of 'retirement homes' were often anxious, sometimes embarrassingly anxious, to play a part in the community. It was they who made efforts to maintain or recreate traditional patterns of village life; the revival of morris-dancing or mumming was almost always the work of middle-class refugees from the cities, the original inhabitants would be more likely to seek their pleasures in the nearby towns. Even the village cricket team was often dependent on the enthusiasm of immigrants or the occasional week-ender. All generalisations are suspect and never more so than in the world of sociology, but it is possible to find in many villages today two distinct communities: the recent arrivals with time and money to spare and an enthusiasm for the picturesque – be it honeysuckled cottages or the delights of folklore; and the original inhabitants, under-employed, under-paid, welcoming the wealth that their new neighbours have brought to the village but resentful of anything that seems patronizing or interfering.

NOT DEAD, BUT HAS IT LOST ITS SOUL?

Most villages have grown in the last sixty years or so. Clyst St Mary, in Devonshire, to take an example at random, had only fifty houses before 1914. Between the two World Wars it expanded, but only modestly. Since 1950 the number of houses has grown five-fold. An enormous carbuncle of modern housing now disfigures the body from which it grew. But Clyst St Mary is no worse than many others and it is considerably better than some. Contemporary village architecture has been too often drear and monotonous, paying little respect to the nature of the original. A church, a pub, a green, a few stone cottages and houses, are marooned amidst a tide of garish brick; slate or shoddy tiles jostle with straw. There is nothing new about this; as long ago as 1878 Francis Kilvert at Clyro complained of 'the hideous huge staring new cottages which dwarf and spoil the village'. But the national growth in population and the need to find homes for the over-spill from the cities has produced results more horrific than anything Kilvert could have dreamed of.

Other villages have shrunk. Those which were particularly remote, which lacked any element of the picturesque, which have lost the mine, or quarry, or fishing ground, that was the original reason for their existence, have seen their population dwindle with striking speed. Others have vanished — swallowed up in the maw of some great city and are now no more than an outer, or even inner suburb. Only the church and, with luck, a cluster of old buildings around it, mark for the casual passer-by the fact that a coherent community once enjoyed its existence on this spot.

But most villages are still recognizably what and where they have been for several centuries. The British village still exists. It will continue to exist so long as millions of people wish to live in a manageably small unit enjoying the benefits of a surrounding countryside. But it is now no more than that — a place of residence which has no obvious economic reason to be where it is and is no longer self-contained or self-reliant. Its body may not yet be mould'ring in the grave, but it is a matter for debate whether its soul will go marching on.

At the turn of the century, country cottages were often allowed to crumble into ruins. In another fifteen years this Herefordshire cottage (1899) ABOVE *(124) could have been no more than a mound of earth — though its stone and brick construction gave it a better chance than if of frailer materials. Gumfreston Mill in Dyfed* RIGHT *(125) was clearly beyond redemption when photographed in 1890.*

Coast & Countryside

THE MOST NOTABLE THING that has happened to Britain's coasts and countryside since the 1860s is that cities and towns, villages and roads, have encroached upon them. If Francis Frith were to survey the countryside today, his first reaction would be dismay that so much had disappeared. Only after he had had time to consider the history of the British Isles over the intervening years might he begin to rejoice that so much had survived.

Between 1880 and 1920 Frith might not so much have feared that the country would be overwhelmed by the towns, as that nobody would be prepared to live there. The agricultural depression led to unemployment or, for the luckier ones, long hours and poor pay. Landlords could

Depressed conditions between 1880 and 1914 meant that landlords could not afford to maintain the cottages on their estates and many country people lived in conditions of unhealthy squalor. The cottage smothered in creepers near Frimley in Surrey OPPOSITE (126), *the crofters' cottages at Glencoe* RIGHT (127), *the farmhouse on the outskirts of Dorchester (now entirely disappeared)* BELOW (128) *— photographed in 1906, 1899 and 1894 respectively — may have looked admirably picturesque but must have been cold, damp and without facilities.*

not afford to put their tenants' houses in order; countrymen often lived in conditions of unhealthy squalor (plates 126-128). The expansion of factories and rail transportation for their products killed cottage industries; there had been thousands of chair-makers scattered around the villages of the Chilterns in 1880, by 1914 there were virtually none. The thatcher, the blacksmith, the peat-cutter, the charcoal burner, all the traditional crafts that had supported the economy of the countryside were losing ground as new techniques and new materials stole their markets (plates 129-132). Thomas Hardy recorded that within a year a third of the pupils at his local Dorset school had disappeared, following their parents to the cities. Between 1911 and 1913 nearly half a million country dwellers abandoned the battle and fled to the cities or abroad; among them many of the most active and ambitious. And this was before the mechanisation of agriculture had really begun to take its toll of employment on the farms.

And yet simultaneously the towns were growing and their surplus population was flowing out, colonizing areas of virgin country, swamping nearby villages. The only obstacle to unending expansion was that the new residents had to get to work, unless a railway line ran conveniently close and a train stopped near enough, the horse, the bicycle or a pair of legs were the only means of transport. It was not till after 1918 that the real invasion of the countryside began. By then Britain had long been the most urbanized nation in the world and, though it did not wholly recognize the fact, had ceased to be an agrarian society. By 1901 only twelve percent of employed men worked on the land and the proportion fell every year as more and more of the nation's food was imported.

The collapse of farm revenues was as damaging to the land-owner as to the farmworker. The big house could no longer play its part in keeping the estate together; it

In many parts of England, even as late as 1910 when this photograph LEFT (130) *was taken, the thatcher was often more in demand than the tiler. Here he was preparing the reeds; for eventual use, probably, on the cottage in the background.*

Collecting seaweed on the sands of Inverary in 1890 LEFT **(129)**. *Probably the weed would have been used for eating, though the value of certain varieties as a source of iodine and potassium was already recognized.*

was not just the farm cottages that grew bedraggled, the roof of the manor house was leaking too. Sometimes the squire struggled on, sometimes he left his house to rot or sold out to a businessman or banker. With so many of the natural heirs dead on the battlefields of the First World War, the urge to hold on at all costs was sadly diminished. With characteristic sentimentality Dornford Yates deplored the fate of Sir Anthony Bagot, who was forced to sell his family estate, Merry Down, to 'a terrible fellow', a wartime profiteer called Dunkelsbaum. 'One of the old school, Sir Anthony had stood his ground up to the last. The War cost him dear. His only son was killed in the first months. His only grandson fell in the battles of the Somme. His substance, never fat, had shrunk to a mere shadow of its former

self. The stout old heart fought the unequal fight month after month. Stables were emptied, rooms were shut up, thing after thing was sold. It remained for a defaulting solicitor to administer the *coup de grâce.*' At the last moment another purchaser appeared, with 'good clean hands' and of English stock, best of all an

Charcoal burning in the New Forest near Lyndhurst BELOW **(131)**. *By 1955, when this scene was recorded, the craft was already becoming something of a rarity.*

Etonian. Merry Down was saved. No doubt Dunkelsbaum bought the next-door estate, and with luck invested some badly needed capital.

THE CONSERVATION CAMPAIGN BEGINS

Depopulation and economic decay on one side, an ever more pervasive invasion from the urban areas on the other, the prospects for the British countryside looked bleak between the wars. But there were forces which sought to resist the trend. As early as 1865 the Commons Preservation Society had been founded to save the commons around London: Hampstead Heath, Epping Forest. Ten years later the protection was extended to rural commons. Rights of way – the immemorial paths which the countrymen had used to go about their business – were another concern of the Commons Preservation Society. It was largely by their doing that hikers organized mass trespasses in the Peak District and that the Rights of Way Bill was introduced in 1932. Today there are well over 100,000 rights of way in England and Wales alone. The National Trust was set up in 1895, at first concentrating on areas of particular beauty which it sought to acquire and preserve for the nation, only later extending its interest to the country houses with which it is now most often associated. The Council for the Preservation of Rural England (C.P.R.E.), dating from 1926, left the ownership of property to the Trust and instead constituted itself a ginger group to make the public aware of how much they were in danger of losing and to press those in power to do something about it before it was too late.

THE AGE OF THE MOTOR CAR HAD COME

It was almost too late. The age of the motor car had come. All over the British Isles main roads ere constructed, minor roads widened and barred; always the motor car filled whatever space was provided for it and demanded more besides. The roads at first had little in the way of markings, lay-bys and lavatories were hardly dreamt of, but the commuting businessman took advantage of his new liberty to thrust out ever further into the countryside. In the short term he found the privacy and open country which he sought; in the longer term he ensured that privacy and the open country were lost to all. On his heels, but pushing ever further onwards, came the week-ender. The term 'weekend' had been coined in the 1880s: till then the sedate Saturday-to-Monday passed in the grand house of some relative or friend had been all that was permissible as a brief break from the city; now the realisation dawned that one could own one's own house or cottage and spend relaxing weekends as temporary country folk. Finally came the retired: still less restricted as to distance from the city but more concerned to be close to decent shops and, as they grew older, hospitals. Unlike most commuters the retired made a real effort to integrate themselves with the community, but their livelihood did not depend on the countryside; they were intruders – well-intentioned, no doubt; a useful source of income; but fragmenting the life of the very community which they believed they were helping to preserve.

Many countrymen disliked the roads and the cars that came with them. In Winifred Holtby's *South Riding* a Yorkshire farmer, told of a plan for a new road, exclaimed angrily: 'Stamp on it! Nonsense! Waste of money. We've got the whole place splintered with motor roads now. Can't keep a horse on its feet. Hopeless for farmers.' But stamp as he might the road still nearly always came. The economic pressure was too powerful. 'As things now stand there would

seem to be no prospect of survival through the coming years, nor will there be any Sussex anymore,' wrote Hilaire Belloc in 1936 with characteristic gloom.

Ribbon development

And with the new roads came ribbon development. The trouble was that a house set back a little way from a main road, in a period when the traffic was still relatively light, with easy access on one side and an uninterrupted view of the open country on the other, was a pleasant solution for the owner who wanted to get quickly to town but still enjoy rustic living. So the houses mushroomed, the trees were cut down, the gaps between houses were lined with billboards. On the fringes of town road-houses offered easily accessible delights to gratify the insatiable appetite of the urban dweller. 'At the present rate,' predicted the Design and Industries Association in 1930, 'the road traveller from London to any important city will be *entirely* cut off from the country (except where the road crosses a public common) within a dozen years or so.'

Virtually no control was exercised over where the developer built or the standards he observed. The result was that shoddy and pretentious houses were run up at the place where it was cheapest to do so and the largest profit could be made – where existing roads made it unnecessary for the developer to construct his own. In Evelyn Waugh's *Vile Bodies* Nina Blount embarks in an aeroplane with her future husband, Ginger. Ginger observes the landscape and began to quote: 'This sceptered isle, this earth of majesty …' Wasn't that appropriate? he asked. 'Nina looked down and saw inclined at an odd angle a horizon of straggling red suburb; arterial roads dotted with little cars; factories, some of them working, others empty and decaying; a disused canal;

some distant hills sown with bungalows; wireless masts and overhead cables … "I think I'm going to be sick," said Nina.'

Not only the roads were ribbon developed. Though the establishments were grander and the inhabitants for the most part richer, the villas which began to spring up along the banks of the Thames and other rivers towards the end of the nineteenth century differed little in spirit from the bungalows along the highway. There was worse to come, the successful stockbroker led the way with a grand façade and spacious lawns sloping down towards the river, his clerk or a local shopkeeper followed suit with what was little more than a shack squashed between the larger properties. As with the developments by the roadside, they destroyed the amenities of the country for all others.

Farmland and forest dwindle

Most of the development took place in the fertile valleys. The farmer, who found it hard to make a living, often jumped at the chance to sell his land to a speculative builder; when a new road was in question he was anyway given little chance to refuse. By the mid-1930s, sixty thousand acres a year were being lost to agriculture. The forests dwindled too. During the Napoleonic Wars the demands of ship-building had led to much prime hardwood being felled, but at least the owners of the forest had seen good economic arguments for planting more. By the late nineteenth century iron had taken the place of timber in ship-building, coke had replaced charcoal in smelting, even the tan bark used in the leather trade had given way to chemical substitutes. Hardwood planting dwindled and ninety percent of Britain's softwood requirements were imported. This led to panic in the First World War – Lloyd George remarked that we were more likely to lose the war for lack of timber than for lack of food – and in 1917 it was recommended that two million acres of softwood should be planted. Vast swathes of conifer began to cover hillsides which had been grazed by sheep or goats throughout the centuries; when oak, beech or elm perished they were replaced by pines, firs and larches. The new forests were envisaged as an economic resource; no thought was given to making them beautiful or providing public access – on the contrary, because conifers caught fire and burnt so easily, the public was often vigorously excluded. The traditional pattern of field, hardwood hedge and copse seemed to be giving way to a harsher landscape of open field interspersed with solid blocks of conifers.

Rather more thought was given to aesthetics when it came to meeting increased demands for water. The growing population and the rapacious appetite of industry meant that the traditional sources of water were proving totally inadequate by the mid-nineteenth century. New reservoirs were needed in large numbers. Compared with the acreage required for buildings, the requirements of the water industry were comparatively modest, but the new reservoirs were often called for in the most tranquil and agriculturally prosperous valleys and, since they were built for the benefit of far-away communities, they were viewed with outrage by the luckless inhabitants whose homes and fields were drowned in the process. Some of the new developments were on a grandiose scale and endowed with building of commensurate magnificence; Birmingham's reservoirs in the Elan valley among the Welsh hills were a statement of civic pride as telling as any Gothic town hall or Grecian art gallery. Such extravagances did little to reconcile those who had lost their homes or fields but they at least provided a striking spectacle for visitors (plates 133-136).

In 1955 Ladybower Reservoir RIGHT (135) *in the Peak District looked well established but only recently the village of Derwent-Woodlands had vanished under its waters. In 1998* FAR RIGHT (136) *sheep were still to be seen, but the new road was a threat to their survival.*

Some of the new reservoirs built towards the end of the nineteenth century were huge in size, and had dams and buildings that were commensurately grandiose. The Vyrnwy (1960) LEFT (133) and the Careg Ddu (1955) BELOW (134) dams, both in Powys, were splendid to behold. But they served the needs of distant Birmingham, and the Welsh farmer who had been displaced could be forgiven for greeting their arrival with something short of total enthusiasm.

ADYBOWER RESERVOIR

1998 LADYBOWER RESERVOIR

Villas on the Windermere lakeside at Biskey How RIGHT (137). *The photograph was taken in 1887, thirty-seven years after the death of Wordsworth. He had inveighed passionately against the creation of such 'discordant objects, disturbing that peaceful harmony'. It is ironic that the Lake Poets should have contributed so much to the area's popularity.*

The pleasure of enjoying the countryside on foot has always been a minority sport, but the size of the minority has grown enormously. The walkers on the Wrekin in 1965 BELOW (138) *were part of an ever-swelling multitude. The picnickers on the rocks near Liskeard in 1890* OPPOSITE (139) *were doing something modestly unusual at that time.*

THE GOVERNMENT COMES TO THE RESCUE

The speed with which Britain's countryside was being contaminated at last convinced the authorities that something must be done to supplement the efforts of private bodies like the Council for the Preservation of Rural England and the National Trust. An Act of 1935 checked, if it did not totally prevent, ribbon development along British roads. In 1930 the first 'Green Belt' was introduced around London, a belated but still welcome measure to stop the relentless spread of the city over ever-wider areas of countryside. The idea spread after the Second World War; the cynic might doubt its efficacy, but without the Green Belt the situation would be far worse and the inhabitants of British cities denied any access to the countryside without first undertaking a lengthy journey. The concept of National Parks, areas of outstanding beauty designated for public use and in which any kind of development was strictly controlled, reinforced the conservationist campaign (plate 137). The idea was first mooted in the 1920s but did

not become law until 1947. It was then quickly implemented and today there are ten parks in England and Wales, with Hampshire's New Forest and the Norfolk Broads as honorary first cousins. The scheme did not apply to Scotland and Northern Ireland, but similar if less stringent rules apply there; in Scotland twelve percent of the country has been listed as being of outstanding beauty and is thus subject to special controls.

THE COUNTRYSIDE AS A PLACE OF ENTERTAINMENT

The establishment of the National Parks recognized officially what was already apparent; that the countryside was not just a place where people lived and worked but was a source of entertainment for the vast urban majority. In the *Architects' Journal* in 1965 Michael Dower suggested that four great waves had broken across the face of Britain in the last two centuries: the Industrial Revolution, the railway, the motor car, and, most recently and perhaps most dangerously of all, leisure. Professor C E M Joad, one of the B.B.C.'s Brains Trust, said of his contemporaries that they had found a land of beauty and left a land of beauty spots (plates 138-151). The Lake District is an early and prime example. Ironically the Lake Poets, Wordsworth in particular, who so prized its wild grandeur, were in part responsible for its popularisation. Thanks to them, pilgrims flocked to the area in the late nineteenth century; but the flocks were small and consisted principally of amateur water-colourists, undergraduates on reading parties, curates in climbing boots. The true influx did not begin until the age of the motor car. Now it seems

The waterfall near Ingleton in Yorkshire (1929) LEFT (140), the mill-pond in Cumbria (1923) OPPOSITE BELOW (142), the small boy perched on the rocks above Ilkley Moor (1914) OPPOSITE ABOVE (141), were all part of the discovery of nature which the urban population of Britain experienced in the early twentieth century. Sadly, like 'W J' on the right-hand rock at Ilkley, too many of them were determined to leave their mark.

uncheckable, in summer covering all the more accessible areas with ant-like hordes of tourists. The Lake Poets have become an industry: 'The Lake District had been turned into Britain's first theme park,' wrote Jonathan Raban. And it was not only the land that was overrun. Fourteen thousand power boats are now registered for use on Lake Windermere, often fifteen hundred or more in action at one time.

Battle was joined between those who used the land and those who wanted only to enjoy it. The tourists, claimed the farmer, trampled crops, left open gates, let their dogs worry sheep, started fires; the farmers, retorted the tourists, put barbed wire and 'No trespassing' signs along traditional rights of way, let bulls or dangerous dogs loose in their vicinity, removed the signs that would have steered the traveller in the right direction. When the tourists took root and began to buy as holiday homes the cottages that the local population needed but could not afford, then resentment became still sharper. In some areas a political dimension was added to the social. It is only a

few years since the homes of English holiday-makers in Wales were targeted for destruction by angry nationalists; no one can be certain a new wave of violence will not recur there or elsewhere. The English had always invaded the Highlands of Scotland in the summer, but they came to fish, to shoot, to stalk in the hills. In their own way they used the land and employed local labour to help them. The new visitors used little except the local supermarket and whatever petrol they needed for their caravans.

TOURISM IS HERE TO STAY

Certain areas of the country are in summer almost overwhelmed by tourism. The shorter working week, longer and paid holidays, rising incomes, increased mobility, have fed the appetites of the British traveller: many go abroad, but so do many foreigners visit British beauty spots. The Lake District is not unique; Devon receives nearly four million visitors a year and the West Country as a whole is a prime beneficiary – or perhaps victim – of the relentless tide. Caravans, some nomadic, many semi-permanent and let by the week to holiday-makers, have taken over former open spaces (plates 152, 153). Well over a million people sleep in caravans every summer night; their encampments are sometimes well concealed but little can blight a landscape so effectively as row upon row of metal boxes, windscreens glinting in the sun, televisions at the ready.

However the nostalgic may deplore the fact, tourism is now an essential part of the economy for many areas. A Cornish farmer told Anthony Smith: 'Well, I'd tried barley in

1891 RHUDDLAN CASTLE

beauty spot must expect
be tidied up and adorned
with helpful notices.
Rhuddlan Castle on the
River Clwyd no doubt
needed some remedial work,
but the sanitized ruins of
1955 RIGHT (144), and
still more of ten years later
RIGHT BELOW (145), lack
the ivied splendour of 1891
OPPOSITE (143).

1955 RHUDDLAN CASTLE

1965 RHUDDLAN CASTLE

this field, and then it was pigs, and then it was beef for fattening. None had been very profitable but I'd heard tell down the road of something that was … I've got nine acres now with tents and I wish I could have another ninety-nine. Then I'd get rid of everything else because it's the best crop I've ever known.' Many thousands of small farms bridge the gap between viability and disaster by offering bed-and-breakfast to the passing visitor. The countryside as leisure centre has come to stay, all one can hope for is adequate control so that

1876 HARLECH CASTLE

greed and irresponsibility are not allowed to destroy the amenity by which they profit.

The problem is that, for the good of the countryside, there are too many people with too much money and increasing expectations. Professor Sir Joseph Hutchinson, President of the British Association, declared in 1966 that 'this country already carried a population as great as the environment can support without degeneration,' and called for a limit to growth. It has taken a long time but something near stability in population seems now to have been achieved – the same is not true, however, of the money and the expectations. Every year huge tracts of land still fall prey to the urban

developer. The government contemplates the construction of some four million new homes; no doubt some of these will be on vacant city sites but many more will be on virgin country. The rumour is that up to a thousand square miles of countryside may be at risk, even the hitherto sacrosanct green belts seem to be under threat.

OPEN SPACES CAN SOMETIMES BE RECAPTURED

There are items on the credit side as well. Large stretches of land have over the centuries been accumulated by the armed services for bases, airfields, training. Conservation was hardly a

The encroachments on Harlech Castle were relatively slight between 1876 LEFT (146) and 1960 BELOW (147), but the farm buildings and piggery on the plain below sadly marred the view.

1960 HARLECH CASTLE

factor in their minds at the time but the result of their benign neglect is that some 600,000 acres, an area the size of Dorset, have been saved from serious development. The land-holding aspirations of the Ministry of Defence have not shrunk in proportion to the size of the services but little by little they have been forced to hand back parts of their empire to its rightful owners, the British people, or at least to share it with them. Travellers across Salisbury Plain from time to time see the red flag flying that indicates tanks are on the move or that shells may fall at any moment, but at least if no flag flies most of the Plain is open. But there are areas which cannot be so readily surrendered. At the end of 1942 Gruinard Island off the coast of Wester Ross was taken over for research into biological warfare and sown with anthrax spores. Fifty-seven years later it is still said to be a minefield of poison. The passing yachtsman or fisherman may wonder whether its innocent-looking pastures

are as lethal as the authorities would have them believe, but few would be bold enough to put their doubts to the test.

Deserted coal-fields, once hideous black scars or buboes on the earth's surface, have been levelled, grassed over and returned to farming or recreational use (plate 392). Gravel pits have been landscaped and converted into lakes. The coast of Durham, once in large part devoted to the extraction and shipment of coal, is now being cleaned up and made a place where human beings might wish to go. Reforestation, which was beginning to languish when the Second World War reminded the authorities how dangerously dependent we were on imported timber, has been vigorously renewed. A third of Britain's standing timber was felled between 1939 and 1945 but subsequently, indeed for the first time in a century, the trend has been reversed.

In the more remoter areas, depopulation continues. Three quarters of rural households

The 'First and Last House' at Land's End stands witness to the march of tourism. In 1893 ABOVE LEFT (148) it was still a simple hut, by 1927 ABOVE MIDDLE (149) it had more than doubled in size and a brash notice disfigured its wall, by 1955 ABOVE RIGHT (150) it had grown again and the dread word 'Gifts' was now added to the list of delights it had to offer. In 1998 LEFT (151) it is superficially much the same, but the crowds around it hint at the vast car park a mile away and the railway that links the various elements of the 'Land's End Experience'.

have a car, but for those who have not, the problems of daily life become ever more intractable. The farm labourer might have been content with his tied cottage several miles from the nearest village but his wife proved less amenable. The labourer left or was made redundant; his cottage decayed or was sold to a would-be week-ender. The pattern was not invariable – overall, rural areas in the South West and East Anglia have grown in population – but in the Highlands of Scotland, the Welsh mountains, even the Lake District, the decline continues.

THE THREAT TO THE COASTS

Coastal areas rarely fell victim to depopulation but they suffered enough damage from other causes. The seas are capricious, they build up as well as destroy. The Wash is silting up, already nearly half its area is visible at low tide and the permanent gains are substantial. But more often the sea takes away (plates 155-157). Dunwich

Bewdley Caravan Park in Worcestershire in 1955 TOP **(152)**. *On the whole caravan parks today are less ramshackle than this nomadic encampment, but as the site at Ladran Bay near Otterton in South Devon* ABOVE **(153)** *attests, row upon row of metal boxes can effectively blight a landscape.*

is the classic example; a once thriving port on the Suffolk coast, it has been eaten away so that now only the most peripheral remains survive. It is said that on stormy nights the church bells can be heard tolling mournfully under the water; they might be tolling for a hundred other vanished ports around the nation's coast. If global warming raises the sea level to the extent predicted by the gloomier prophets, a hundred could become a thousand. More often the damage was done by men. For centuries they have treated the sea as a convenient bin in which sewage and every kind of refuse could be deposited, the beaches were encrusted with flotsam and jetsam, slicks of oil escaped from passing ships, fouled the rocks and sand, and destroyed every kind of creature that lived among them. As with the former coal-fields, things are getting better. The authorities are now more responsible about the discharge of waste products untreated into the water, some of the worst rubbish dumps and dilapidated buildings have been swept away. But the coasts of Britain would be healthier and more beautiful if man had never come there.

Behind the beaches things were little better (plates 158-161). The coast proved a magnet for many thousands who felt they deserved a place beside the sea but lacked the money to install themselves in a seaside resort, still less to build a proper house elsewhere. The newcomers squatted on, or perhaps rented, a piece of land within easy reach of the water. There they built some sort of squalid shack, or brought a disused bus or railway carriage to the site. Peacehaven, on the Sussex coast, was the most notorious example; a shanty town populated originally by veterans from the First World War. Little tarred bungalows with tin roofs paraded backwards, gardens scratched in the chalk, dry flower beds like Saxon emblems carved on the

downs …' wrote Graham Greene. The village 'dwindled out against the downs; half made streets turned into grass tracks'. But Peacehaven was a stately metropolis compared with some of its imitators scattered along the south coast, and in the north of the country too.

In her novel *South Riding*, Winifred Holtby described one of these settlements on the cliffs of Yorkshire. It consisted of 'two railway coaches, three caravans, one converted omnibus, and five huts of varying sizes and designs. Around these human habitations leaned, drooped and squatted other minor structures, pig-sties, hen-runs, a goat-house and, near the hedge, half a dozen tall narrow cupboards like up-ended coffins, the cause of unending indignation to the sanitary inspectors.'

That was in 1936, and by then the sanitary inspectors were not the only officials to be

The Downs just behind Beachy Head, photographed in 1912 BELOW (154), show that even a renowned beauty spot need not necessarily be overwhelmed by visitors. But the moth-eaten appearance of the Downs makes it clear how vulnerable the thin layer of soil above the chalk was to the depredations of both man and animal.

1924 HALLSANDS

In the twenty years or so before 1924 when this photograph of North Hallsands on Start Bay in Devonshire ABOVE (155) *was taken the sea had drowned the neighbouring village of South Hallsands. By 1998* RIGHT (156) *the sea had chipped away at the cliff face, but this does not appear to have deterred some bold owner from extending his premises. May his faith be rewarded.*

1998 HALLSANDS

oncerned about this invasion of Britain's coastline. Increasingly the authorities tried to check the incursions, but though they slowed them they could not control them altogether. Some of the new settlements, indeed, graduated to respectability; acquired permanent houses, shops, roads, even a church; were formally registered on the map.

Then came the Second World War. The coast became Britain's front line, the army moved in and temporary settlements were obliterated to make way for defences. For several years the beaches were festooned with rolls of barbed wire; monstrous concrete bollards were erected to impede the advance of enemy tanks; pill boxes lined the adjacent cliffs. Some of these proved difficult to get rid of at the end of the war, but one problem at least had been solved. In the course of time some of the former settlers tried to return but, except in a few selected sites, found their way blocked. The Town and Country Planning Act precluded temporary structures and it strictly controlled the building of anything more permanent.

The coastline was not saved. No government had the right to deny the British people access to the sea, and the caravan camps that lurk a little way inland behind so many of the most beautiful cliffs and beaches show that no government was going to be foolish enough to try. Nor could there be a total ban on the growth of seaside towns or the creation of new settlements. But much was achieved. The designation of certain areas as 'Heritage Coasts' ensures that more than a thousand miles of particularly beautiful coastline were guaranteed protection; the National Trust's 'Operation Neptune' is dedicated to adding more threatened areas to the tally. Things could be a great deal worse. Frith would think about the coasts as he did about the countryside as a whole: how tragic that so much has been lost but how remarkable that so much survives.

One of the greatest of the South Coast's headlands, Beachy Head LEFT **(157)**, *has withstood the winds and storms with more conviction, but even here rock falls are not infrequent.*

The twentieth century encroached on even the most sacred scenes, here at Dover. The great view along the front at Dover to the castle on the cliffs beyond was pretty well maintained between 1899 ABOVE (158) and 1908 OPPOSITE ABOVE (159) and again until 1924 RIGHT (160), but by 1965 OPPOSITE BELOW (161) a block of flats, offensively out of proportion with the other buildings, marred the prospect. On the other hand, people had shed their hats, so something had improved.

1924 DOVER

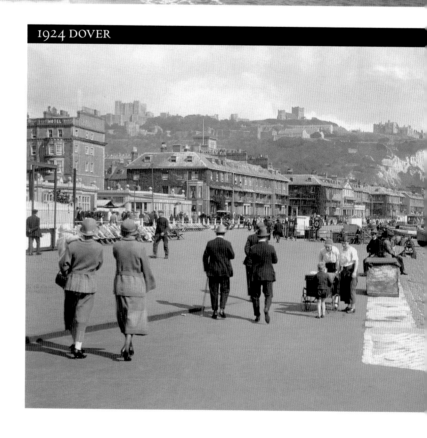

PART TWO

The British

at work and play

4

Advertising

ADVERTISING, on anything approaching the scale which is implied by the word today, requires a market of some size and sophistication. The street vendor who called out to tell potential customers of his presence, the pawnbroker or barber who hung the symbols of their trade outside their shop, were advertising, but they were not prepared to spend much money on it or to devote any thought or effort into devising original ways of attracting people to what they had to offer. Only when there were large quantities of goods to dispose of as well as rival products to compete with did it become necessary for the merchant to go out into the world actively to sell his wares.

In the eighteenth century, as newspapers became more widely distributed, the practice grew of inserting discreet announcements about a new consignment of tea or a fresh range of patterns, that were available through some local retailer. Next came the bill-poster, a larger version of the newspaper advertisement which could be stuck on a wall for all to see. Then, in the 1870s, technical developments made it reasonably cheap to reinforce the text of such announcements with eye-catching coloured designs. At first manufacturers bought up the rights to pictures by celebrated artists – Pears Soap, for instance acquiring and energetically exploiting Sir John Millais' 'Bubbles' – but paintings which were both apposite and dramatic were hard to come by, and more and more manufacturers commissioned artists to prepare posters intended from the start to promote a particular product. Once the posters existed, competition became feverish to capture the best sites in which to exhibit them. By 1872 two hundred men in London alone were jostling for space on the walls of the city, 'ladder men', who specialized in placing their posters high up where everybody could see them, were especially prized and well paid (plates 163, 164).

Posters were not the only device available; sandwichmen or 'boardmen' were, sometimes still are, to be seen on city streets (plates 165-167). They were miserably paid and generally despised; there were no such creatures in the Five Towns, wrote Arnold Bennett: 'in that democratic and independent neighbourhood nobody would deign to be a sandwichman'.

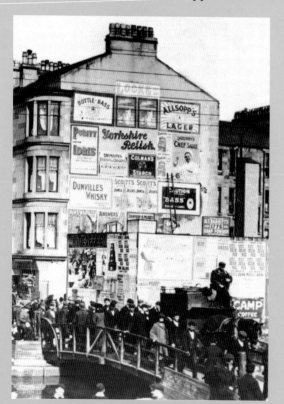

In the late nineteenth century 'ladder men' were hired to cover the walls with posters extolling certain products. In Kilbowie Road in Clydebank LEFT **(163)** *posters, in 1900, were orientated towards varieties of alcohol. At the Alhambra Theatre in 1899* OPPOSITE **(164)** *advertisements for tobacco, table salt, newspapers and boots and shoes rubbed shoulders with announcements of new plays and musicals.*

The horse and cart at Skegness PREVIOUS PAGES **(162)** *was used to ferry passengers dry-shod from the boat in the background to the dry sand. The boys in the picture took a more robust attitude to wet feet.*

A London 'boardman' in 1877 BELOW **(165)**. *They were miserably paid and generally held to be among the lower forms of working life — a view confirmed by this melancholy picture. They still survive today — as the somewhat tacky specimens from Bournemouth* RIGHT **(166)** *and* FAR RIGHT **(167)** *make all too evident.*

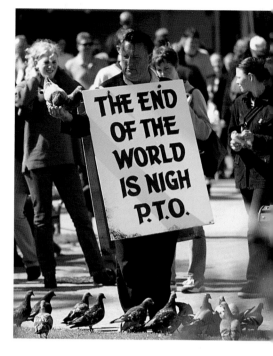

Enamel signs were more expensive to produce than paper posters but lasted for longer. Horse-buses were deemed particularly suitable. The bus nearest to the camera in 1900 RIGHT **(168)** *concentrated on a single product, but its rival to the right preferred a measure of diversity.*

Nor was the poster the ideal medium. It was vulnerable to the assaults of unscrupulous rivals and deteriorated fast in bad weather. Though more expensive and less flexible, the enamel sign was easy to install and would still be there months or even years later. Horse-buses were particularly suitable for this treatment and looked quite as much like an itinerant advertising hoarding as any bus on city streets today (plates 168-171).

THE RETAILERS ENDEAVOUR TO GET ADVERTISING ON THE MOVE

It was the buccaneer entrepreneurs of the retail trade who gave advertising its greatest stimulus. No one was more innovative or more energetic

This horse-drawn bus in the City in 1897 RIGHT (170) advertised a bewildering variety of soaps, pills and powders. Its modern Edinburgh equivalent ABOVE (169) shows that the value of a bus as an advertising medium is as great as ever.

than the great grocer, Thomas Lipton. It was he who pioneered advertising on the sides of trains and buses, he who first substituted for the restrained and dingy signs above his rivals' shops, a bold and eye-catching fascia board that read 'LIPTON'S MARKET'. He introduced American techniques and seemed to initiate a new stunt almost every week: the world's largest cheese, cheeses which every so often contained a golden sovereign; processions of thin men carrying banners reading 'Going to Lipton's' crossing processions of fat men whose banner read 'Coming from Lipton's'. Certain posters were so wide-spread and so well-known that they became a part of natural life; the jolly fishermen extolling the virtues of bracing Skegness and Tom Browne's red-coated

Johnny Walker were everywhere at the beginning of the twentieth century. Soap was a commodity which made particularly effective use of advertising, so was tea – it seemed that no grocer's window or railway platform, however insignificant, was complete without its tribute to Twining, Lyons or, of course, the inevitable Lipton's (plates 172-176).

The very success of the new medium caused it problems. The free-for-all on urban walls and the tendency to embellish every rural highway with intrusive hoardings, alarmed those who were concerned for the appearance of the country. The object of advertising was to make placards visible to as many people as possible; not surprisingly advertisers picked sites which would be conspicuous, with scant regard to the

Soap was a commodity pushed particularly hard by advertisers. Lever's Sunlight Soap led the market; here BELOW (**171**) *its glories were extolled on a horse-drawn bus in Sheffield in 1870 .*

Lever's Sunlight Soap was even more prominent on bathing machines on the North Beach at Blackpool in 1870 ABOVE (172). 'Sensation' Soap also figured in Blackpool twenty years later, this time on the South Pier RIGHT (173).

Tea was another intensively competitive market; retailers were sometimes rewarded handsomely for their loyalty to one particular brand. Lyons, Twining, and Lipton's were frequently displayed; seen here respectively at Chawton in Hampshire in 1928 ABOVE LEFT (174); at a grocer's in Bridge Street, Leatherhead in 1899 ABOVE (175); at Witley Station in Surrey in 1908 LEFT (176).

Advertisers strove to make their signs as conspicuous as possible, with scant regard to aesthetic considerations. Examples show the impact of Brooks & Sons, Drapers, on Glastonbury High Street in 1909 TOP **(177)**, *Ind Coope's beer in Milford, Derbyshire in 1955* ABOVE **(178)**, *and Fry's Cocoa on the post office at Clandon in 1911* OPPOSITE TOP **(179)**.

surrounding scenery or any other aesthetic consideration (plates 177-180). In 1893 a National Society for Checking the Abuse of Public Advertising was set up; it failed to secure the passage of a bill which would have prohibited the posting of bills in public places in rural areas but it managed to secure powers for local authorities which enabled them to curb excesses like the projecting of advertisments on to Nelson's Column in Trafalgar Square or on to the dome of St Paul's. In 1907 the Advertisments Regulation Act gave local authorities the power to refuse permission for hoardings to be erected – it only applied to hoardings more than twelve feet high but at least it was a start.

By then advertising had been accepted by even the stuffiest of manufacturers and retailers as a legitimate and necessary part of marketing. The advertising agency had become an acceptable alternative to the Bar or journalism

The plethora of signs and advertisements which adorned the Old Oak Tree restaurant in Cobham, Surrey, in 1911 RIGHT (180), was a fine example of the sort of mess which dismayed anyone concerned about the appearance of Britain's roads. The old oak tree itself was pretty much a mess too.

for the bright young graduate with a gift for words, a hundred thousand people were employed some way or other in the fledgling industry. But it was not until the First World War, when advertising was enlisted to work in the national interest, that it ceased to be a slightly raffish and peripheral undertaking and entered the mainstream of public life. For four years the walls of Britain were bestrewn with placards enjoining citizens to be economical, diligent, patriotic. One image more than any other evokes the atmosphere of that period:

the poster of Lord Kitchener, eyes glaring madly, moustache luxuriantly menacing, hand raised in exhortation, calling on BRITONS to rally to the nation's flag in the hour of need: 'JOIN YOUR COUNTRY'S ARMY! GOD SAVE THE KING.'

THE AGE OF THE HOARDING

Between 1918 and 1939, when the industry still enjoyed the respectability earned by its wartime service and a huge variety of new products became available to stimulate the

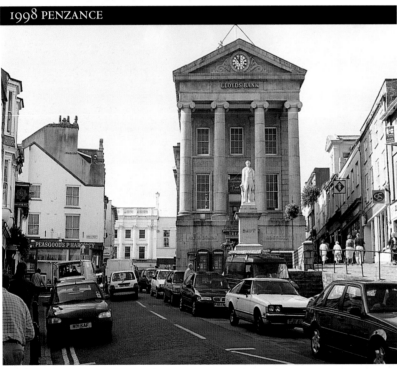

But on the whole things have got much better over the years. In 1925 Market Jew Street in Penzance TOP *(181) was besmirched by obtrusive advertisements;* *today* ABOVE *(182) it has been cleared up — even the intrusion of Lloyd's Bank above the colonnade of the central building has been handled with dignity.*

appetite of consumers, advertising enjoyed its period of most rapid growth and most minimal supervision. It was above all the age of the hoarding. Any site which was likely to catch the public's eye was fair game for the advertiser. 'The King's highway is becoming of increasing value as an advertising station,' proclaimed the monthly magazine of a leading agent. 'Advertising along the roads cannot be stopped any more than Canute could stop the waves.' In *Brighton Rock* Graham Greene described how, miles from the outskirts of the town, the motorist encountered 'the long parade of posters … "Guinness is Good for You", "Try a Worthington", "Keep that Schoolgirl Complexion": a long series of adjurations, people telling you things: "Own Your Own Home", "Bennett's for Wedding Rings".' Horrified at the damage being done to Britain's landscape, the architect and crusader Clough Williams-Ellis called for a tax on roadside hoardings — 'The tax to be graded in inverse ratio to the rateable value of the land or building.' So advertising in an inner city would be taxed relatively lightly, a remote moorland or crumbling barn would become prohibitively expensive. His pleas were ignored; not least because the farmers and country land-owners battling against agricultural depression, were eager to grasp any chance of extra income.

A few companies — Shell and Guinness being conspicuous examples — produced posters of such wit and attraction that their intrusiveness could almost be forgiven. Most were mediocre or crassly vulgar. New products — or products that at least were new to the mass market — were sped on their way by energetic promotion: the jingle of the garish ice cream van penetrated to the remotest rural fastness. An ill-placed poster or shop sign could destroy the homogeneity of an entire street. Even if a local authority was sufficiently enlightened to wish to do so, it had little in the way of powers to curb excesses. The 1930s in particular were the age of unbridled free enterprise and adventurous experimentation: banners towed behind aeroplanes, slogans printed on the side of balloons or written in smoke across the sky, or flashed on to the clouds at night. Dorothy Sayers' Lord Peter Wimsey went sleuthing in an advertising agency and was entranced:

'All over London the lights flickered in and out, calling on the public to save its body and purse: SOPO SAVES SCRUBBING – NUTRAX FOR NERVES – CRUNCHLETS ARE CRISPER – EAT PIPER PARRITCH – DRINK POMPAYNE … DON'T SAY SOAP, SAY SOPO! Whatever you're doing, stop it and do something else! Whatever you're buying, pause and buy something different. Be hectored into health and prosperity! Never let up! … Keep going – and if you can't, TRY NUTRAX FOR NERVES!'

THE SQUANDERBUG IS BRIEFLY VILLAINOUS BUT SOON REVERTS TO TYPE

In 1939 the advertising industry was once again called up for national service. There was no image so powerful as that of Kitchener – on the whole the touch was lighter and the illustrations the work of cartoonists – but the exhortations were no less memorable. 'Dig for Victory', 'Is Your Journey Really Necessary?', 'Careless Talk Costs Lives', are phrases that will always have a special resonance for survivors of the wartime generations; the Squanderbug, that sinister yet comical little beast who was supposed to discourage spending in favour of National Savings, was the creation of a profession whose usual preoccupation was to persuade people not to save but to spend, spend, spend.

The war once over, the Squanderbug reverted from villain to Prince Charming. The Labour government, partly from puritan instincts but more in recognition of the need to clamp down on home consumption, deplored this spendthrift approach. They threatened to limit the amount of advertising

Some areas especially favoured by advertisers caused little pain, even to the most ardent conservationist. Who cared whether the motor race track at Oulton Park in Cheshire RIGHT *(183), photographed in 1960, was smothered in hoardings?*

Piccadilly in 1890 ABOVE (184), though an advertisement for beer had crept on to the parapet of the corner tower of the London Pavilion, was still relatively uncluttered and even dignified. By 1955 RIGHT (185) scarcely a square inch was left to the north and east that did not stridently proclaim the qualities of some drink, cigarette or chewing gum. Here too, however, there has been improvement; today OPPOSITE (186) the Pavilion has been swept clear of advertisements and is even more virginal than was the case a century ago.

1955 PICCADILLY

expenditure that could be set against profits; it never came to legislation but, fearful that it might do so, most manufacturers exercised voluntary restraint. It was not till the mid-1950s that advertisers threw off the last curbs of austerity and set out with increasing vigour to conquer the world.

Within the next twenty-five years the amount spent on advertising increased almost twenty-fold. The size of hoardings became ever more enormous, the ingenuity employed to make them eye-catching presented an ever greater menace to any easily distracted motorist. The exploitation of some venues caused no distress – who cared whether a motor racing track was smothered with advertising matter (plate 183)? Others were more regrettable: Piccadilly Circus, for one, was notably more dignified in 1890 than it was sixty-five years later. By 1998, however, it had regained some part of its former sobriety (plates 184-186).

But though far more thought and money was being devoted to advertising, the impact on the appearance of the nation if anything diminished. Local authorities enjoyed greater powers to control advertising: hoardings could still be unsightly and obtrusive but the threat that they would one day line every highway in the country has mercifully receded; the high streets of most towns and villages are today noticeably less cluttered with signs and posters than thirty or so years ago (plates 181, 182).

Most significant of all, a huge proportion of advertising revenue is now channelled into television, which is believed to be the most effective, as well as the most expensive way of winning public support for a new product. Whether the frugality and moral fibre of the British public has been adversely affected by this new onslaught is a question for the economist or the moralist; those who care about the appearance of the country have good reason to rejoice at this development.

1998 PICCADILLY

Beside the Seaside

THE BRITISH HAVE ALWAYS CONSIDERED themselves a sea-faring race, though only a tiny proportion of them actually went to sea and, until the mid-nineteenth century, most of them had never even glimpsed it. Between going to sea and going to the seaside, however, there is a wide gulf, both physical and psychological. At the time of Trafalgar most British males would have been aware of the possibility that they might be caught up in the machinery of war and be forced to go to sea. The idea that they might go to the seaside would have seemed a far more remote possibility.

Most people would have felt there was scant purpose in undertaking a journey that would probably be both laborious and expensive, and had little to offer at the end of it. In the eighteenth century one went to the seaside, if at all, for the sake of one's health. Even then, it was not primarily to enjoy or, at least, endure the bathing. Immersion in salt water was to be undertaken only with caution; as late as the 1860s Dr Spencer Thomson was warning that a bathe of more than twenty minutes might be hazardous. It was the sea air that did one good. The belief persisted. In 1886 James Forsyte said that he thought of visiting Bath for his health. "'Bath!' said Nicholas. "I've tried Harrogate. *That's* no good. What I want is sea air. There's nothing like Yarmouth!'" The most celebrated of all advertisments for a seaside town did not claim that it had a marvellous climate, splendid beaches, lavish entertainment or accommodation: Skegness was 'bracing'.

Even by 1805, however, holidays beside the sea were not unheard of if a family was reasonably prosperous and lived within easy carriage distance of the coast. By then Brighton, Margate, Southend, Weymouth and Scarborough were all established as bathing resorts. The first day-trippers were beginning to arrive at Blackpool, where 'genteel accommodation' with the use of a bathing machine thrown in had been on offer for twenty years or more. But so far this was on a trivial scale; the 'resort' element being at first a minor ancillary to the proper role of the seaside town as a port. Only with time, and the demand for a holiday in which the sea was an essential element, did the harbour give way to a resort, the Marine Parade or Esplanade replace the shabby houses and inns along the waterfront and the jetty become a pier.

BRIGHTON LEADS THE WAY, BOURNEMOUTH FOLLOWS

It was Brighton which first made acceptable the idea of a fashionable seaside resort, existing of its own right without reliance on fishing or maritime trade. It was not merely the oldest but also the grandest, made fashionable by the Prince Regent and retaining thereafter the slightly seedy smartness to be associated with that most raffish of monarchs. In the mid-nineteenth century it was four times larger than Hastings, thirty times larger than the fledgling Blackpool and still expanding fast (plates 187, 188). At that time Bournemouth was no more than a cluster of cottages at the end of a gorse-encumbered chine.

1894 BRIGHTON

Brighton was for many years the largest and grandest seaside resort in the British Isles. By 1894 ABOVE (187) challengers were threatening its supremacy, in size at least, but as this photograph of the promenade attests, it still possessed unique distinction. The same view a century later RIGHT (188) shows sadly how much that distinction has been marred.

1998 BRIGHTON

As with so much else in the British Isles, it was the railway that provided the catalyst for change. Those seaside towns which were the first to be linked by train with the great metropolises not merely grew the fastest but often took a lead that they never forfeited. Blackpool and Scarborough were endowed with a railway station before their potential rivals, Morecambe and Whitby, and their pre-eminence was never challenged. For a long time progress was slowed by the Sabbatarians, whose Anti-Sunday Travelling Union tried to stop the visitor returning home by train on Sunday evening – a facility essential for those working men who had to be at their office or factory on Monday morning. In the end, however, the profit motive triumphed over religion and propriety. The results were dramatic. When there was no nearby rival already established with a railway station, it was possible to expand at an astonishing speed. By the 1860s

Bournemouth attained modest renown as a select and salubrious resort where the rich could relax without any risk of intrusion from the proletariat. The residents knew that this exclusiveness could never survive the coming of the railway as one of them wrote:

'But not let Bournemouth, health's approved abode
Court the near presence of the iron road.'

Not all the neighbouring land-owners, however, were so high-minded or so snobbish, and in 1870 the iron road duly arrived. Even then the retreat from vulgarity was hard-fought. It was 1914 before Sunday trains were provided, until 1929 the pier was closed on Sundays, no band played and no excursion steamers were allowed to sail. But though a few battles might have been won, the war was lost from the start. A population of seven hundred in 1850 had

In 1908 Bournemouth Pier BELOW (189) *still had a jolly clock tower. By 1933* OPPOSITE ABOVE (190) *it had gone, and the elephantine bulk of new developments loomed monstrously above the Pavilion on the right. Today* OPPOSITE BELOW (191) *it is even worse. The old Pavilion, for what it is worth, is still there, but otherwise only the church spire remains as a reminder of the Bournemouth of ninety years ago.*

1908 BOURNEMOUTH

1933 BOURNEMOUTH

1998 BOURNEMOUTH

grown to 16,800 in 1881, 78,700 by 1911, and to 116,000 by 1931. The farmers and land-owners had too much at stake to resist the trend. George Liversedge of Branksome loved his pine woods, but when his old friend, Soames Forsyte, set up a company to develop the area in 1887, he had no hesitation in sacrificing the woods and pocketing the cash. For him it meant a handsome profit, for the public it meant the possibility of pleasure, but for the aesthete and the conservationist it was desecration. From the Purbeck hills, wrote E M Forster in *Howard's End*, 'Bournemouth's ignoble coast cowers to the right, heralding the pine trees that mean, for all their beauty, red houses, and the Stock Exchange, and extend to the gates of London itself' (plates 189-191).

THE MIDDLE AND LOWER CLASSES TAKE TO THE SEA

Except for Blackpool, which started resolutely vulgar and grew ever more so, the usual tendency for the seaside town was to begin as a resort for the middle classes and only gradually sell out for the superior rewards offered by the mass market. Some, like Scarborough or Southport, managed to cater for both worlds, encouraging the wider public yet preserving enclaves where the gentry or would-be gentry could feel that they were among their own kind. A few, like Frinton, retained their exclusiveness

1897 ABERYSTWYTH

1921 ABERYSTWYTH

1965 ABERYSTWYTH

Aberystwyth was a seaside resort which resisted the encroachments of the mass market. By 1897 LEFT ABOVE (192) the funicular railway was already in place, but the hills behind the great crescent of the beach were almost entirely bare. By 1921 LEFT MIDDLE (193) a few buildings had sprouted on the slopes and one building in the crescent was being demolished, but substantially the sea front was unchanged. By 1965 LEFT BELOW (194) development on the slopes had again increased and the demolished building had been replaced by a hall with a tower of uninspired design, but no Victorian inhabitants of Aberystwyth could have doubted exactly where they were.

at the expense of growth. And then there was a fringe of lower-middle to middle class resorts which had no pretensions to smartness but clung with obdurate determination to their respectability. Aberystwyth was a purpose-built seaside town which jealously preserved its atmosphere of solid decency (plates 192-194). The Pooters always holidayed at 'good old Broadstairs'. Lupin Pooter, who hankered after something a little more dashing, refused to walk down the Parade with his father because 'I was wearing my new straw helmet with my frock coat'. To Mr Pooter's dismay, Lupin went to 'a common sort of entertainment, given at the Assembly rooms,' where he saw 'Polly Presswell, England's Particular Spark'. So perhaps even 'good old Broadstairs' had to make some concessions to the demands of the mass market.

If the railway had given the first great impetus to the growth of the seaside town, Sir John Lubbock's Bank Holiday Act of 1871 consolidated the advance. A day, or weekend at the seaside for the August Bank Holiday became a fixed point in the year of the city

New Brighton in 1900
LEFT (**195**). *Kilvert had visited the resort twenty-eight years earlier and had found the sands covered 'with middle class Liverpool folk out for a holiday; digging in the sand . . . and enjoying themselves generally'. Little seems to have changed.*

worker. The limited facilities were put under impossible pressure, people would sometimes wait for two hours before being able to board one of the excursion trains to the coast. Even resorts that at that time considered themselves exclusive were swamped by visitors; Kilvert in 1872 found the sands at New Brighton 'covered with middle-class Liverpool folk and children out for a holiday; digging in the sand, riding on horses and donkeys, having their photographs taken and enjoying themselves generally' (plate 195). The August Bank Holiday was increasingly extended to include a few days before and after it – the Lancashire tradition of Wakes Week had its origin in this innovation. The idea of holidays with pay was still in the future, but the concept of the week's holiday as of right, for which the worker would save up throughout the year, was well established before the First World War. Many of the seaside hotels were often far from luxurious, sometimes the week was passed in surroundings which were depressing if not actually squalid, but the family was beside the seaside so it *must* be having fun (plate 196).

Griffiths' Temperance Hotel in Tenby on Carmarthen Bay in 1890 RIGHT (**196**) *might have been expected to cast gloom on any except the most resolutely jolly of holiday-makers. The, presumably local, children around its door certainly look somewhat cheerless.*

THE PLEASURES OF THE BEACH

The horses and donkeys which Kilvert saw at New Brighton were – and indeed still are – a regular feature of the British beach (plates 197-199). In the eighteenth century the beaches had been a convenient venue for an informal race-meeting, then less aristocratic members of the horse family found employment towing bathing huts on wheels to and from the water line. Donkeys for children's rides, however, did not become popular until well on into the nineteenth century. These shaggy and often cantankerous beasts formed part of a curious seaside sub-culture, most of which has now vanished. Brass bands were a conspicuous feature. They were usually described as 'German', and though the men who played in them might not have been authentically Teutonic, they did their best to look the part; Osbert Lancaster described them as 'plump elderly gentlemen with long hair and thick glasses clad rather improbably in tight-braided hussar

Donkeys for children's rides have been a regular feature of the British beach since seaside towns first became popular resorts. Skegness in 1910 LEFT (197) and 1955 BOTTOM (198) showed how the practice of rides along the beach never lost favour. The photograph of the donkeys at Rhyl BELOW (199) is undated but probably came from the 1890s; the side-saddle of the donkey to the left was an unusual feature.

uniforms'. Their chief rivals were nigger minstrels, even less authentically negroid than the bandsmen were German, who blackened their faces, donned straw hats, and played along lustily on cornets, concertinas and banjos. They were well established by the mid-nineteenth century; pierrots did not start to perform until the 1890s, when the railway age had brought multitudes to the coastal resorts. Punch and Judy shows – vulgar, violent, politically incorrect and adored by children – were prominent on almost every beach for the best part of a hundred years, only in the last two or three decades have they gone out of fashion. But surprising things could be met with on a beach, including a light sea plane on the sands at Paignton in 1918 (plate 202).

It was not enough merely to be on the beach and to enjoy such simple pleasures; the fact of one's presence had to be recorded too. The era of the 'happy snap' was still far away, only the most technologically evolved of families would have possessed a camera in the 1870s or 1880s. It was the birth of a new profession; any self-respecting beach boasted a scattering of tents or kiosks where the photographer lurked, offering to record for posterity the visitors to Brighton or New Brighton, Southport or Southend (plate 201). Few if any had the skills of Francis Frith, but the frozen and embarrassed images that peer from a million faded photographs are mute testimony to the delights experienced by those who were enjoying their annual, perhaps their first ever, holiday away from home.

The heyday of the pier

The delights, but also the expense ... Arnold Bennett's Derry Machin took his girl-friends to Llandudno in 1887. 'He simply could not stay out of the house without spending money, and often in ways quite unforeseen. Pier, minstrels,

New Brighton in 1887
LEFT (201), *in common with any other self-respecting beach, boasted an array of tents or kiosks where the professional photographer — there were only a handful of amateurs at the time — offered to record for posterity the visitors' seaside holiday.*

Unless the Avro light seaplane was a native of Paignton, on whose sands it was resting in 1918 RIGHT (202), *it must have caused something of a sensation. Seaplanes — or any other planes for that matter — were still a rarity at the time.*

Punch and Judy, bathing, buns, ices, fruit, chairs, row-boats, concerts, toffee, photographs, any of these expenditures was likely to happen whenever they went out for a simple stroll.' The 'simple stroll' usually took place along the far from simple Promenade, or Parade, or Esplanade; an avenue set between the front and a line of hotels, restaurants, shops, where women could display their finery and men their generosity (plates 203-206). At some point any such walk along the sea-front was bound to approach the pier. The idea that a man-made projection into the sea might be more than a functional protection against high tides or a convenient point from which a would-be passenger might embark on the packet boat, was

1904 WESTON-SUPER-MARE

1998 WESTON-SUPER-MARE

The Esplanade at Weston-super-Mare in 1904 ABOVE (203) *was a fashionable area. Today* LEFT (204) *it has been lightly vulgarized, but it is the contrast in dress between the photographs of 1904 and 1998 that is most startling.*

1897 DUNOON

The Quay at Dunoon in 1897 ABOVE (205) was dominated by the Argyll Hotel, a grand if somewhat dour establishment opened in 1837 and remodelled by Alexander 'Greek' Thomson in 1876. It was much patronized by prosperous Glaswegians who would come across the Firth of Clyde from Gourock. The hotel still stands proudly RIGHT (206) but no longer on a quay; the port has been pushed back to provide a car park for the ferry.

1998 DUNOON

first tried out in Brighton. The Old Chain Pier of 1823 was, as its name implies, made of metal; it was austere and largely free from buildings, but its principal object was to provide a platform down which the visitor could venture out to sea without the inconvenience of taking a boat. If the pier provided an extension of the Esplanade, then logically it should offer some of the same facilities. Soon there were restaurants, dance-halls, games, slot machines where the would-be voyeur could, for a modest sum, share in What the Butler Saw. The most characteristic style of pier architecture was richly rococo, crowned with domes and minarets, and

the grotesquely ornamental silhouette picked out at night with a plethora of coloured lights (plates 207-209).

The end of the nineteenth century was the heyday of the pier; of the fifty odd that survive today, over thirty were built between 1870 and 1910. The trouble was that they were expensive to build and even more expensive to maintain. Corroded by salt water, battered by winter gales, in need of constant repainting, the piers were almost entirely neglected during the Second World War and many never recovered from this inattention. Once they had been substantial money-spinners, today most of

The New Pier at Yarmouth in 1902 OPPOSITE (207) was simple in its entrance buildings but exploded into bravura baroque in the main pavilion at the end. By 1908 ABOVE (208) it had acquired a sprightly helter-kelter in the middle. Its appearance in 1998 RIGHT (209) is, almost literally, too awful to contemplate.

1998 YARMOUTH

Total immersion in salt water was not at first considered an essential, or even a desirable feature of seaside life. The schoolboys at Hartlepool in 1903 ABOVE (210) clearly had no intention of getting more than their feet wet, any more than the two ladies at Inverary in 1890 LEFT (211). The party being towed ashore on Filey Sands in 1927 ABOVE RIGHT (212) obviously preferred not to risk getting wet feet.

them at the best break even and are kept up, if they are kept up at all, by a town council which think they add a cachet to the sea-front. The ornate metal-work of the original has often been replaced by mean plastic, the band has departed, the butler sees no more, the glory has departed.

The essential for a seaside resort is the sea

But though piers and pierrots might be desirable embellishments, the basic essential for a seaside resort was the sea. Total immersion was not essential – paddling was quite as far as some were prepared to go and many did not wish even to get their feet wet (plates 210-212), but at first for therapeutic reasons, then for the fun of it, the idea took root that bathing was desirable. A problem was that it was felt indelicate for a member of one sex, particularly of the weaker sex, to expose any significant part of its anatomy to a member of the other. Bathing machines at the water's edge were to be found on almost every beach, even those reserved for women only (plate 213). Segregated bathing was indeed the norm until the end of the nineteenth century; conversely, nude bathing among men was by no means unusual. Kilvert was

The bathing machines at Paignton in 1896 RIGHT (213) were towed to the edge of the water by horses and moved from time to time to accord with the tides. Would-be bathers would step fully dressed into the back and emerge, wearing bathing dresses but already half under water, in the front. This elaborate procedure was still followed on the remoter beaches, even those reserved for women, where no prying male could licitly be observing the scene.

indignant when he found that at Shanklin in the Isle of Wight in 1874 'one has to adopt the detestable custom of bathing in drawers. If ladies don't like to see me naked why don't they keep away from the sight?' But with the acceptance of bathing drawers for men and light-weight costumes for women, both nude bathing and segregation went out of fashion. Bexhill, in 1901, was one of the first to introduce mixed bathing; soon, to do anything else was an old-fashioned oddity. For most people, at any time, simply messing around on

the beach was what mattered most. The elaboration of the clothing might diminish but the essential activities – paddling, poking around in rock pools, making sand castles, sitting and reading, sitting and not reading – remained the same (plates 214-219).

Cheap electricity, with all the stimulus which it gave to seaside lighting and entertainment, was the next important factor in the growth of the seaside town. Blackpool led the way, by its brash energy and determination overcoming the limited assets with which it had been

The Victorians had the sense to distinguish between children and adults when it came to bathing. These small boys in Newlyn in 1893 ABOVE (214) saw no need for all-embracing costumes, let alone bathing machines, and to judge by their presence in the centre of the harbour, their parents took the same view.

1890 LLANFAIRFECHAN

These two views of Llanfairfechan, though taken in 1890 LEFT (215) and 1960 BELOW (216), do not suggest that peoples' attitudes to beach life had altered greatly. A desultory but enjoyable mucking about was characteristic of both periods. The town seems to have altered even less.

1960 LLANFAIRFECHAN

On the beach at Rhyl in 1913 ABOVE (**217**) these elegant wicker shelters provided some protection against a stiffish breeze. Bathing machines had disappeared, though it seems unlikely that the solitary bather undressed on the beach. At Towyn, in Clwyd (1925) LEFT (**218**), it was a bucket-and-spade holiday of a kind still to be witnessed wherever there are children, sand and rocks.

endowed by nature (plates 220-222). J B Priestley visited the town in 1933. 'Compared with this huge mad place,' he wrote, 'with its miles and miles of promenade, its three piers, its gigantic dance-halls, its variety shows, its switch-backs and helter-skelters … its army of pierrots, bandsmen, clowns, fortune-tellers, auctioneers, dancing-partners, itinerant singers, hawkers; its seventy special trains a day, its hundreds and hundreds of thousands of trippers; places like Brighton and Margate and Yarmouth are merely playing at being popular seaside resorts.' Its Esplanade in 1890 was sedate compared with the view that Priestley saw forty years later, but even then a different world to that at Cromer in 1899 (plate 223).

THE ADVANCE CONTINUES AFTER THE FIRST WORLD WAR

The First World War had imposed a short check on the irresistible advance of Blackpool and its rivals; August 1919 proved that the setback had been temporary. That Bank Holiday fifty thousand people went from London to Yarmouth; Clacton received 35,000 more visitors than it could accommodate; 300,000 went to Blackpool.

Over the next decade the working week was shortened and by then the idea of paid holidays had become a commonplace for most. The British worker for the first time had more money to spend, as well as more time in which to spend it.

A strikingly high proportion elected to spend both the money and
time at the seaside. A Parliamentary Committee, which in 1937
considered the desirability of making holidays with pay compulsory,
found that an overwhelming majority of the working classes agreed that
the only proper vacation was one spent at the seaside. By that date one
in every three people was spending a week a year away from home.
Blackpool alone attracted seven million visitors between June and
September and was investing fortunes on new and improved facilities:
£1.25 million on the promenade, £1.5 million on the Winter Gardens,
£300,000 on an indoor swimming pool. The numbers of day-trippers
grew no less dramatically. 'They came in by train from Victoria every five
minutes,' wrote Graham Greene in *Brighton Rock*, 'rocked down Queen's
Road standing on the tops of the little local trams, stepped off in
bewildered multitudes into fresh and glittering air: the new silver paint
sparkled on the piers … a race in miniature motors, a band playing,
flower gardens in bloom below the front, an aeroplane advertising
something for the health in pale vanishing clouds across the sky.' To the
lure of sea air and salt water had now been added the pleasures of the
sun: for centuries the British had cherished their pallid complexions and
lurked beneath straw hats and parasols, now tans were all the fashion and
resorts vied with each other to boast about the glories of their climate.
The train was still the favoured means of transport but the coach
progressively eroded its supremacy; especially for the day visitors the
chara-trip — for the Women's Institute, the school, a company outing —
became almost an end in itself with its own songs and games and jollity.

THE GOOSE THAT LAYS THE GOLDEN EGG SUFFERS FROM INDIGESTION

So great was the congestion, so intense the pressure, that it seemed the goose that laid the golden eggs might stuff itself to death. The Second World War saved the resorts from that fate; saved them, indeed, with a thoroughness that the resorts could well have done without. Again people feared the worst – again it did not happen. The war was barely over before business as usual was resumed. The first July Wakes holiday in 1945 saw over 100,000 visitors carried by train to Blackpool in a single day; every resort was quickly attracting crowds as large or often even larger than they had known before the war. Yet the traditional pattern of seaside life was changing.

One factor was the caravan. As much a harbinger of summer as the first swallow, the caravan had become a common sight on Britain's roads even before 1939, but nobody had anticipated how rapidly its numbers would increase. By the late 1970s one in four holiday-makers was travelling by

Cromer from the beach in 1899 RIGHT **(223)**, *a view dominated by the fifteenth-century tower of St Peter and St Paul which for centuries acted as a lighthouse. Sober, dignified, serious, Cromer was in a different world to the brash and uninhibited modernism of Blackpool. A century later* OPPOSITE ABOVE **(224)** *and the aspect of the town is remarkably unchanged. Only the people have altered, and even there the development is purely sartorial.*

caravan. Many of these aimed for sites on the fringes of seaside towns; every night five thousand visitors slept in caravans within a mile or so of Scarborough's centre. Their desertion was a blow to the lodging-house keepers and restaurateurs, but at least they were still bringing some money into the town. More serious from the point of view of the established resorts was the multitude of caravan dwellers who took their vehicle to, or rented a semi-permanent home in, some relatively remote coastal area. Bill Bryson cast an acerbic American eye on the caravan holiday-makers in North Wales. 'It seemed an odd type of holiday option to me, the idea of sleeping in a tin box in a lonesome field miles from anywhere in a climate like Britain's and emerging each morning with hundreds of other people from identical tin boxes, crossing the rail lines and dual carriage way and hiking over a desert of sinkholes in order to dip your toes in a distant sea full of Liverpool turds.' Put like that, it does sound a little odd (plate 225).

The threat from 'abroad'

But 'a climate like Britain's' was the cause of a more significant defection from the traditional seaside holiday. Even before the war Britain's ever more substantial middle-class had been forming the habit of taking its summer holiday abroad. In the 1960s the new affluence and the increasing range of package holidays meant that more and more sun-worshippers took to the Continent. The Costa Brava, Torremolinos, areas of the world which the British had not even known existed a few years before, became as much part of the national consciousness as Blackpool or Southend. Of course, the flow was not all one way, twenty-five million foreign visitors came to Britain in 1996. But though this did wonders for attendance figures at the Tower of London or sales at Harrods, it was precious little help to the seaside resorts.

No foreigner in his senses would travel to Britain to bask on the beaches, except possibly an Eskimo who thought that twenty minutes

of watery sun represented a heatwave, or an equatorial African who hankered after temperate coolness. The blow was far from terminal – the nation's great resorts continued to do a booming trade – but the days of seemingly irresistible growth were over.

No one can be sure that the economic and political factors which have made 'abroad' so attractive and accessible, will continue indefinitely; the golden age of the British coastal resort may yet return, unlikely as this may seem. But in the meantime, the Brightons and Blackpools, let alone the weaker members of the seaside fraternity, realize that they are going to have to work most energetically even to hold their own.

Perran Sands Holiday Camp, Cornwall in 1960 ABOVE **(225)**: *'sleeping in a tin box in a lonesome field miles from anywhere'.*

Communicating

I F, IN THE MID-NINETEENTH CENTURY, you wanted to make contact with somebody who lived a long way away, there was little alternative to sending him or her a letter. Telepathy, it is true, might have been cheaper, but it was also a good deal less reliable and, anyway, the postal services provided astonishingly good value for money. This was the doing of Rowland Hill, an administrator so fanatically devoted to the expansion of the service that his brother once remarked: 'When you go to Heaven I foresee that you will stop at the gate to enquire of St Peter how many deliveries they have by day.' Against the advice of the economists and almost all his staff he forced through the principle of the penny post, insisting that the flow of letters would quickly expand to more than compensate for any temporary loss of revenue. In fact it took well over twenty years for revenue to rise to its former level, but by the time Hill retired his creation was a cherished national institution and the Post Office had become one of the main forces binding together the country and opening the way for ever faster modernisation. He could not have done it without the railways; the two services co-operated so closely that they became almost inter-dependent. As early as 1839 ingenious gadgets were being installed at wayside halts, making it possible for express trains to drop off the mail without losing speed, let alone stopping.

From then on it was a process of continuous refinement and innovation. The first letter boxes on the British mainland (oddly enough, the Channel Islands had led the way) were installed in Carlisle in 1853. They were solid, square constructions with a ball on top. Soon they gave way to what was literally a 'pillar' box, fluted and Doric in style, and it was not until the 1880s that the circular red model became standard (plate 226). In 1871 Francis Kilvert recorded proudly: 'Today I sent my first postcards … They are capital things, simple, useful and handy. A happy invention.' These were pre-stamped cards manufactured by the post office. It was to be another twenty years before the authorities countenanced the idea that postcards could be printed privately and despatched with the addition of a halfpenny stamp. The day of the picture postcard had dawned. Tuck, Valentine and, of course, Frith, were quick to exploit the genre; within another decade the celebrated *risqué* seaside cards of Donald McGill were sweeping all before them. Well before then the postal order had been

This pillar box, photographed in Birmingham New Street in 1890 LEFT **(226)**, *was the Penfold model, which had gone out of production ten years before. A few hundred still survive — though today this one has been destroyed or possibly moved.*

From the sublime to the ridiculous, or the palace to the cottage. The Post Office in Leeds (1897) ABOVE (227) was on the grandest scale (it also accommodated the Revenue Office). The Post Office at Tintagel, two years earlier RIGHT (228), was one room in a dilapidated cottage. But both served the same master and were proud of it.

Though the Post Office at Rosneath on the Gare Loch ABOVE (229) *seems to have been maintaining its independence in 1893, not many villages could provide enough business to support an office operating in its own right. More often it settled in a wing of the local general store, as in Nutfield in Surrey, photographed in 1908* ABOVE MIDDLE (230). *A more modern example is Hixon in Staffordshire* ABOVE RIGHT (231), *a typical little post-Second World War box which, in spite of its lack of charm, was in 1955 providing an essential service to the village.*

introduced; this, and the Post Office Savings Bank pioneered by Gladstone, enormously increased the responsibilities of the individual post office and confirmed its status in the high street of every town and village.

A POSTAL SERVICE THAT WAS THE ENVY OF THE WORLD

By the end of the nineteenth century Britain had a postal service that was the envy of the world. In West Central London there were twelve deliveries a day; the first at 7.20 am, the last at 8.15 pm. At Soames Forsyte's house in Montpelier Square the last post did not arrive till after dinner was over and Soames' father had left for home. It was among the most active postal services too, the British sent more letters per head than any other people except inhabitants of the USA. Of course, central London was not typical of the whole nation. At Flora Thomson's Lark Rise 'Old Postie' did not arrive till about 10 am; 'On wet days he carried an old green gig umbrella with whalebone ribs, and, beneath its immense circumference, he seemed to make no more progress than an overgrown mushroom.' But he always got there in the end; it was rare for a letter to take more than two days to get from one end of the country to another, for an item to be 'lost in the post' was an almost inconceivable catastrophe.

The service remained uncommonly good value for many years – became still cheaper, indeed, for the weight that could be carried for a penny was raised from half an ounce to four ounces. Not until 1918 was the cost increased. Successive Postmaster Generals battled with Chancellors of the Exchequer to avoid a tax on stamps. Shortly after the end of the First World War motor lorries were introduced to ferry the mail from station to station or from station to post office; they were obviously quicker than horses but it was 1949 before the last horse-drawn mail van was withdrawn. The telephone made rapid deliveries less essential, but even in the 1930s there were four deliveries on weekdays in London and one on Sundays.

A VAST NETWORK OF POST OFFICES

To operate this vast enterprise post offices sprang up in every town and village in the land. The description 'post office' covered a multitude of variations: from the grandiose palace in Leeds, whose splendours rivalled those of even the most prestigious bank or town-hall, to the — literally — cottage industry at Tintagel (plates 227, 228). The fusion of post office and village shop was desirable wherever the business could not support a full time postmaster (plates 229-231) and ensured that the establishment became the centre of local life. There were some four thousand post offices in 1848, by 1913 there were nearly 27,000, many of them run by sub-postmasters working on commission who might earn only a few pounds a year. In Flora Thomson's Candleford Green the post office shared premises with a blacksmith's forge; no doubt by 1955 it would have followed the example of Ludford Magna (plate 232) and linked its fortunes to a garage. It was equally likely that it would have closed altogether. Up till 1939 the post office held its own (plate 233) but from

The alliance between sub-Post Office and blacksmith's forge was by no means uncommon; it seemed only logical that when, as in Ludford Magna in Shropshire ABOVE (232), *the forge gave way to a garage, the Post Office should renew its alliance with the new owner. Today the Post Office has withdrawn to the other end of Ludford — the building is still there but the structure has become a desirable residence and it is now called 'The Old Post Office'.*

Until after the Second World War the Post Office retained its position as an essential element in British life. In Hindhead ABOVE (233) *it provided the pivot around which society gyrated.*

the end of the Second World War it was downhill all the way, business mail swelled but private correspondents increasingly transferred their loyalties to the telephone or, later, to the Fax and E-mail. As the village shops crumbled before the competition of the supermarket, so the post offices closed with them; as automation reduced the number of workers needed to sort the mail, so the enormous establishments of the cities became redundant.

Until 1922 the Post Office had been the largest employer in the country. It took itself and its standards immensely seriously; before Flora Thomson's Laura was accepted as a clerk she had to swear before a justice of the peace: 'I do solemnly promise and declare that I will not open or delay or suffer to be opened or delayed any letter or anything sent by the post,' and went on to pledge secrecy in all things. The postmen, or woman letter-carrier — the

The postman, 'postie' to all the world, at first did most of his work on foot, as at Elstead in Surrey in 1906 ABOVE **(234)**, *where he spoke, perhaps rather enviously, with a passing rider. By then many of his colleagues would have been on bicycles, as in the Dorset village of Pymore in 1909* RIGHT **(235)**.

distinction was to be marked more in their pay than in their responsibilities – whom Laura fed with letters, worked mainly on foot, then came the bicycle, finally the van (plates 233-236). Postmen had begun to wear uniforms as early as the eighteenth century but the practice did not become universal until the 1870s and even then was confined to full time workers rather than the casual employees in rural areas. Under his green umbrella 'Old Postie' was *probably*

By 1936 the motor van had become standard for distribution to branch offices, though feet or bicycles were often still resorted to for the final stage. On the *precipitous streets of Clovelly in North Devonshire* ABOVE **(236)** *a donkey was recruited to carry the load – they still help out as pack animals.*

wearing uniform but it would not have been surprising if he had stuck to his ordinary clothes, and remarkable if he had been correctly dressed in every way. The main object of putting the postman into uniform had been to make him immediately recognizable; since in the country everyone knew who he was anyway, the need seemed less pressing.

THE TELEGRAPH AND TELEPHONE

The telegraph was not integrated with the postal service till 1870 and even then remained largely autonomous. Miss Watkins took Kilvert into her telegraphing room at Hay in 1871 'and initiated me into the mysteries of her craft. So many turns to the right, so many turns to the

1925 PENTRAETH

The square in Pentraeth,
Gwyned, in the 1920s
LEFT (237) and the 1960s
BELOW (238). *Though the
centre of the square had been
adorned with a flower bed,
the most conspicuous
improvement was that the
Post Office had acquired an
external telephone box.*

1965 PENTRAETH

C. 1955 MUNDESLEY

left … the needle went jerking from side to side so that I could hardly follow it.' So far as the outward and visible aspect was concerned the most significant development was the proliferation of telegraph wires (plate 233). At first the delivery of a telegram more than three miles from a post office cost the substantial sum of 3/6ᵈ, but soon an army of telegraph boys was recruited to carry the telegrams by bicycle around the towns or countryside. The telegraph boy, like the lift attendant in the smart hotel, became the paradigm of everything that was cheekiest and most morally suspect; the reputation was not entirely unmerited, when the notorious male brothel in Cleveland Street was raided by the police in 1889 it was found that it was staffed largely by telegraph boys. Then, their service was bought

to an end when they became sixteen; gradually the rules were relaxed and when motor-cycles were introduced for telegram delivery, the minimum age for using them was seventeen.

Next came the telephone. Though Bell did not perfect his system till 1877, there had been previous sighting shots that came somewhere near the mark. Even at the very end of the nineteenth century, however, it was still a novelty – its mention usually prefaced by the adjective 'new-fangled'. Neville Cardus encountered his first telephone when he joined an insurance office in Manchester in 1910. It was attached to the wall. 'To communicate with the Exchange you turned a handle (it was the age of handles). Sometimes it was possible to obtain a slight electrical shock, temporarily stiffening the finger joints.' Cardus's office was

At first glance the spruceness of the windmill at Mundesley on the Norfolk coast in the second of these two pictures (c. 1965) OPPOSITE (**240**) *might suggest that it was the earlier of the two; the television aerial that had sprouted from the roof of the adjacent house, however, proves that it was the later and that the mill had been drastically tidied up in the years since c. 1955* ABOVE (**239**).

C. 1965 MUNDESLEY

unusually well equipped; not many could boast a telephone before the First World War. It was not till the mid-1920s that they became commonplace; there were 176,000 personal telephones then, more than 1.4 million by 1930. By the 1940s and 1950s, anyone unfortunate enough to lack a telephone at home would probably be within range of a public call box (plate 238); whether this would necessarily be in working order was another matter. For a time its main function seemed to be to provide a target for the trainee vandal before he moved on to bigger things. Except in certain particularly benighted areas things seem to be better. Today, *not* to have a telephone is considered a mark of extreme poverty or eccentricity; in certain circles *only* to have a telephone is proof that one is technologically disadvantaged and pathetically out of date.

The only thing today that is odder than being without a telephone is to eschew television. The photographs of the windmill at Mundesley taken *c.* 1955 and *c.* 1965 (plates 239, 240) possess a special interest. The fact that the windmill is notably sprucer in one than the other might suggest that the second picture is the earlier, the fact that a television aerial has intruded on the roof of the house to the left proves that it is the later. Thus the conservationist took back with one hand what he had given with the other.

At first it was only the BBC whose aerials besmirched the sky-line, then Independent Television began to intrude, then it was the turn of the satellite dishes. There seems no end to the number of excrescences that bristle on

The grander monuments of modern British communications possess a certain surreal splendour. The 620 feet of the Post Office Tower — or, as one should now say, the 186 metres of the British Telecom Tower LEFT (241) — contrast pleasingly with the tranquil backwater in Regent's Park, while the radio telescope at Jodrell Bank BELOW (242) would excite anyone except the most phlegmatic.

the nation's rooftops; a line of telegraph poles or pylons can mar a landscape but no more thoroughly than the demands of television can wreck the appearance of a house.

Not all modern communications are ugly in their by-products. The Post Office Tower and the radio telescope at Jodrell Bank possess a certain surreal splendour; so do the monster golf-balls of Forest Moor or British Telecom's dish on Goonhilly Downs (plates 241-244). On the whole, though, the wish of human beings to talk to each other when they are apart and to know what is going on in the wider world has done inestimable damage to the appearance of the country. Rowland Hill had no idea what he was doing when he encouraged the British on their way down what is apparently an endless path.

So, photographed only in
1999, do the monster golf
balls that adorn the
American radio station near
Blubberhouses in Yorkshire
ABOVE **(243)** *or the*
British Telecom station on
Goonhilly Downs in
Cornwall RIGHT **(244)**.

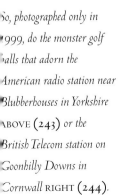

Dressing

THE PURPOSE OF CLOTHING is to keep the wearer warm in winter and cool in summer, to cover what is unseemly or unattractive and leave as much as possible exposed, above all to be comfortable. Towards this ideal the British have taken considerable strides since the days when Francis Frith donned his long sack coat or Norfolk jacket, thick tweed trousers, woollen socks and stout boots, woollen underwear, shirt of heavy Egyptian cotton, stiff and upstanding white collar, knotted tie held in place by a pearl tie pin, waistcoat of the same material as the jacket accommodating a gold watch and chain, and a deer-stalker or round-crowned brown hat which in a few years was to evolve into the bowler. Only when he was thus equipped did he feel ready to sally forth for a day's photography under the August sun.

Fashion in the 1860s was, of course, still a luxury reserved for the middle and upper classes. Frith's dress was markedly different to what he might have been wearing a hundred, or even fifty years before; most of the men he saw working in the fields or around the villages would still have been in the long cover-all smock, probably with leather breeches, in which their grandfathers and great grandfathers would equally have felt at home (plate 245). But already things were changing. New materials, mass production, improved means of transport, were making more convenient if less long-lasting dress available even in the remotest villages. Richard Jefferies wrote to *The Times* in 1872 to report that in the countryside today 'Corduroy trousers and slops are the usual style. Smock-frocks are going out of use except for milkers. Almost every labourer has his Sunday suit, very often really good clothes, sometimes glossy black, with the regulation "chimney pot".' In Lark Rise leather breeches had disappeared by the 1880s. The carter, shepherd and a few of the older labourers still wore traditional smock-frocks topped by a round felt hat, but most men wore suits of stiff, dark brown corduroy or, in summer, corduroy trousers and an unbreached drill jacket known as a 'sloppy'. The farm labourers photographed at Looe and Beaminster in 1906 and 1907 (plates 246, 247) would have looked much the same twenty years before or, for that matter, twenty years later. So would the Cornish fishermen (plates 248-250). There was not much scope for indulging the vagaries of fashion if one was any kind of manual labourer particularly in the countryside; at the most there was a general drift towards the cloth cap in preference to any other kind of headgear.

An elderly farm labourer in a cornfield near Coltishall, Norfolk, in 1902 ABOVE (245). His long cover-all smock was already something of a rarity; his grand-daughter — if that is what she was — would have been too young to notice, but within a few years she would have been urging him not to cover her with shame by looking so embarrassingly old-fashioned.

The farm labourers
photographed at Looe,
Cornwall LEFT ABOVE
(246), and Beaminster,
Dorset LEFT (247), in
1906 and 1907
respectively, belonged to the
post-smock generation. They
would have looked much the
same twenty years later,
though the veteran at Looe
would probably have
changed his hat for a cap
something like that worn by
the younger man.

The unknown fisherman of 1896 ABOVE (249), though his pipe looked decidedly Victorian, would not have been dressed very differently a generation later. The Newlyn fishermen of 1924 ABOVE LEFT (248) would probably have changed their headgear for the cloth caps worn by most of the group seated on the beach at Mevagissey LEFT (250). The bowler hat worn by the man on the left, as in plate 269, probably indicated that he was a cut above the rest.

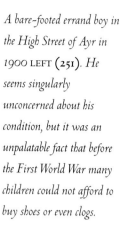

A bare-footed errand boy in the High Street of Ayr in 1900 LEFT (251). He seems singularly unconcerned about his condition, but it was an unpalatable fact that before the First World War many children could not afford to buy shoes or even clogs.

On the whole Frith eschewed the miserable. His working class subjects were usually selected as being picturesque rather than squalid or bedraggled. Most of his children were well fed and well-dressed. Occasionally he features one who is barefoot but his photographs generally leave the impression that the child was shoeless by choice rather than necessity (plate 251). It is impossible to imagine the children on the beach at St Ives or playing with boats on the Isle of Wight being without shoes in any other circumstances, while the group at Lyme Regis clearly came from prosperous homes and could easily have been encountered in the catalogue of some purveyor of youthful fashions (plates 252-255).

A PERIOD OF GREAT YET MODERATING FORMALITY

For the upper and middle classes the last decades of the nineteenth century were a period of great yet slowly moderating formality. Clothes symbolized one's status in society. In the group walking down Queen

The shoelessness of the
children playing with boats
at Shanklin on the Isle of
Wight in 1913 LEFT (252)
or on the beach at St Ives in
1890 BELOW (253) is, on
the other hand, clearly part
of the holiday atmosphere —
the Shanklin parents are
irredeemably middle class.

Victoria Street in the City of London (plate 256), the two men in top hats and frock coats clearly spring from a higher level of society than the intensely respectable bowler-hatted and short-coated figure on the left, who in his turn is from a different world to the bearded news-vendor in the centre. It would have been perfectly possible for the man on the left to have exchanged his bowler and short coat for a top hat and frock coat, but it would not have occurred to him to do so.

Of course, the rules changed from place to place, for not everywhere endured a hierarchy as rigid as the City of London. It would be rash,

These children in the street at Lyme Regis in 1906 LEFT (254) *could easily have stepped straight from the catalogue of a purveyor of youthful fashions.*

Boys outside Shrewsbury Old Market Hall in 1911 BELOW (255). *The small boy on the left had presumably been posed so as to introduce an element of 'them and us' into the picture.*

however, to deduce from the headgear alone which are the more affluent of the citizens of Penryn and Norwich (plates 257, 258); it would appear that on the whole the more elderly seem to affect top hats but even that is not invariable. Though on holiday there might be some slight relaxation of the rules, the basic

*Clothes, in the late
nineteenth century were a
symbol of one's status in
society. In the group walking
down Queen Victoria Street
in the City of London
shortly before the Jubilee of
1897* BELOW (256), *the
man on the right in top hat
and frock coat was clearly
from a higher level of society
than the intensely respectable
bowler-hatted and short-
coated figure on the left, who
in his turn was from
a different world to the
bearded news-vendor in
the centre.*

framework was still observed vigorously;
nobody could have been more triumphantly
middle class than the young couple with the
baby on the bench in Sandown on the Isle of
Wight (plate 260).

Dress was an armour, as emblematic as that
of any medieval knight. Sometimes it was
almost literally armour: the boiled shirt and
stiff upright collar of the male, the corsets of
the female, exhibited the rigidity of the caste
system at its most unyielding. The structure of
corsets was peculiar, wrote Neville Cardus,
'they were erected on a girder of steel, and the
secret was to begin at the bottom, at the waist-
line. One clip was fastened down there, then
you walked upwards. Often when connection
had been made at the top, the lowest clip would
burst asunder.' There was some room for
individuality within this framework – a dandy

might wear a monocle or stridently chec[ked]
trousers; the more daring woman abandone[d]
the bustle or experimented with extravagant[ly]
flounced sleeves – but the parameters o[f]
fashion could not be altered. Wasp waists we[re]
ordained for the young woman, and whateve[r]
agonies of congestion might be involve[d]
waspish the waist would be. Informality wa[s]
permitted only within the most formal o[f]
frameworks. Whether one was on the Parade a[t]
Torquay or Worthing, or picnicking abov[e]
Reigate, the same *tenue* was always resolute[ly]
observed (plates 259, 261, 262).

But almost imperceptibly things wer[e]
changing. Youth was not yet in revolt but it wa[s]
growing restive. The frock coat was no longe[r]
an essential uniform for London, in Marlo[w]
the vicar found it necessary to entreat his floc[k]
'Please do not permit the matter of dress t[o]

Market Street, Penryn
ABOVE **(257)** *and*
Rampant Horse Street in
Norwich RIGHT **(258)**
(both 1891) pose more
complex problems for the
sociologist. It would be
dangerous to attach as much
importance to the headgear
as could safely be done in
the City of London. In both
photographs the bowler-
hatted gentlemen look quite
as affluent as those who
effect top hats. Top hats tend
to go with age, but even that
is not invariable.

Some relaxation was permitted on holiday. The choice of hat by the man with his wife and baby at Sandown, Isle of Wight, in 1895 RIGHT (260), was a tiny concession to informality but his middle-class status was conspicuous. The baby could easily have become the young man on Princess Parade in Torquay in 1920 ABOVE (259): the garb was more festive, the hatlessness unusual, but the social statement was the same.

keep you away, come in your flannels and boating dress.' H G Wells's Mr Kipps owned and managed an unsuccessful small gentlemen's outfitters in a provincial town: 'He was dressed in a shabby black morning coat and vest … His collar was chosen from stock and with projecting corners, technically a "wing-poke"; that and his tie, which was new and loose and rich in colouring, had been selected to encourage and stimulate customers … His golf cap, which was also from stock and aslant over his eye, gave his misery a desperate touch.'

THE FIRST WORLD WAR SHATTERS THE SARTORIAL UNIVERSE

The First World War shattered this universe for ever. For four years uniform was the smartest thing that could be worn (plates 263, 264), women worked in factories and on farms and wore trousers and their hair short, cloth was scarcer so skirts perforce got shorter.

Once the war was over fashion resumed its sway but the old despotism was never restored. Short hair with what would once have been an unacceptable display of ankle became *de rigueur*

In what might have seemed the most informal circumstances the late Victorians and Edwardians dressed as if the eyes of the world were on them. On the parade at Worthing in 1903 RIGHT **(261)** *(how that wretched small boy must have loathed the outing), picnicking above Reigate in the same year* RIGHT BELOW **(262)**, *always a perfect tenue was maintained. Possibly the girls above Reigate had made a special effort for the benefit of the photographer, but even if Mr Frith had not been present they would have looked much the same.*

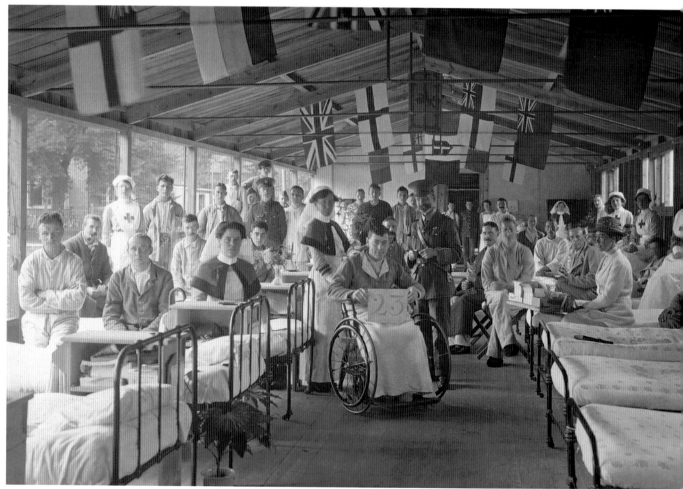

among the young (plate 265). The ladies on the promenade at Weymouth in 1923 may not seem wholly liberated compared with their counterparts today but they were freedom itself if contrasted with their predecessors at the same spot only five years before (plates 266, 267). Cosmetics, deemed by the more censorious before the war to be a sure sign of the harlot, were now tacitly condoned; even, by the 1930s, the more daring might make up in public, though this would still be enough to cause raised eyebrows among the traditional. Trousers for women were another battlefield. In 1930, in Evelyn Waugh's *Vile Bodies*, Agatha Runcible wore trousers in a roadside hotel and the party was rapidly ejected (though Miles Malpractice touching up his eyelashes in the dining room may have given even greater offence).

The various stages in the sartorial hierarchy became more blurred. After visiting Wigan in the mid-1930s, George Orwell remarked that cheap sharp clothes were now readily available; for £2.10.0. a young man could buy a suit on hire purchase which 'for a little while and at a little distance, looks as though it has been tailored in Savile Row'. For women the transformation was still more striking. The introduction of artificial silk and rayon made it possible to produce at relatively low cost clothes which bore a more than passing resemblance to the creations of *haute couture*. As well as being cheaper, they fell to pieces quicker and thus needed replacement; new styles were rapidly copied and spread throughout the country. If skirts went up in Mayfair it would not be long before a similar phenomenon was observed in Wigan.

Sabre drill on the parade ground of the Cavalry Barracks in York in 1886 ABOVE (263). *In the minds of civilians these were the 'licentious military', to be regarded with some suspicion, even hostility, if encountered in the street.*

These were the survivors, the lucky ones, at a Cambridge hospital after the end of the First World War LEFT (264). *The strict uniform of the nurses contrasted with the much more casual overalls of the convalescent men.*

A fashion display at Southbourne, Bournemouth, in 1922 BELOW (265). *The line of the dress worn by the girl on the right was no doubt challenging enough, but it was the haircut and the indecent display of ankle that would have seemed most shocking to the Victorians.*

Even male fashions change — though sluggishly

Unsurprisingly, the change in men's clothing was more sluggish. By the mid-1920s they were beginning to dress casually when on holiday; even, perhaps, to dispense with a tie, but they would not have contemplated presenting themselves in such a guise at their place of work. In the cities and towns narrow trousers, high-buttoned jackets and stiff collars were still worn by every man who had any pretensions or claims to respectability.

The hierarchy of hats was modified but retained in its essentials. The tall silk hat became a rarity except in certain sectors of the City of London and for Eton school-boys but the bowler ruled supreme as the ultimate symbol of respectability. It was a sign of status too, the man standing so proudly in front of the gates of the park at Aberdare was making it clear to everyone that *he* was the boss and the rest his underlings (plate 269). But though supreme, the bowler hat was not unchallenged. Even before 1914 King Edward VII had been known to favour a soft Homburg; in the 1930s Anthony Eden usually wore a black felt hat with the brim turned down in front. What was good enough for the Foreign Secretary was good enough for the Foreign Office officials, and the Foreign Office was felt by those who knew no better to be the very seat of fashion.

By the time of the Second World War the bowler hat was generally considered by the young to be slightly dowdy, suitable for army officers in mufti or a senior bank clerk. The straw Panama hat, too, which had in 1918 been an essential piece of equipment at the seaside, also slipped from fashion to be replaced by the ubiquitous trilby. But though the appearance of the hat was modified, its reign was unchallenged.

The promenade at Weymouth in 1918 above *(266), 1923* opposite above *(267) and 1998* opposite below *(268). The ladies of 1923 may not seem particularly liberated compared with their contemporary equivalents, but they would have appeared almost revolutionary to their predecessors of only five years before. For men, the early 1920s was the golden age of the straw hat.*

Until 1939 it was unthinkable for a man at almost any social level to venture out bare-headed when in town, and frisky to do so even when he was in the country.

King George V, unlike his father, set no new trends in clothing but he kept his beard, a rarity in the inter-war period when beards were increasingly associated with the more farouche practitioners of the arts and crafts. The bearded were greeted by the young with cries of 'Beaver!', and a beard-spotting game was devised in which an ordinary beard earned one point, a white 'polar' beard two points, and so on. The ultimate in scores was presumably gained by spotting the King himself.

His son, later to be King Edward VIII, was almost embarrassingly clean-shaven – enemies claimed that this was as much a deficiency on the part of nature as by his choice. He was in the van of fashion and invariably championed

the novel and informal – preferring zips to buttons, dinner jackets to tails, suede shoes to the more traditional brogues.

Sport brings its own sartorial revolution

Because it was so difficult to play games in formal or constricting clothes, the spread of sport in the second half of the nineteenth century increased the pressure for liberalisation. The top hat disappeared from cricket; the photographs of women playing tennis in 1886 and 1928 show how gradually but irresistibly the fashion was changed (plates 270, 271). A few years later they might well have been wearing shorts. Before the First World War the closely fitting woven bathing dress for women caused some concern to the Mrs Grundys, by 1933 it was taken for granted (plate 272). While bicycling had been a hobby for the rich a curious variety of costumes had been devised which were deemed both decorative and suitable (plate 273), but as the habit spread so the dress became more utilitarian. Richard Church as a small boy in 1900 or so was amazed to see two lady bicyclists wearing bloomers in Battersea Park: 'I was puzzled, that

grown-ups could have separate legs like men, yet retain piled-up hair, veils and sweet voices.' Thirty years later it would have caused him no surprise at all.

Then came the Second World War, to deliver another hammerblow to tradition and formality. Once again uniform became the most acceptable form of dress, even the best-stocked wardrobe grew ragged as the war dragged on. For the civilian, to be shabby was to be in vogue, 'utility' clothes were introduced in 1942 to provide serviceable but resolutely unstylish suits or skirts for those who could find the clothing coupons to buy them. The British emerged from war to a bankrupt victory, longing for colour and variety yet knowing that their economic plight made it unlikely that they would quickly secure them. For the fashionable, Christian Dior's New Look, with its strikingly lengthened skirts, provided the first great post-war opportunity. The Chancellor of the Exchequer was horrified at the amount of extra cloth that would be needed if the New Look were to be generally adopted; he urged the Prime Minister to prohibit it, but the sagacious Attlee knew that it would be easier to dam Niagara and decreed that fashion should be

The gates of the park at Aberdare in South Wales in 1937 ABOVE LEFT (269). *The bowler hat worn by the man in front was a proud assertion that he was the boss and the rest his underlings.*

In 1886 at Buxton ABOVE
(270) women still played
tennis dressed as if they were
attending a garden party
given by a duchess.
By 1928 in Newquay LEFT
(271) a sensible cloche hat
and a shortish, though still
not short, skirt was
acceptable. Ten years later
they might even have been
wearing shorts.

First the idea of mixed bathing caused a frisson of dismay among the Mrs Grundies of the pool and seaside; by 1925 on the beach at Penrhyn Bay LEFT (**272**) *this line had obviously been breached.*

The lady bicyclists in Oyster Lane, Headley, in Surrey in 1906 ABOVE (**273**), *must have found their voluminous skirts something of a liability, but at that time* *anything more practical would have been deplored. At least the turn-out was uncommonly decorative, and the bicyclists seem confident enough.*

allowed to take its course. Rapidly the New Look spread across the country; affecting the clothes of those who had no pretensions to fashion and who had in many cases perhaps not even heard of Dior (plate 274).

JEANS USHER IN THE AGE OF UNISEX

The standards that had prevailed before 1939 would never be reinstated. Blue jeans became all the rage from about 1947, they were informal, they were flattering to the figure, they were worn by women as well as men. Jeans ushered in the age of unisex, soon pedestrians would find themselves speculating whether the slim and long-haired androgyne walking in front was male or female. The bathing dress allowed no such misconceptions and anyway became more exiguous by the moment. 1947 was the year of the bikini. It was predictably greeted with outrage by the conservative, equally predictably it was soon taken for granted and the cries of dismay reserved for topless bathing. Total seemed less shocking than semi-nudity. The nudist had long been accepted as a crankish but respectable figure who was probably a vegetarian as well. Vegetarianism in time became more main-

stream than nudity, but the latter throve and most resorts had some part of the beach reserved for its practitioners.

Even in the most entrenched bastions of tradition, the short black coat and striped trousers vanished as office wear, hair grew longer, shoes became suede, in time certain establishments even encouraged their staff to appear on Fridays in jeans and sandals. A few self-consciously antique establishments – like the bankers, Coutts – kept and still keep their staff in frock coats, but this is in the spirit of the theme park, as remote from reality as the Ruritanian generals who guard the doors into London's classier hotels and night clubs. A stout rearguard action was mounted to stop women wearing trousers at work, but as women increasingly reached positions of authority it became obvious that men would not be able to dictate the sartorial code for the new arrivals. Illogically, the conservatively minded male employer had taken equal exception to women shrouding their legs in trousers and exposing too much of them in mini-skirts. In the second case, too, they were defeated: mini-skirts offered little protection against the cold and, except in the case of the long-legged and

extremely slender, were aesthetically deplorable, but if that was what women wanted to wear, then wear it they would.

The most striking casualty in the gallop to informality was the hat. On London Bridge at rush hour in 1946 virtually all the pedestrians would have had something on their head. For men it might have been a bowler, trilby or cloth cap, for women something flannel and substantial or the most aethereal suggestion of a hat – but headgear was a necessary part of life. Within fifty years it had become the exception, the bowler an oddity to be gawped at by tourists and giggled at by teenagers. In the harsher days of winter a crop of Russian-style fur hats might blossom, but vanished again as soon as a flicker of watery sunshine appeared.

Fashions came and went, women's skirts continued to go up and down, the suns of the Mods and Rockers rose and, mercifully, set. But to a greater extent than ever before, people wore whatever it was convenient for them to wear, without undue consideration of the statement they were thereby making. Fashion was not dead, fashion will never die, but its stranglehold on the saner sections of society has at least temporarily been loosened.

Eating & Drinking

I F FRANCIS FRITH had wanted to eat outside his home, or, still more ambitious, to take his wife or lady-friend out for a meal, he would not have found many places to choose from. In London things would not have been too bad. All the larger hotels had dining-rooms that welcomed guests from outside, and though hotel dining-rooms, then as now, tended to be expensive and singularly staid, they were at least suitable for mixed entertaining of any kind. There were plenty of restaurants in London too, but here care had to be observed. Many of them verged on the raffish, more suitable for an illicit rendezvous than a sedate family outing. Who would dare surmise what was happening within the curtained recesses of a restaurant like Rules in Covent Garden; the thought that the Prince of Wales himself might be entertaining Lily Langtry in an upstairs room would have added a frisson of the improper to the most chaste of meetings. Other restaurants were wholly respectable but looked with some distaste on women; Simpson's in the Strand, associated until the mid-nineteenth century above all with cigars and chess, only allowed women to eat downstairs in 1984.

Other cities offered still less scope for gracious dining; in towns and the larger villages one was thrust back upon the coaching inn or, with luck, an 'eating house' (plate 275). Sometimes these were spacious and well decorated; more often they were like the 'coffee room' to which the young David Copperfield was ushered – a 'large long room with some large maps in it' – where he was given no alternative to chops, potatoes and a batter-pudding. In the typical pot-house, anywhere in the country, one would have been offered similar fare in murkier surroundings – certainly they were not a place to take a women with any claims to respectability.

For the most part, the British ate at home; a retreat to which Frith's camera – with one unexplained exception (plate 276) – was too discreet to pursue them. There was at least no difficulty in procuring the raw materials; any village worth its salt would have had at least one baker and butcher, one general grocer, one shop for fruit and vegetables. For the most part they were restricted to local products, but by 1870 refrigeration was beginning to change the pattern of British shopping. Meat from abroad, oranges, pineapples, were first luxuries found only in the larger centres but soon spread around the country. Bananas were hardly to be seen before the late nineteenth century, but consumption increased six-fold between 1900 and 1913. The British were convinced that food bought at stalls in the open air was both cheaper and more fresh than the same article procured in a shop. In the case of the Newlyn Fish Market they were probably quite right, but the fruit stall at Walberswick was unlikely to have offered any significant advantage over the local shop (plates 277, 278). With the exception of bread and cakes it was generally assumed that customers would procure the raw materials and do the rest themselves – often they baked at home as well. London was to some extent an exception; William Pitt's last words in 1806 are supposed to have been: 'I think I could eat one of Bellamy's veal pies' (a more convincing *envoi* than the

One of Frith's very few domestic interiors RIGHT *(276). The dining-room in Pinehurst, Surrey in 1925, was clearly the result of much loving care and attention. The telephone next to the door had probably only been installed within the last two or three years.*

The British tended – and tend – to believe that food bought in the open air would be fresher and cheaper than in a shop. In the case of the fish market at Newlyn in 1906 RIGHT (**278**) *they were probably right – fish went straight from boat to market and bargains were to be had at the end of the day. The fruit and vegetable stall at Walberswick, Suffolk (1919)* ABOVE (**277**) *looked less promising.*

grandiloquent version preferred by his doting biographer: 'My country! Oh, my country!'). The Old Original Bakewell Pudding Shop (plates 279, 280) suggests that even in the provinces one did not have to rely entirely on home cooking. But the concept of pre-cooked

foods was still hardly contemplated before the First World War; even in the 1960s somewhat unsavoury mixtures that could be extracted from a tin and heated up or, if one was lucky, fish and chips, were the best on offer for those who wanted a quick, hot and trouble-free meal.

*The Old Original
Bakewell Pudding Shop,
photographed in 1955
RIGHT (279) but on that
site for a great deal longer,
provided something as close
to the pre-cooked take-away
meal as could be looked for
in the nineteenth century.
In 1998 RIGHT BELOW
(280) it still enjoyed good
trade and was little changed
– bar a few extra placards
and floral decorations.*

1955 BAKEWELL

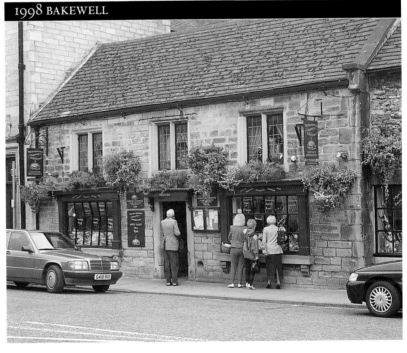

1998 BAKEWELL

THE FEMALE OFFICE WORKER DEMANDS BETTER THINGS

As prosperity spread downwards and the female office worker became an accepted feature of the business world, it became obvious that something other than a pot-house or a grand hotel was needed where a light – or lightish – mid-day meal could be obtained. A movement was fostered by a holy alliance of the temperance movement, which wanted to get people out of the pubs, and the tea and coffee importers, who wanted to boost their sales. They found an ally in the Aerated Bread Company, the ABC, who in 1884 first conceived the idea of offering customers to its bakeries the chance to have a cup of tea and light snack as well.

Originally the plan had been to attract people to its shops, soon the new enterprise became an important source of profit in its own right. The Express Dairy quickly followed suit; in 1894 the tea wholesaler Salmon and Gluckstein opened the first of its Lyons tea-shops at 213 Piccadilly. By 1910 there were nearly a hundred branches of Lyons to be found in London and, given the immense increase in the numbers of office workers in every city and major town, there seemed to be no limits to the demand for these clean, cheap, genteel and profoundly unadventurous institutions. The Lyons 'nippie', as the waitresses in their black dresses and neat white shirts were nicknamed, became a symbol of middle-class respectability; by the 1930s they were serving half a million meals a day.

Not everyone was content. 'We five-to-ten pound-a-weekers aren't well served in the way of eating places in London,' grumbled the hero of George Orwell's *Coming up for Air*. 'If your idea of the amount to spend is 1/3ᵈ, it's either Lyons, the Express Dairy or the ABC, or else it's the kind of a funeral snack they serve you in the saloon bar.' One response was the milk bar. From 1928, with enthusiastic backing from the Milk Marketing Board, 'milk bars' sprang up, offering quicker, lighter meals than the other restaurants. With their glittering expanses of glass and chrome, their high stools, their complicated gadgetry for producing American-style milk shakes with exotic names like Honolulu Dreamboat, or Passionflower Special, they offered a flavour of cosmopolitan glamour lacking in their staider rivals. Cheap Italian cafés also began to proliferate, staffed by an army of expatriates who were accepted as part of the local scene but then, in 1940, were arrested as spies and placed in internment camps. For the most part expensive French and cheap Italian restaurants provided the only foreign cooking available for the Briton, but between the wars the Chinese restaurateur began to venture from his redoubts in Liverpool and London's docklands, to open up to a wider clientele. Casanova's Chinese Restaurant, which Anthony Powell's Nick Jenkins patronized in the 1930s, catered for a clientele that was 'predominantly male and Asiatic, with a backbone of Chinese businessmen and Indian students', but employed English staff and was delighted to welcome English diners.

THE CULTURE OF THE TEA-ROOM

Tea, a fashionable drink since the seventeenth century which had grown immensely popular by the end of the nineteenth, generated its own culture. The very phrase 'tea-room' conjures up an image of prim respectability, middle-aged and be-hatted housewives contentedly shredding the reputations of their neighbours while they sipped their tea and ate cucumber sandwiches or daintily presented buns and cakes. In fact tea-rooms came in many guises:

Tea-rooms came in many shapes and sizes, but the Coombe Valley Mill in Cornwall (1929) LEFT *(281) was as good example of the rustic idyllic as could be asked for.*

the picturesque rural, the olde-world country town, the river-side terrace, the brash little hut dumped on the fringes of a village for no particular reason except that the site and, with luck, the demand was there (plates 281-283). The tea-room was the teetotaller's version of the pub, as much a social centre as a place of refreshment; it had passed its zenith by the time of the Second World War, but there are still few decent-sized villages and no towns that do not boast at least one of them today.

Apart from the mass internment of the Italian waiters, the war was notable for the first incursion of the government into catering. Concerned to provide a sustaining if frugal meal for workers who could not afford expensive restaurants, the Minister of Food, Lord Woolton, decided to open his own establishments. 'I hope the term "communal feeding centres" is not going to be adopted,' wrote Churchill anxiously. 'It is an odious expression, suggestive of Communism and the workhouse. I suggest you call them "British Restaurants". Everybody associates the word "restaurant" with a good meal, and they may as well have the name if they cannot get anything else.' There were eight hundred British

Another popular variety of tea-room was the 'Ye Olde' school. These tended to be in old, or at least quaint, buildings, as here in Rye in 1912 LEFT **(282)**.

Tea-rooms, houses or gardens might spring up anywhere it seemed possible that there would be a passing trade. The Copper Kettle in the New Forest, photographed in 1955 BELOW **(283)** *and now demolished, was rather more substantial. It is included for no reason except that the author used to spend his pocket money on sweets there when he was a child.*

It was not only in the great cities that ethnic restaurants flourished. In Kirriemuir, north of Dundee, a Chinese take-away rubs shoulders with an Indian restaurant, the Curriemuir RIGHT *(284). Nor is this all; behind the camera is Visocchi's Coffee Shop and Ice Cream Bar.*

Restaurants by the end of the war; they withered rapidly thereafter, but they had accustomed a new social class to the idea that it might be fun, from time to time, to eat away from home.

NEW APPETITES AND NEW PLEASURES

The coffee bar now came into vogue, nearer in spirit to the milk bar than the tea-shop but seeming to the youth of the period more engagingly up-to-date than either. The potted palms and flashy decorations, a fit setting for the glass and chrome Gaggia machine which spluttered and expectorated in the middle, were cosmopolitan, colourful and comfortingly cheap. Rather more recently the British way of eating began fundamentally to change. The consumption of eggs fell by nearly a half – a process speeded by dark rumours of contamination and sermons on the perils of cholesterol. Red meats were viewed with increasing nervousness; cream became a dirty word to all but the greedy or stout of heart; skimmed milk was soon the norm; fruit and vegetables were consumed in ever greater quantities, and people who had once thought it daring to eat a banana now rejoiced as a matter of course in lychees and kiwi fruit, mangoes and kumquats.

This new spirit of adventure spread to the restaurants. The Chinese restaurants, which had begun to escape from their ghettos before the war, in the 1950s burst the boundaries and within twenty years were ensconced in almost every town in Britain. In the wake of immigration a flood of Indian restaurants followed, claiming parity with their Asian neighbour. The Thais too took over a large slice of the market. From Europe, the Cypriot invasion began in the 1960s and accelerated after the civil war of 1974. The Greeks had already a foothold before the war; the British rarely distinguished between them and the Cypriots but patronized one as happily as the

There was always room for 'traditional' restaurants catering for a nostalgia for a largely imaginary past. The Hautboy Hotel at Ockham in Surrey (1938) LEFT (285) was a baronial great hall with swords and antlers. One would be lucky not to be served with mead and venison by wenches in fancy dress. The Galleon, at Seaford in Sussex (1965) BELOW (286), was as nautical as its name implied, with ship's wheels and lanterns prominent among the fittings.

other. And then there were the Lebanese and the Egyptians, the Mexicans, the Jamaicans and the Japanese: in London more than a hundred ethnic styles of cooking could be identified (plate 284). The familiar restaurant, however, did not disappear: there would always be a corner in British hearts for meat and two veg or soggy puddings.

Nostalgia was a powerful force, and oak beams and mock-Jacobean furnishings, swords and antlers, evoked an atmosphere which the diner-out would never have encountered in reality but which still seemed reassuringly familiar (plates 285, 286). Yet even in such fastnesses of tradition, the cooking became more ambitious. The British expected more and were also prepared to venture more when they ate out. No longer could they fairly be accused of insularity.

The growth of the fast food industry was still more phenomenal. Ever since Lord Sandwich made his celebrated breakthrough in

the late eighteenth century his creation had been an accepted feature of the British lunch, but with the 1980s and 1990s it became an art form, with specialized shops producing scores, even hundreds of exotic variations on the theme. Mineral waters achieved a similar success. Malvern had been exporting its waters for generations (plate 287) but now it seemed that every country town or stately home was bottling its water, putting on a fancy label and selling it at a high price to a clientele who were too gullible or too proud to insist on tap water in a restaurant.

Then there was the hamburger, a speciality of McDonald's and Burger King; and of course there was always the fish and chip shop, once dominating the world of take-away food, and still enjoying a substantial share of the market. Pizza Hut and Pizza Express popularized Italian food among millions who had never encountered it in more authentic surroundings. The Wimpy Bar and the Little Chef (plate 288) produced serviceable meals for the multitudes who had neither the time nor the money – perhaps not the inclination either – to dine more graciously.

Mr J H Cuff's Mineral Water Factory at Holywell, Great Malvern, in 1904 ABOVE (287). *Malvern produced one of the longest-established brands of mineral water which was held, by the bottlers at least, to be a sovereign remedy for a plethora of complaints.*

Take-away, or eat in, these popular, quick and inexpensive establishments, caught the spirit of the age as surely as any other national institution; more surely, indeed, than most.

THE PUB HAS CHANGED LESS RADICALLY THAN THE RESTAURANT

The pub has changed less radically than the restaurant; even though the government has interfered far more to try to direct its running. Since the fifteenth century the authorities have made spasmodic efforts to control the numbers and opening hours of public houses. In the eighteenth century gin was seen as the most potent menace, by the end of the nineteenth it was beer. There were then thirty percent more pubs than there are today, well over twice as many in terms of pubs per head of population. The big brewers were hard at work, buying up and refurbishing old pubs, building new ones, all dedicated to the sale of their own particular brand of beer (plates 289, 290). The temperance movement complained that the situation was growing out of control; at

A Wimpy Bar in Bexhill in 1965 ABOVE (**288**). *Wimpy produced quick food — preferably hamburgers — at a low price; and several million customers can't all be wrong.*

1890 SUTTON

1898 SUTTON

A development typical of what was happening all over Britain as the big brewers bought up old pubs and refurbished or rebuilt them. In 1890 the Cock Hotel at Sutton LEFT *(289) was a small, dignified coaching inn; eight years later it had been swamped if not totally pushed from the nest by the monstrous great cuckoo that had been built almost on top of it* LEFT BELOW *(290). The cuckoo itself perished when the street was widened in 1950.*

much happened, though there were more closures than new openings in the years before the First World War.

The brewers had got a point when they argued that the pub played an important social role. To sit in the pub or outside it with their beer and their pipes, and to chat with their friends, was one of the few forms of entertainment open to the lower classes at the end of the nineteenth century. The Bull and Bush — the 'Old Bush and Bush' where the music hall star Florrie Ford urged her admirers to 'Come, come, come and make eyes at me' — really was a valuable centre of local life. In remote hamlets pubs provided a rallying point where a scattered and rural community could find a measure of cohesion. In village life the pub was often indispensable (plates 291-296).

THE GOVERNMENT DECIDES TO INTERFERE MORE ACTIVELY

Between 1914 and 1918 the government made its most determined effort yet to regulate the beer trade. Lloyd George was convinced that

least thirty thousand pubs should be closed; the brewers retorted that this would be an outrageous infringement of liberty and that if even one pub was condemned the owner would expect lavish compensation. The Conservatives, by and large, backed the brewers; the Liberals, the temperance movement. In the end nothing

1899 HAMPSTEAD

The men seated outside a London pub, the Wall Worker BELOW (293), seem almost improbably content, but to sit in the sun, drink their pint and chat with their friends was one of the few forms of entertainment open to the working man in 1885. Anyway, Frith had probably bought them a drink, which would explain their contentment.

1998 HAMPSTEAD

The Bull and Bush (1899) ABOVE TOP (291) was a Hampstead pub that was celebrated as being the place where the music hall star, Florrie Ford, urged her followers to 'Come, come, come and make eyes at me'. Nobody would be likely to make eyes at her in today's 'Old' Bull and Bush ABOVE (292).

essential industry – ship-building in particular – was being put at risk by drunkenness among the work-force. 'We are fighting Germany, Austria and the drink,' he pronounced, 'and as far as I can see, the greatest of these deadly foes is drink.' Total prohibition was not declared, Lloyd George knew that he would have had a revolution on his hands if he had tried anything so drastic, but the King was bullied into renouncing alcohol until the war was over and in certain areas of particular importance – around Carlisle, for instance, where important armaments works were concentrated – the government acquired by State purchase all breweries and licensed premises and ran them under strict control. In Gretna the authorities actually bought a redundant post office and re-opened it as the Gretna Tavern. Lloyd George would probably have liked to continue the experiment after the war, but the Conservatives would have none of it, and this early and improbable foray into nationalisation was abandoned once the war was over.

Between the two wars a Royal Commission was set up to consider the effects of alcohol on

1929 COUNTISBURY

the British public. Its conclusions were broadly satisfactory to the brewers. 'The present century has seen a distinct advance in sobriety,' the report stated. Many people still drank more than was good for them but drunkenness was a rarity. The view of the Salvation Army was that, in the poorer parts of the cities, gambling was a greater threat to the fabric of society than heavy drinking.

The idea was beginning to spread that a pub ought to be more than just a place where men could congregate and drink. The new pubs built by the brewers in the 1920s and 1930s had billiard rooms, playgrounds for children, and often a restaurant attached. They were usually built in sternly contemporary style and could as well have passed for a post office or bank. One source of inspiration was the German beer-garden; the pub, it was maintained, should be an equally suitable venue for a family outing where a good time would be had by all.

Yet simultaneously there was a vogue for the picturesque. A new pub built from scratch would probably be modernistic; an old pub rehabilitated might well be endowed with fake Tudor half-timbers and quaintly leaded windows on the exterior and, inside, a plethora of spurious horse brasses and other such indications of antiquity. The Six Bells Inn at Billingshurst, decently unpretentious if a little drab, renewed life as Ye Olde Six Bells and by 1998 had been yet further tarted up (plates 297-300). The theme pub came into vogue, dedicated to the tin miner, the farm labourer, the angler and adorned with appropriate artefacts to evoke the atmosphere that might have prevailed a hundred years before.

THE DRINKER ABANDONS THE PUB FOR OTHER VENUES

The number of pubs continued to fall after the Second World War – from seventy thousand or so in 1956 to not much over sixty thousand twenty years later. The trend was towards fewer but larger pubs, and as the number of rival attractions grew – television to keep potential customers at home, cheap restaurants or amusement arcades to allure them once they ventured out – so the pub found it harder to survive unless it had extra facilities to offer. In country areas, where the permanent population dwindled and the young had access to cars or motor-cycles to carry them to the neighbouring town, attendance at the traditional 'local' fell away. Where there had been two there was now one; in time that too sometimes closed.

Fewer pubs did not mean less drinking. The new affluence, the end of national service, an explosion in the number of teenagers, together meant that the 1960s were marked by a notable amount of drunkenness. Barbara Castle's imposition of a drunk-driving law in 1967 would not have been so readily accepted if the need for it had not been obviously urgent; it weakened still further, however, the country

The Blue Ball Inn at Countisbury, on the fringes of Exmoor ABOVE LEFT **(295)**. *In remote hamlets like this the pub was one of the few places where a rural community could find a measure of cohesion. By 1998* ABOVE **(296)** *it had become the Exmoor Sandpiper but otherwise seemed to prosper.*

pub whose clientele had often come by car. But the drinking against which Barbara Castle was particularly guarding was not primarily of beer and for the most part did not take place in pubs. Far more alcohol was now being drunk off the premises; vodka for the first time joined whisky and gin as a major alternative to beer, sales of wine doubled, doubled again and then redoubled. As early as 1934 J B Priestley had been surprised to find that Southampton 'shared the taste of Fleet Street and the Strand for wine bars'; by 1970 it would have come as no surprise; any town of even minor consequence would have boasted a wine bar, probably more than one. Many women still found the atmosphere of the wine bar more congenial than a pub. The pubs recognized and accepted the new trend: whether the style was classical antiquated or austerely clinical, the late twentieth-century publican anticipated requests for wine as well as beer and spirits.

Today there are still more than fif thousand pubs and the decline in numbe seems to have been slowed if not yet altogeth arrested. Though there will always be anxie about the amount of alcohol consumed an Chancellors of the Exchequer will no doul relentlessly force up the price of drink ye after year, the leading public enemies now see to be drugs and smoking, and drink ha become a secondary bugbear to both th authorities and the public.

If present trends continue Britain's diet wi become ever more ethnically varied, mo people will become vegetarians, more peop will drink wine and less beer and spirits. But only because so many new tastes and fancie have been experimented with over the last fe decades, it seems likely that the pace of chang will slacken. Certainly future change coul hardly be more dramatic than it has been ove the last 130 years.

The Six Bells Inn at Billingshurst in 1912 ABOVE LEFT (297) was decently unpretentious if a little drab. By 1923 ABOVE MIDDLE (298) it had renewed life as Ye Olde Six Bells. By 1960 ABOVE RIGHT (299) it had been further tarted up and equipped with a multitude of tables and umbrellas in the garden. An extension on the left, an outside lamp and some desultory bunting completed the process by 1998 RIGHT (300).

1890 MAPLEDURHAM

1998 MAPLEDURHAM

The mill at Mapledurham on the outskirts of Reading in 1890 ABOVE (301). The cart was in the water not just for the sake of the horse but so as to keep the wood of the wheels damp and prevent it contracting and separating from the iron cladding. This mill has been kept in working order for the benefit of visitors in 1998 LEFT (302).

Farming

I N THE 1870s, when Francis Frith first began seriously to turn his attention to the farms of Britain, he would have been hard put to it to tell whether he was working in the nineteenth century or a hundred years earlier. There had, in fact, been an agricultural revolution in the 1770s and 1780s, when enlightened landlords like Coke of Norfolk began to apply themselves to the problem of making a profit out of their farms, but though the expert would have spotted many significant changes as a result, to the townsman it would have appeared that things were much the same. The barn still soared triumphant, unchallenged chieftain of the farm buildings that clustered around it, the lowing herd still wound slowly o'er the lea, the ploughman's way was no less weary. One of the few noticeable changes was the abundance of new hedgerows. Those who deplore the wholesale destruction of hedges over the last twenty or thirty years tend to think of them as an immemorial feature of the landscape, established by our medieval forbears. So some of them were, but many more were introduced in the mid-nineteenth century, when the need to produce more food led to the enclosure of much traditionally common land. Frith could have seen thousands of miles of hedging which would have seemed strange and out-of-place to Gray; otherwise the two men were looking at much the same things in much the same place.

But this tranquil scene — tranquil, at least, to the casual observer, who never suspects the state of almost continual crisis in which the average farmer lived and lives — was on the verge of a century and more of turbulent change. The British farmer had survived the repeal of the Corn Laws with greater ease than he had expected, but now the storm broke over his head. Wheat produced on the great prairies of the New World was already vastly cheaper than its home-grown counterpart; only the cost of transportation had kept it at bay, and between 1873 and 1883 the charges for carrying grain from Chicago to Liverpool fell by a third. At the same time imports of meat from Australia and New Zealand vastly increased; a hundred-fold within a period of five or six years. British farming had been devastated by the introduction of the steamship. In 1870 there was a greater acreage under plough in Britain than ever before or since; within twenty years the area had been halved. The spring countryside changed colour, from brown to green, as three million acres of arable farming were abandoned and the land put out to grass. The small mills around the country which had for centuries ground the corn of the land around them could not compete with their huge rivals handling imported grain at the ports where it arrived: one by one they closed, fell into dereliction, disappeared or were converted into houses (plates 301-304).

THE DEMAND FOR LABOUR FALLS AWAY

The rural population suffered. Even before mechanisation began to make serious inroads into the employment market the decline in arable farming had reduced the need for semi-skilled labour. Membership of the National Agricultural Labourers' Union fell by nearly three quarters between

The mill at Mundesley on Sea in North Norfolk LEFT (303) *was evidently still deemed useful enough in 1921 to justify some patching up; by 1950* BELOW (304) *it had disappeared.*

1950 MUNDESLEY ON SEA

1872 and 1879; partly because farmworkers could not afford to pay their dues, more often because they had given up the battle and left the land. The depopulation of the farms had begun and was to continue inexorably until the First World War. Landlords, who found it hard to compete with new conditions, built virtually no new cottages and spent as little as possible on shoring up those which already existed. Buildings which were surplus to requirements began to crumble. Rural slums became a commonplace; almost, indeed, the norm.

The farmer adapted, but not in a way which did much to increase the demand for labour. His wheat and meat might have been priced out of the market, but there was one product at least which was largely free from foreign competition. Though butter and cheese might be imported, the market for fresh milk remained secure, and as the new railway network provided facilities for carrying it into the urban areas, so demand doubled and redoubled. The milk train, chugging its early morning course into the heart of the city, became a vital factor in the economics of

agriculture, the great dairy herds more and more dominated the farming landscape. Milk, and the new vegetable gardens that were set up to serve the ever-growing population of the towns and cities, provided an increasing part of the farmers' income (plates 305, 306).

But it was mechanisation that did most to depopulate the countryside. At first the process did not displace the horse. The mechanical

The Highland cattle above Loch Long in 1901 LEFT (305) might still be seen there, for there are many reasons beyond the economic for keeping these most picturesque of beasts. The sort of scene photographed at Pyles Farm in Addlestone near Chertsey three years later BELOW (306), however, becomes increasingly rare in the farming landscape.

reapers and hay-mowing machines, which became common towards the end of the Victorian era, were for the most part drawn by horses. Steam was increasingly used to power the static machines that were being introduced back at the farmyard, but in the field its value was limited. Steam traction engines drew ploughs on a cable to and fro across a field, but though the system had its partisans, it was in general found to be ineffective. The ploughing machine was so heavy that it frequently bogged down; the horse was altogether cheaper, more reliable and more efficient. What could not be done by hand was done with the help of a horse. There were almost a million horses at work on British farms in 1911, substantially more than there had been thirty years before (plates 307-313).

The Strand Horse Fair in Barnstaple in 1923 ABOVE **(307)**. *Though the mechanisation of farming was already advanced the horse population on Britain's farms had hardly begun to drop off.*

Lord Bathurst's team of oxen at Cirencester Park in Gloucestershire were an anachronism even in 1898 LEFT (309). Not even their proud owner suggested they were a sensible alternative to the horse.

At Hawes in North Yorkshire they used a sledge for haymaking in 1923 ABOVE (308); though tractors were increasingly available, only the most go-ahead farmer used them for such purposes.

Ploughing near Leatherhead, 1925 LEFT **(310)**. *Tractors got bogged in the heavy soil; tractors broke down; tractors were expensive to run; tractors were nasty, smelly things; above all tractors weren't horses.*

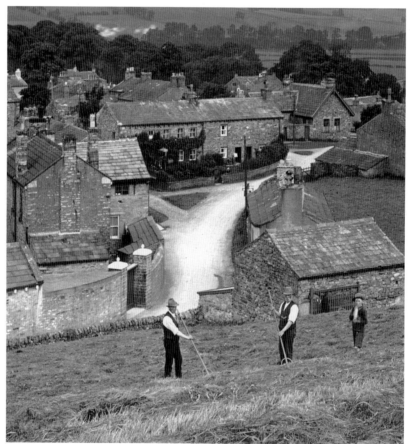

What the horse couldn't do, manual labour could. In Bainbridge, North Yorkshire (1924) RIGHT **(311)** *the farm ran almost into the village; the farmhands would have been at home within a few minutes of stopping work.*

The farm hands riding home after a day's harvesting on Lullington Hill near Alfriston, Sussex, in 1894 LEFT (312) had no other source of motive power except their legs, but, by 1955, when the harvest was being brought in at Garboldisham in Norfolk BELOW (313), the farmer could easily have acquired a tractor if he had wanted one. But who, he might have wondered, needs a tractor when a horse can pull loads like this?

THE MARCH OF THE MACHINE

But already they were under threat. In 1902 Dan Albone of Biggleswade had produced a petrol-driven tractor; the following year he set up a company to manufacture these devices. At first there was scepticism; even if the tractors worked, it was argued, they suffered from the fatal weakness of not producing any manure. Even as late as 1939 there were ten times as many horses on British farms as there were tractors – but already the tractors were producing around two-thirds of the mobile force (plate 314).

The combine harvester was still an expensive novelty at the outbreak of the Second World War, but only the sentimentalist or the reactionary doubted that this too must be the way of the future. By 1960 there were a hundred for every one that had existed before the war. It rendered the role of the horse still more peripheral. Increasingly, those noble animals, so inevitable a part of life for anyone over the age of sixty who when young had witnessed a farm at work, have become an antiquarians' toy or an advertising gimmick for traditionally minded brewers (plate 315).

The march of the machine was not unopposed. The novelist, Rider Haggard, who prided himself on his generally progressive approach to farming problems, maintained as late as 1899 that no reaping machine could ever match the manual labourer for flexibility and reliability. Nor did the manual labourer himself always accept his incipient redundancy with becoming meekness. The Luddites might have perished on the scaffold at York in 1817 but their soul went marching on. Even at the end of the nineteenth century ploughing machines and self-binding reapers were being destroyed by indignant labourers; in 1878, a Kent farmer pursuing suspected saboteurs was attacked at night and murdered for his pains.

If those labourers had been able to look ahead they would have known that the milking machine would pose an even deadlier threat to their livelihood. Like the combine harvester, the milking machine was still a relative rarity in 1939 – perhaps one in seven cows was by then served by a system that was often erratic and wasteful in its operation as well as being disproportionately expensive to install and run. Like the combine harvester, it swept all before it in the decades after the Second World War; by the late 1970s manual milking would have been considered an oddity on anything except the smallest homestead.

THE FARM BEGINS TO LOOK LIKE A FACTORY

The larger herds that were essential if expensive milking systems were to be justified made necessary new buildings. So did the need to house the ever larger machines. The physical appearance of any farm that had pretensions to being up-to-date was transformed in the fifty

Four years earlier, in 1951 in Llansilin, west of Oswestry ABOVE (314), *th break had already been made. Tractors had replaced the horses. The farmer in Garboldisham who stuck to his horses was beginning to seem old-fashioned.*

The heavy horse, so much a part of the farming scene for anybody over the age of sixty or so, has almost completely vanished, surviving only as an antiquarian's toy or, as here in Devizes LEFT *(315), as an advertising gimmick for some traditionally minded brewers.*

years after the Second World War. Some changes, of course, had been visible far earlier. Silage had been introduced by the more avant-garde farmers as long ago as the 1880s. At first the silos were in pits or primitive stacks held in place by strained rope wires, but these were abandoned as inefficient. Briefly, silage went out of fashion, but soon a new system was appearing: towers, based on American designs, built in wood, concrete, steel or brick. The silo

This noble stone barn
LEFT *(316) cannot be*
traced. Does it still exist?
If so, has it suffered the fate
of so many of its peers and
been converted into a bijou
country home?

Cromwell's barn at St Ives
in Cambridgeshire BELOW
(317) already looked rather
frayed in 1931 but it was
still very much at the heart
of the farm's activities. Now
it has been destroyed.

was the first building of the modern age to challenge the barn as the most prominent feature on the farmyard.

The traditional barn, indeed, was in trouble. For centuries, often since the Middle Ages, these majestic cathedrals of the agricultural world had been at the centre of the farm's activities. Increasingly, they had become irrelevant to the daily routine; operating as little more than store houses in which could be dumped anything that needed a roof over its head and had no more specialized building at its disposal. Their vast extent and huge timbered roofs made them expensive to maintain; the only thing that saved them from mass destruction in the years before and after the Second World War was the fact that many farmers lacked the money to demolish and replace them (plates 316, 317). When the funds did exist, Dutch barns, unsightly constructions of steel and corrugated iron, rose in their place; when they did not, the barn was suffered to crumble, often to collapse. Since 1980 the preservation of the barn has become a prime target for conservationists. Many have

been saved. Some still fulfil the functions for which they were originally created. More have survived at the price of conversion into country retreats for the week-ender. The conversions have often been carried out with

By 1953 Kithurst Barn in Storrington RIGHT (318) had been sadly neglected; it did not look as if the gate in the centre had been opened for a year or more. Unlike Cromwell's barn, however, it survived and in 1972 was converted into a private house. Today RIGHT BELOW (319) it is once more in the process of refurbishment.

taste and discretion, and it is anyway better that the barn should continue in this adulterated form than perish altogether. It is difficult, however, to survey its spruce exterior, with windows elegantly inserted and flower beds clustered around the walls, without experiencing the vague dismay which one feels when seeing an ocean-going liner converted into a static gambling casino or dormitory for tourists (plates 318, 319).

Cornstacks and haystacks, by the 1960s and 1970s were becoming as obsolete as windmills. Here were a group of stacks on the outskirts of West Lulworth, Dorset, in 1904 LEFT *(320), and at West Dean, near Seaford, in 1921* BELOW *(321). The rick yard in West Lulworth is now 'Rickyard Cottages'; the view of Seaford is unrepeatable because of the activities of the Forestry Commission but the ricks themselves have long since vanished anyway.*

Corrugated iron, so prominent in the Dutch barn and many other twentieth century farm buildings, vied with cement as being the single most important element in the first wave of the farmyard's transformation. It was cheaper than thatch, tiles or timber, quicker to install, easier to maintain. The fact that it was also liable to rust, however, made it both unsightly and – more importantly in the eyes of most farmers – in need of regular replacement. In the early 1930s asbestos-cement sheeting began to take its place; then, as asbestos became a dirty word and plastic more adaptable, plastic sheeting of various weights, shapes and colours. The wood, stone and brick which had been ubiquitous when Frith took his first photographs, were now rarities, used mainly by the rich with an eye for the picturesque.

The gap between farm and factory was being whittled away. Facilities for storing and drying grain became more substantial and grain-stores took over from silos in challenging the barn for pride of place. The quantities of liquid fuel

that were used every year by the larger farms called for massive tanks, usually rearing on piers beside a cement roadway. Cornstacks and haystacks, for so long a visible manifestation of what the farm was all about (plates 320, 321), became as obsolete as windmills; if crops remained outside at all it was in squared-off blocks swathed in black plastic sheeting.

LIVESTOCK FIT RELUCTANTLY INTO THE MECHANISTIC PATTERN

With the exception of the sheep, which, together with its traditional companion, the goat, has remained relatively free to continue its immemorial existence (plates 322-326), the animals which survive in the farming world today have had to fit into the new mechanistic pattern. Recently the pace has quickened. Until well after the Second World War the pig, even when farmed intensively, still led a recognizably porcine life. To inhabit a huge field, pimpled with corrugated iron arks, was not as good as roaming the forests in search of acorns, but it was at least a life in the open air. Gradually, however, it dawned on the expert that it would be more efficient if the pig were to pass the whole of its life in a controlled environment, confined to a pen where it, and several thousand others, could be fed regularly and protected from excessive heat or cold by one man pressing a switch at the appropriate moment. Another long pre-fabricated building was added to the industrial complex that made

Almost alone among farm animals, sheep are allowed to live much as they did 140 years ago. The descendants of the sheep photographed somewhere in North Yorkshire in 1865 ABOVE (322) or at Tintagel in North Cornwall in 1894 LEFT (323), could well be there today.

up the modern farmyard; usually a scanty run existed alongside where the pigs could occasionally see the light of day, but this was more a sop to the sentimentalist than a serious contribution to the pig's quality of life.

The chicken was still more vulnerable to this sort of treatment. Cod liver oil could provide birds with Vitamin D, so they were deprived of daylight. The battery system was first tried out in the United States and was found in Britain by 1930, but the broilerhouse did not really establish itself until the early 1950s. Then it grew explosively. By 1970 a hundred million birds a year were spending their brief, cheerless lives caged in long windowless sheds; diligently fed and watered but offered no vestige of freedom. The distinguishing feature of these sinister barrack blocks was the tall hopper where food was delivered. Belsen had come to the British countryside.

Cattle could not be treated with quite such ruthlessness but a nineteenth century farmer would notice with surprise how rare it is today to see herds grazing at any distance from their yard. Whether they were kept for milk or meat a herd of any size would be congregated in a cowhouse complex, perhaps three hundred to a building. They were allowed brief outings in an adjacent paddock – in summer a dust bowl, in winter a sea of mud – but the luxury of grazing was not permitted. Instead, a carefully controlled portion of food was presented to them each day. No doubt their diet was better balanced as a result, though the BSE epidemic has shown dramatically what fearful blunders can be committed in the name of science.

Of course there are still plenty of farms with a well-stocked duckpond, a yard where hens pick busily between the cobbles and a goat surveys arrivals with supercilious disdain

In 1965 sheep-dipping from
a coracle was obviously
something of an oddity even
in Cenarth, Dyfed ABOVE
(325) – hence the group of
onlookers. Shearing, though
the equipment has been
modernized, still follows
much the same procedures as
it did in Coldbeck, Cumbria
in 1955 RIGHT (326) or,
for that matter, a century
before.

(plates 327, 328, 331). But usually these belong to small-holdings or are an indulgence allowed by the farmer to his nostalgic wife. Farming today is big business. To survive, the farmer must come to terms with present-day demands – and resist the depredations of the developer and the town planner if his land is close to a town or village (plates 329, 330).

HEDGES AND SET-ASIDE

Outside the immediate environs of the farmyard the requirements of big business have not so clearly left their mark, though rape and flax have added an exotic and sometimes garish note to the traditional greens and browns of the British countryside. One sign of the time is the vanishing hedgerow. The hedges so

Old Ford Farm, near Bideford, in 1890 LEFT *(327), was typical of the traditional farmyard where hens picked busily between the cobbles. They are still to be found today, but usually belong to a smallholder or are no more than an indulgence allowed by the farmer to his nostalgic wife. This one, in 1998* BELOW *(328) still recognisable but no longer serving as a farmyard, is in fact part of a house which once belonged to a steward of Sir Richard Grenville and is one of the oldest structures in the neighbourhood.*

1998 BIDEFORD

aboriously put in place in the first half of the nineteenth century are now being swept away, not to allow a reversion to common land, but so as to produce prairies in which giant machines can operate more efficiently. Road-widening schemes and housing projects speeded the destruction; 350,000 miles of hedgerow in 1984 have fallen to under 200,000 today, and though legislation is promised to check or even reverse the process, a further 7,500 are still being lost each year.

With the hedges go their inhabitants: there are today only half the linnets that were to be found a quarter of a century ago, and little more than a tenth the number of tree sparrows. The barn owl – mown down by motor cars and

1890 BIDEFORD

1998 BIDEFORD

Harvesting across the river from Bideford in 1890 ABOVE (329). By 1998 LEFT (330) the town had struck across its bridge and the cornfield was covered by the villas of Salternes Terrace. On the other hand, the railway line protected by the fence in the earlier picture has now been closed and converted into a long-distance footpath.

Ovey's Farm at Cookham in 1914 RIGHT (331) — *a site memorable to John Cleare, the photographer who has been taking the up-dated views, as being the only one in the British Isles where the owner demanded a fee in exchange for allowing the property to be photographed: hence no modern photograph.*

deprived of its natural nesting places — is perhaps the most conspicuous victim of progress on the farm, but the small brown birds which we have for so long taken for granted have suffered quite as severely (plates 332, 333).

The problem of over-production is now added to the farmer's woes. There are quotas for this and quotas for that — but these are not the traditional totalitarian quotas which lay down some impossibly distant targets for yields that must be reached, but they are quotas forbidding the farmer to produce more than a certain amount. To the layman it seems odd that, when so much of the world is patently short of food, it should be thought desirable to pay the British farmer to set aside part of his cultivated land as a reserve in which nothing may be grown, but such are evidently the dictates of economic necessity today.

Even the most untutored eye can see the obvious consequences as once prosperous farmland returns to the wild. Occasionally the results are scenically successful; some farmers take advantage of the restrictions to encourage wild flowers and contrive suitable habitats for threatened species of birds or animals.

THE INDUSTRIAL FARM IS NO THING OF BEAUTY

No one would claim that the industrial farm, with a concentration of large pre-fabricated buildings, most of the livestock permanently under wraps, and prairie-like expanses of beet or wheat, has much attraction for the casual visitor. Factory farming is as aesthetically unappealing as any other kind of factory.

Many smaller farms, however, desperately casting around for fresh sources of income, are offering their activities as a tourist attraction. For children on holiday or on a school excursion to visit a traditional farm and to experience the pleasures — even the pains — of a manner of life which their grandfathers took for granted, must be a welcome widening of their horizons. Probably it is one largely irrelevant to the life that they will lead themselves, but it is none the worse for that.

To the farm as funfair can be added the farm as 'bed-and-breakfast'. All over Britain, where country lanes meander away from the highway, can be seen the – usually mercifully discreet – signposts bearing the inscription 'b-and-b'. This carries the promise of a quiet night at a modest price, followed by the sort of breakfast, outrageous with carbohydrates, which the right-minded town-dweller would never contemplate at home but will eat with relish at somebody else's table. The farmer and his wife will never grow rich by providing such a service, but for a small and struggling farm the b-and-b market can make the difference between bankruptcy and survival.

There are, of course, many farms where the pace of change is far less marked. If Francis Frith were to visit today a hill farm in Argyll,

Westmorland or Powys, he would see little except a battered tractor, telephone and electricity wires, a television aerial, to tell him that well over a hundred years had passed since he had first photographed the scene. The sheep still roam the hillside, the dogs perform their policemen duties, the walls have rarely been replaced by wire. What new buildings there are may be in alien materials, but there will be

precious few of them: certainly no broilerhouses, grain-storage units, mega-cattle sheds. The primary objective of all farming remains the same – to produce, usually, food, sometimes other raw materials. In the case of the great lowland farm, however, methods have changed so radically as to render it, to all intents and purposes, a new form of industry. In the Argyll hill farm there have been only minor modifications of technique.

It is possible to accept the evolution of British farming as inevitable and yet still to deplore the uglification of the countryside. The vast majority of the changes made since 1870 have been aesthetically for the worse. Some sacrifices were necessary – the picturesque cannot always be saved at the expense of efficiency. Many more were not. The controls which are working reasonably well in the countryside as a whole are signally failing to curb the farmer. Often he gets away with what, in a visual sense, is close to murder. If the deterioration is allowed to continue at its present pace, then one can be certain that the average farm in fifty or a hundred years will be a grisly spectacle.

North Devon does not compare with East Anglia when it comes to the destruction of hedges so as to create the prairies in which the new giant machines can work to the best advantage. Nevertheless, the contrast between Taddiport in 1923 LEFT (332) *and in 1998* ABOVE (333) *shows how, even on this miniature scale, the hedge has lost out to the agrarian developer.*

Fishing

To COMPARE THE ACTIVITIES of the solitary angler with those of a fleet of deep-sea trawlers may seem far-fetched. One involves the exercise for pleasure of an individual craft, or perhaps art; the other is a profit-making industry. Both, however, involve the extraction from water of creatures that are slimy and, with luck, edible; neither merits a chapter on its own. This, therefore, deals with fishing as an industry, with fishing as a sport added as a by no means inconsiderable coda – one moreover which is growing as its big brother shrinks.

Britain, it was once said, enjoyed the singular advantage of being an island made out of coal and surrounded by fish. Today the coal is largely exhausted and what is left is often neglected; fish stocks have been depleted and competition for what remains is more intense. Both industries throve and expanded dramatically in the nineteenth century, both have retracted sharply in the twentieth. But while coal mining is now confined to a few areas and is under pressure even there, fishing is still widespread and the main activity of many thousands. It seems in no imminent peril of decease.

Until the 1840s or thereabouts the fishing industry operated on a scale and by methods that had evolved gradually but imperceptibly over the centuries. The fishwives and fishermen whom Frith photographed so lovingly, lived, for the most part, at the end of the nineteenth century, but give or take a few items of clothing, they would have been doing the same things in the same way a hundred years before (plates 334-337). Nor had the fishing vessels photographed at the same time changed to any marked degree (plates 338-343). But though the old world survived, it was increasingly by-passed by a revolutionary new wave which made demands with which the veterans could not cope, yet offered rewards far greater than any they had been accustomed to enjoy.

RAILWAYS AND REFRIGERATION CHANGE THE FACE OF FISHING

As with so much in the British nineteenth century, it was the railways that precipitated change. Until the 1840s and 1850s fresh sea fish was virtually unknown in inland areas; smoked or salted it might be available but salted and pickled herrings were both expensive to produce and not particularly tempting to the palate. The railways were able to ensure that regular and sufficient

The group of fishwives in
Tenby in 1890 ABOVE
(334) was timeless both in
their costumes and in their
countenances – a few details
of dress might betray the date
but in essence they could
have been sitting in the same
place doing the same thing in
1800 or even earlier.

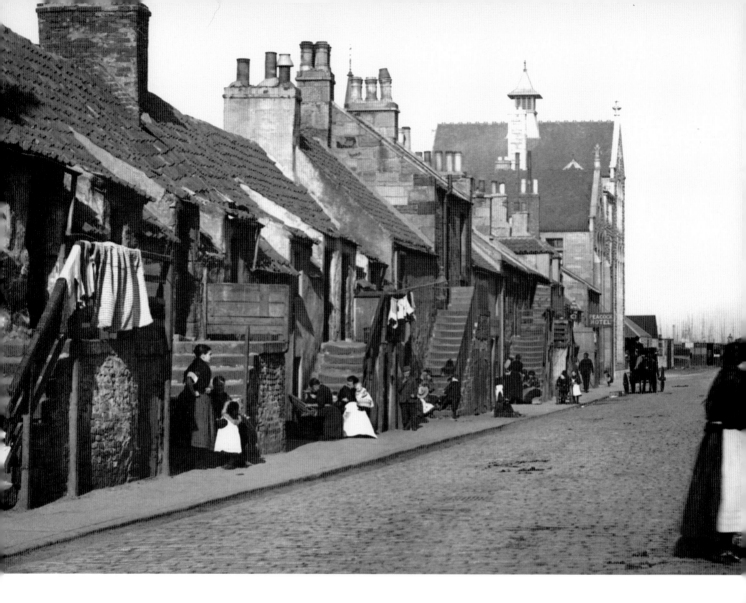

A row of fishermen's
cottages at Newhaven,
Lothian, in 1897 ABOVE
(335). The steep steps
leading up to the doorways
suggest how exposed the
houses were to the sea
which also furnished the
inhabitants here with
their livelihood.

The fishermen casting their nets from their coracles at Cenarth in Dyfed were photographed in 1960 LEFT (337), but their equipment and techniques had not varied for centuries.

The fishermen mending lobster pots at Sheringham in 1906 ABOVE (336) were as hard to date as the fishwives at Tenby in plate 334 sixteen years earlier.

1998 MEVAGISSEY

Fishing fleets in the harbours of Mevagissey (1890) LEFT ABOVE (338) *and Newlyn (1895)* ABOVE (340). *As the contemporary photograph of Mevagissey attests* LEFT (339), *it is still an active fishing port, though the number of boats engaged in full-time fishing has diminished.*

The fishing fleet in Scarborough in 1890
RIGHT (341). *An excursion steamer has bustled up in the midst of them.*

The herring fleet in Stornoway on the island of Lewis in 1890 LEFT (342). *For a small community of this kind the success or failure of a fishing season was of vital economic importance; the heavy fishing smacks seen in Sutton Pool, the original port of Plymouth, in the same year* LEFT BELOW (343), *counted for much in the lives of their crews and owners but were only peripheral to the prosperity of the city.*

supplies of fresh fish were available for sale in every inland town. But though the train could transport fish far more rapidly and efficiently than barges or horse-drawn transport, it could not guarantee that its cargo would be eatable once it had been distributed to the retailers and offered for sale for a day or two or even longer. Ice was the second vital factor in the expansion of the trade; its use on board the trawlers meant that the boats could spend longer at sea and larger catches could be accumulated; its use on land gave the traders a chance to distribute

the catches far more widely. At one time Essex farmers used to flood their fields in winter and sell the resultant ice for storage underground, but this proved unreliable; by the 1850s large cargoes of ice were being picked up in Norway by trawlers that used the ice at sea and delivered what was left when they finally reached their home port.

The demand for fresh fish grew with amazing speed (plates 344-346). Within thirty years landings at Grimsby rose from 450 tons a year to very nearly sixty thousand.

Sheffield opened a wholesale fish market almost entirely dependent on Grimsby's products, from there the fish was distributed over the whole region. Thirteen trains a day were dedicated to the transport of Grimsby's catches. By 1890 the average Briton was eating twenty-five pounds of fish a year, by 1910 the figure was thirty pounds. A quarter of this was consumed in the form of fish and chips. The boats that supplied this new demand also changed radically. The development of steam power in the second half of the nineteenth

Railways and refrigeration led to enormously increased demand for fresh fish. The fishing fleet at Grimsby grew more rapidly than that of any other port; part of it seen here ABOVE (344) *in the docks in 1893.*

Within thirty years landings of fish at Grimsby rose from 450 to the best part of 60,000 tons a year. The display of part of its catch on the fish pontoon dates from 1906 ABOVE TOP *(345). Other ports, like Fraserburgh at the mouth of the Moray Firth, whose herring fleet is seen here in 1898* ABOVE *(346), also expanded rapidly, but not on the same industrial scale.*

century increased both the size and the range of the trawler. It also increased the cost. One sailing boat could operate successfully from a tiny port; if the steam boat was to work at full efficiency it needed facilities that could only be justified by the existence of a fishing fleet. More and more the industry was concentrated in a number of ports which left the rest far behind and in the end forced many of them to

close. Hull led the way; by the 1930s it was the leading fishing port of Britain; bringing in well over 200,000 tons a year, above all of cod. Grimsby was only a little way behind. But, measured by value, more than half Britain's fish came ashore in Scotland; Aberdeen was the only port that competed for pride of place with Hull and Grimsby, but Fraserburgh, Leith, Ullapool all landed important catches.

THE SMALLER FISHING PORTS COME UNDER PRESSURE

But though the smaller fishing ports were weakened by the competition from their more thrusting and successful rivals, most of them survived until well into the twentieth century and many, though on a reduced scale, to the present day (plates 347-350). In social terms, the effect of the changed economic climate was

St Ives in Cornwall (1908) ABOVE (**347**) *was once so dominated by fishing that the vicar complained that the smell could stop the church clock. Fishing still goes on, but the clock is in no danger from the smell today.*

in some cases catastrophic. For many ports fishing had been their principal source of livelihood, to the same extent as a coal-mining village or a wool town might be dependent on a single product for its existence. The Vicar of St Ives once remarked that the smell of fish there was so potent that it sometimes stopped the church clock. No doubt at times he would have wished the smell away if he had not known that, without it, his clock might have run better but the life-blood of his parishioners would soon have drained away. Fishermen supplemented their earnings by taking summer visitors on trips around the lighthouse or

1899 INVERARY CASTLE

The smaller Scottish fishing ports were subject to the same pressure. There are no fishing boats to be found now below Inverary Castle as there were in 1899 LEFT (348). In 1998 the Arctic Penguin Historic Ship Museum BELOW (349) is the only vessel to be seen regularly afloat.

1998 INVERARY CASTLE

Arctic Penguin
Historic

offering outings to private anglers but this was still a by-product of their real occupation. The small and often improbably picturesque fishing villages that still abounded after the Second World War survived, but only just. The lifeboats on whose existence their safety might depend dwindled in number but still provided a basic service (plate 351). What changed them most was competition from abroad, the depletion of fish stocks that resulted from the free-for-all, and the efforts of governments to prevent the extinction of certain breeds by imposing strict quotas on the amounts that could be caught. For many small fleets, not to

The boats on the beach before Arran Castle (1890) ABOVE (350), if they survive at all, are more likely to be taking tourists for trips in the vicinity than engaging in fishing. Where fishing still takes place it will probably be done privately and on a domestic scale.

mention single vessels, fish became more difficult to find; when they did track down a shoal, they were often not allowed to catch them. There were 984 fishing vessels registered at Yarmouth in 1920; by the 1970s there were none.

REPORTS OF THE DEATH OF BRITAIN'S FISHING INDUSTRY ARE PREMATURE

In spite of such real setbacks, reports of the death of Britain's fishing industry are mercifully premature. We still catch well over half the fish that we consume each year, there are over nine thousand registered fishing vessels, the trade is worth many millions of pounds a year to those who bring in the fish and to those who sell it. But year on year the number of vessels dwindles, as does the tonnage of fish brought ashore. The future, if not necessarily calamitous, is certainly bleak. The small fishing village that might have boasted half a dozen boats in 1950 is now down to one or two, and they are often mainly used for entertaining tourists. The fishermen have moved away to make a living in some other way, their cottages have been converted into holiday lets or bought by people from the town who want a seaside base.

There have been gains, too. The farming of salmon, which in the early 1970s was yielding a thousand tons of fish a year, now produces getting on for a hundred times as much; connoisseurs claim that farmed salmon cannot compare for quality with the wild fish, but nevertheless what was

The small boys who were dangling their lines into Weymouth harbour in 1913 RIGHT (352) were perhaps exercising less artistry than the fly fisher on the Test or the salmon fisher on the Beauly but they were having just as much fun. Today OPPOSITE BELOW (353) the stone bollard remains but the boys have gone, and the waterfront opposite with them.

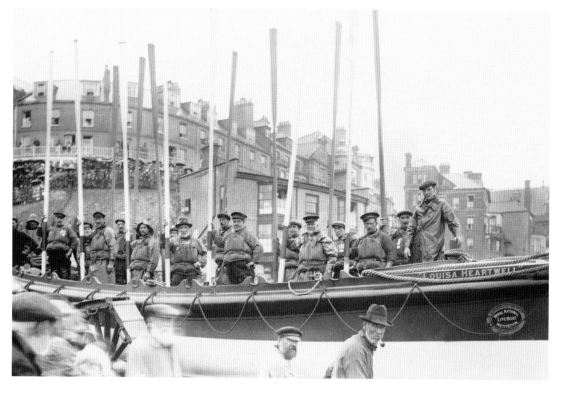

The Cromer lifeboat in 1922 LEFT (351). By the 1960s and 1970s fewer fishing ports could maintain their own lifeboat, but a basic service was still maintained.

913 WEYMOUTH

once a luxury is now no more of a rarity than cod or plaice. Lobsters, crabs, oysters are all being subjected to the same regime. If the trade continues to expand at its present rate it may recoup much of the loss which the fishing industry has suffered on the high seas. Aesthetically, however, the damage will be irreparable: the pens in which the farmed salmon are confined are at the best inoffensive; the beauty of a fishing fleet under sail as it leaves its harbour can never be matched by the methods of today.

Whether men extracted fish from the sea or from the lakes and rivers, the primary purpose was at first the same — to eat the product. No one can state with precision how it happened that, while the catching of fish at sea has, for the most part, become an industry, angling for fish in fresh waters has developed into a sport. Nor is it clear exactly when it happened, though when Izaak Walton published *The Compleat Angler* in 1653 the sport was already well established. As so often the early practitioners tended to be rich or well connected. Even today, fishing for salmon in one of the more celebrated Scottish rivers, or with dry fly for trout on the Hampshire Test or Itchen is not a pursuit for the generality

1998 WEYMOUTH

of mankind. As so often, however, the less rich and well connected have showed that it is possible to have as much fun, at vastly smaller expense. The small boys dangling their lines into Weymouth harbour (plate 352) enjoy the thrill of the sport as intensely as the solitary angler or deep sea game fisherman.

'A WORM AT ONE END AND A FOOL AT THE OTHER'

Dr Johnson would not have agreed. Fly fishing might be a pleasant amusement, he conceded, 'but angling or float fishing I can only compare to a stick and a string, with a worm at one end and a fool at the other'. If he was right, there are an awful lot of fools today. Angling is the most popular single sport in the British Isles, followed by more than three million devotees.

Few of these are in pursuit of the aristocratic trout or salmon; the roach, the eel, the uncouth catfish are more likely victims. The fisherman for trout or salmon boasts that his is a solitary sport, which takes him to beautiful places (plates 354, 355). No one who has seen a long line of green umbrellas along the side of a canal or river can believe that those beneath them are in search of solitude. Nor are the places where they forgather necessarily of great beauty (plates 356-359). But the sport takes people into the open air and provides excitement and competition. The cynics watch with interest to see whether, once the opponents of blood sports have had their way with hunting and shooting, they will pause to draw breath and then attack this vastly more popular diversion.

The fisher for trout or salmon is accustomed to claim that his sport takes him into remote and beautiful spots. The fisherman near Bodmin in 1906 ABOVE (**354**) *had certainly found tranquillity; Byron's Pool at Grantchester* OPPOSITE ABOVE (**355**) *was a little more frequented but the spot could hardly be more seductively rural.*

The same could not be said
for the riverbank at
Kingston, though the anglers
of 1890 BELOW (356)
presented a peaceful scene,
with the flat-bottomed
Thames sailing barge in
the background.

The Thames at Richmond, where the anglers were congregating in 1947 ABOVE (357), might have had some scenic appeal, but Anderby Creek in Lincolnshire (1955) OPPOSITE ABOVE (358) must have been among the most charmless fishing spots. No doubt the fishing was equally enjoyable.

No one could claim that this fisherman LEFT (359) — a seventy-eight year old veteran of the Royal Malta Artillery — has found himself a secluded rural spot in which to pursue his hobby, but he seems profoundly contented and the perch, bream and pike for which he is fishing will be none the worse for being caught in the shadow of Canary Wharf.

Learning

To CLAIM THAT MODERN EDUCATION began in Britain in 1870 would be unfair to England and Wales and grossly unfair to Scotland, whose standards were traditionally superior to those in the south. There is a nugget of truth in the statement, however. Before the Education Act of 1870 schooling in England and Wales was erratic and ill-organized; every child could get some sort of education if its parents wanted it to, but the quality differed widely from area to area and it was easy to slip through the net of the system if the family could not be bothered or felt that their progeny would be better employed elsewhere. The literacy rate was in theory something over seventy-five percent but 'literacy' guaranteed little more than an ability to sign one's name. In large areas of the country, particularly in the burgeoning cities where the growth in population had by far outstripped the services on which the people depended, serious education was a luxury enjoyed by few.

The Act of 1870 changed all that. Every school district, it insisted, should provide 'a sufficient amount of accommodation in public elementary schools' to accommodate any child who was not otherwise provided for. Where a deficiency existed, a school board should be set up charged with ensuring that the gap was filled. In theory these 'Board Schools' were supposed to keep a child until the age of thirteen but there was provision for the education being only part-time after the age of ten and in practice ten often became the accepted leaving age. Not till 1893 was the age raised to eleven and almost the twentieth century before it was increased to twelve.

'I attended what was known as a Board School,' wrote Neville Cardus, who was a boy in Manchester, 'a place of darkness and inhumanity. I learned scarcely anything there except to read and write.' But he *did* learn how to read and write, skills that might well have eluded him twenty years before. By 1891 the literacy rate had risen to ninety-three percent, a remarkable improvement over the figure of twenty years before. 'A place of darkness', however was not too far from the mark for many of the new Board Schools. Beauty was not an element taken seriously in their planning. Mark Girouard has pointed out how they were often built on constricted sites and reared aggressively above their surroundings: 'The cliff-like façades and high multi-paned windows of their classrooms, rising above the little houses, became a new feature of the townscape.' Often, too, they were built of the dreariest and cheapest types of brick; they exuded an air of gloom that must have chilled the spirits of the luckless schoolboy on his first arrival. But they were a great deal better than the nothing which had been available before. Sherlock Holmes, viewing them from a railway

Stone, in Staffordshire (1900) RIGHT (361), had something altogether more pretentious which dated from 1848. The architect seems to have felt that a little bit of everything was what was needed — or the building may just have grown.

Grammar schools, or their near equivalents, come in many different forms. In Hawkshead, Cumbria, in 1892 LEFT (360), it was small, dignified and, in its quiet way, extremely handsome — as befitted the school where Wordsworth was a pupil. Today it is a museum.

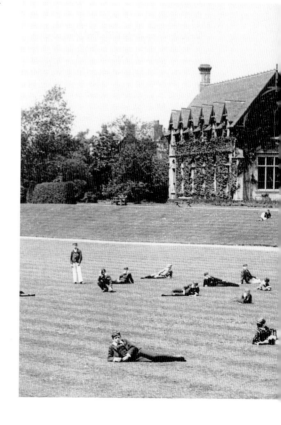

carriage between Clapham Junction and Victoria, observed rapturously to Watson: 'Lighthouses, my boy! Beacons of the future! Capsules, with hundreds of bright little seeds in each, out of which will spring the wiser, better England of the future.'

THE RESORTS OF THE MERITOCRACY

Many of the country towns were not so keen on lighthouses. Most of them had their own endowed grammar schools, which in some cases had been allowed to run to seed in the early nineteenth century but were staging a strong comeback by the time of the 1870 Act. Grammar schools, and other similar establishments which were grammar schools in all but name, came in all shapes and sizes (plates 360-364), some large, some small; some in ancient buildings, some dimly Victorian, some reconstructed towards the turn of the century in prosperous Edwardian or mock-Tudor. All had one thing in common: they were the resort of the meritocracy, the chosen educational tool of those who, though unlikely to be more than comfortably off themselves, wanted their children to have good careers and, if possible, become rich. The public schoolboy sneered at the grammar school as dowdy and *petit bourgeois*, the board schoolboy thought it the acme of toffee-nosed snobbishness, the grammar schoolboy just did what was called for and got ahead. ('Schoolboy' was the appropriate word in the 1870s and 1880s. Few girls were thought to require more than the most rudimentary education and high schools for girls were almost unheard of until the 1890s – Lincoln being one of the first examples.)

The grammar school at Farnham in Surrey FAR LEFT (362) was on a very different scale and would yield pride of place to no one. It had only been completed in 1906, the year Frith photographed it, so its brashness was at its most assertive. At Ilminster LEFT (363), set against the noble tower of the fourteenth-century St Mary's, the boys relaxed in front of a building which clearly knew its place in the town's hierarchy and did not rate itself particularly high.

Whether the boys at the Abbey School, Beckenham LEFT (364), habitually lolled on the grass in such curious isolation from each other, or whether Frith arranged them thus in 1899, their clothes and demeanour, not to mention the lawns and the flag, proclaim the institution's claims to gentility.

Country villages would not have been eligible for a Board School, even if they had wanted one. Given a conscientious squire and parson, however – or at least squire's wife – the village school could offer an excellent grounding from which the brighter pupil could – theoretically at least – progress to the nearest grammar school (plates 365-367). The children from Flora Thompson's Lark Hill walked a mile and a half each morning to the village school at Fordlow, a small, grey one-storied building accommodating forty-five or so pupils with one large classroom and moth-eaten playground. Reading, writing and arithmetic were the core of the syllabus, with a scripture lesson given every morning by the rector and needlework every afternoon for the girls. Most boys left on their eleventh birthday; a few stayed on for an extra year. Only a handful of boys and no girls went on to any sort of further education but the system was flexible enough to offer a chance to those who were both intelligent and ambitious.

BALFOUR LAYS A FOUNDATION FOR THE FUTURE

The next step forward came with Balfour's Education Act of 1902. With its acceptance of the principle that the state had an obligation to provide primary and secondary education, in theory at least available to everyone, it laid the foundation on which subsequent generations were to build. The administration of the system was entrusted to the county and borough

Though the book clutched by one of the Evesham school-boys in 1892 BELOW (365) indicated some pretensions to scholarship, gentility was hardly the impression he was seeking to create. The group on the left, indeed, looked like Bill Sykes accompanied by some of Fagin's more promising pupils.

The more grandiose school
buildings are often
associated with so-called
'public' schools, but as
Nottingham High School
RIGHT (366) with its
fancy castellation and
mullioned windows, and
the Holmscroft School at
Greenock in Strathclyde
(1904) RIGHT BELOW
(367) made clear, it was
not only the fee-paying
boarding schools that could
put on a fine show.

authorities; if they accepted the highest level of grant-in-aid from state funds then they were committed to offering a quarter of their places to winners of scholarships from the elementary schools. The number of pupils moving on from primary to secondary education was already rising steeply by the time of Balfour's act, in the next twenty years this figure had almost quadrupled (plate 368).

It had not been intended that the new system should weaken the system of church education but that was the result. In 1902 there

The County Intermediate School at Machynlleth in Gwynedd LEFT (368) was a fine example of the kind of school from which, theoretically, the brighter pupils should have emerged for further education. It is unlikely that many did so when the photograph was taken in 1900.

were 3.5 million children in church schools, of all denominations but predominantly Church of England. Progressively those schools found that lack of funds prevented them keeping pace with their state-controlled competitors, by the time of R A Butler's great Education Act of 1944 there were still nine thousand church schools in existence but only a handful of the best endowed could be said to be thriving or anything near it. Butler's solution was brutal and, as it turned out, almost terminal. If the church wanted to retain control then it would have to find half the cost of any alteration or improvement; if the state was to provide the money then it was the state which would exercise control. The result was inevitable, the nine thousand schools dwindled to two thousand and almost as many of these were Roman Catholic as Church of England.

In 1918 the school leaving age was raised to fourteen with no exemptions permitted. To make this work, however, more, or at least larger schools were needed. The government launched on a building programme; then, three years later, ran into financial difficulties. Work on the new secondary schools was slowed down or cancelled altogether. As late as 1923 three-quarters of Welsh and English children never got beyond the elementary school which they had entered at the age of five, less than one in fifteen went on to further education. Three years later the concept of an 'elementary' school was abolished altogether: the new word was 'primary', to be followed at the age of eleven by 'secondary'. In effect, it was to be grammar schools for the more academic and 'modern', a category which included the senior departments of the old elementary schools, for the unfortunate but numerous remainder.

THE PREPARATORY AND PUBLIC SCHOOLS SOLDIER ON

Meanwhile the private preparatory and public schools continued much as they had always been. These ran the gamut between the excellent and the appalling. Dr Fagan's Llanabba Castle, from Evelyn Waugh's *Decline and Fall*, was certainly a caricature of the sort of school which taught its pupils nothing except how to be snobbish with very little ground for such pretensions, but was still horribly close to the reality. *Decline and Fall* was also memorable for

The newer public schools thought it necessary to build in a style which would over-awe potential parents and conceal their lack of antiquity behind a dignified facade. Cheltenham College, founded in 1841 LEFT (369), could have passed for one of the grander Victorian railway stations; the main hall of the associated and pioneering Cheltenham Ladies' College BELOW (370) was, in contrast, portentously medieval.

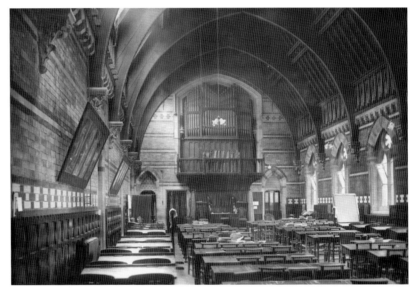

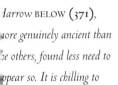

Harrow BELOW (371), more genuinely ancient than the others, found less need to appear so. It is chilling to speculate how many of the boys parading for the 'Bill' in 1914 would have been killed within the next few years.

Sedbergh LEFT (372), *as befitted both its reputation and its rugged setting, was bleak and uncompromising.*

Paul Pennyfeather's resigned conclusion that 'anyone who has been to an English public school will always feel comparatively at home in prison'; a comment redolent of the malign cocktail of chilblains, bad food and incarceration which were among the more disagreeable features of the system. Acute discomfort in buildings that were often beautiful and historic and almost always up to a point imposing, seemed to be endemic to the British public school (plates 369-373). Some of the public schools, Marlborough being an example, graduated from grammar school status in the nineteenth century. It was an example which others were much later to follow when the move towards comprehensivation began to gather force and they chose to opt for independence. In 1945, after the sweeping Labour victory in the general election, it was widely assumed that fee-paying schools would be abolished, or at least confronted with so many difficulties as to make their demise inevitable. The threat never materialized, however – or the opportunity was missed, depending on the way one views the issue. Though some of the smaller boarding schools are experiencing difficulties, the public school system as a whole is today as strong as it has ever been in the past.

R A BUTLER RESHAPES THE NATION'S EDUCATION

By 1945, however, the educational system had been decisively recast – by a Tory Minister of Education whose instincts were quite as radical as those of his Labour counterparts. R A Butler adopted the principle that, as soon as possible, the school leaving age should be raised to

Noblest of all was Stowe ABOVE (373), *which made no attempt to create its own environment but fitted snugly into one of Britain's greatest stately homes, the seat of the Grenvilles in Buckinghamshire.*

xteen, but he accepted that not all children ould benefit by continued academic education. selection would be made at the age of eleven, hereafter the elite would be sent on to grammar chools, the rest divided between those who were eemed suitable for special training in technical olleges and the rest. In the decade after the econd World War more than five hundred new

secondary modern schools were built; the buildings were both spacious and reasonably well equipped, the trouble was that the pupils within often felt themselves to have been left behind in the academic rat race and had little motivation to make good use of their time (plates 374-376). The technical schools withered for much the same reason: parents felt

R A Butler's Education Act was followed by a spate of school building between 1945 and 1970. Typical of the unpretentious village schools of the period was Alderholt in Dorset LEFT *(374); equally typically it was closed down as being too small to be viable and converted into a village hall. It was burnt down by some mindless vandal shortly before the second photograph* BELOW *(375) was taken.*

1960 ALDERHOLT

1998 ALDERHOLT

Bromsgrove high school ABOVE (376) *was an example of the glass and brick, or glass and concrete boxes which were so much the fashion in the 1960s. Nobody could say it had charm but it served its purpose well enough.*

that they lacked the prestige of the grammar school, the local educational authorities resented the high cost of providing special facilities for a small number of not particularly grateful youths. In 1950 more than seventy thousand pupils attended technical schools, by 1985 the number had fallen to a mere 2,500. Some of the most grandiose educational buildings of the twentieth century – and of the nineteenth for that matter – have been dedicated to technical training (plates 377, 378) but they have been designed above all for the young, or not so young, adult. If schoolboys or girls are to be given such specialist education, it is now felt that it should be fitted within the framework of conventional schooling.

It was the conviction that any attempt to carve up pupils after the age of eleven into separate groups would be bound to lead to discrimination and a sense of rejection, that fostered a new experiment. What was needed, it was decided, was a school large and flexible enough to accommodate everyone and to cater for every normal need. The 'comprehensive' school was pioneered at Windermere in 1945; the first purpose-built fully fledged comprehensive was opened in London, at Kidbrooke, in 1954.

Ten years later the Labour government formally adopted a comprehensive system as its preferred form of education; from then on intense pressure was brought to bear on grammar and other semi-independent schools to come within the framework. There have been changes of emphasis since, but the trend has never been reversed; today the vast majority of state secondary pupils throughout the British Isles obtain their education in comprehensive schools.

*The Technical Institute at
Redhill (1906)* LEFT
(377) *was grimly
forbidding; it does not seem
likely that the children on the
pavement would ever be
tempted to climb those steps
in the pursuit of knowledge.
At least it is architecturally
more imaginative, however,
than the Technical College at
Camborne* BELOW (378)
*— though the latter probably
provided lighter and more
congenial working space.*

GROUPS ON THE FRINGES OF THE SYSTEM

On the fringes of the educational system, jealously guarding their independence yet knowing that their success must largely depend on working smoothly with the established order, were the various youth movements which had been set up, usually by inspired individuals, to keep the young occupied, teach them skills, and instil in them a sense of duty and self-discipline. Most prominent were the Boy Scouts, a movement conceived by Robert Baden-Powell, hero of the siege of Mafeking.

He held his first camp on Brownsea Island in Poole Harbour in 1907; the idea quickly proved popular; with his sister Agnes he extended the concept to girls and founded the Girl Guides. At their zenith the Boy Scouts numbered nearly half a million (plate 379). The Boys' Brigade, strong on religion where the Scouts favoured patriotism, was established earlier but was somewhat overshadowed by its more glamorous rival; still, at the outbreak of the First World War, the Boys Brigade and the Church Lads' Brigade together had more than

By 1921, when this photograph was taken in Lord Street, Southport LEFT (379), there were nearly half a million Boy Scouts in Britain. Their shorts, ending an inch or so above the knee, were as much subject to regulation as were the women's skirts, four inches below the knee.

100,000 members. Even more avowedly militaristic than the Boy Scouts were the cadet groups that were run, or at least sponsored by, the armed services.

Links between the cadets and their parent forces were close; the great majority of the boys who trained aboard the *Helensburgh* at the mouth of the Gare Loch in 1901 and most of the boys parading beside the *King Alfred Training Brig* at Reading nine years later would have been on active service with the Royal Navy in the First World War (plates 380, 381).

The Army and Navy were eager to catch boys young and train them so that they would get used to the life and later join the services. The

Helensburgh Training Ship at the mouth of the Gare Loch (1901) ABOVE (380) and the King Alfred Training Brig at Reading

(1910) LEFT (381) provided the Royal Navy with much needed manpower in the First World War.

THE CENTURY OF THE UNIVERSITY

When Frith took his photograph of Aberystwyth College in 1903 it was just that; splendid though its appearance might be, the days when it was to achieve university status were far ahead; Glasgow University had been founded in 1451, though rebuilt in the late nineteenth century (plates 382, 383), but though Aberdeen and Edinburgh were also ancient there was only a sprinkling of English universities outside Oxford and Cambridge and none of those was of great antiquity. In 1900 only twenty thousand students received full-time education in British universities. Then came a breakthrough: the Imperial College of Science and Technology was welded together from various units and joined the University of London, while Birmingham, Leeds, Sheffield, Bristol and Liverpool transformed technical colleges or similar institutions into fully fledged independent universities. It proved to be a false dawn. Between the two wars certain so-called 'red-brick' University Colleges were founded, which awarded London University degrees, but

Reading was the only full university to be opened in this period; 'red-brick' is a description usually employed with a note of contempt and is often strikingly mis-applied; few buildings could be less red or less brick-like than the University College of Nottingham (plate 384).

By 1939 only a tiny 1.7 percent of eighteen-year-olds went to university. When a flood of demobilized would-be students and the products of the enlarged sixth forms created by R A Butler swamped the existing system, it was clear that something had to be done and done quickly. The universities that were already there were expanded; new universities were founded at Nottingham, Southampton, Hull, Exeter and Leicester; by the late 1950s the student population had crept up to about four percent of all school leavers. This was an improvement, but the comparable proportion in the United States was five times as great, in France nearly twice as great. The Robbins Report of 1965 called for further expansion and a fresh wave of university creation began, many of the new

When Frith photographed Aberystwyth College in 1903 LEFT (382) *it was very far from enjoying the status of being a university, let alone of the University College of Wales. Glasgow* ABOVE (383) *on the other hand had been founded in 1451, though its memorably Gothic buildings, mainly the work of the London architect George Gilbert Scott — had only been completed a few years before this photograph was taken in 1897.*

The University of Nottingham LEFT **(384)**, *when this photograph was taken in 1928, was no more than a university college. It gained full university status in 1948 as one of the post-war universities which were lumped together by some of the older seats of learning as 'red-brick'; though few buildings can have been less red or brick.*

arrivals being not extensions of existing institutions but built on virgin sites and sometimes of considerable architectural distinction (plate 385).

The promotion of polytechnic and art colleges to the status of universities in 1992 had no comparable effect on the physical appearance of the country, since the buildings for the most part were there already, but this change enormously increased the number of those who could properly style themselves dons or undergraduates.

Today there are eighty-six universities in Britain with nearly a million students – among them a proportion from overseas which, though still substantial, sadly continues to diminish year by year.

NOT ALL EDUCATION TAKES PLACE IN SCHOOLS OR UNIVERSITIES

Not all education takes place within schools or universities. Since the mid-nineteenth century local authorities had been empowered to set up public libraries but few got round to doing so for forty or fifty years. Then, suddenly, they became the fashion; every town of any consequence felt that it must endow its citizens with this cultural resource and did so in a variety of styles as eclectic and imaginative as had been seen in the new town halls a generation before (plates 386-390). A significant contributor to the process was Andrew Carnegie, a Scottish ironmaster who made a vast fortune in the United States and devoted a large part of it to the founding of

The University of Sussex ABOVE (385) *was architecturally one of the most interesting of the post-Second World War universities. It was opened in 1961, thus preceding the Robbins Report, and was for a time the most fashionable of the new wave of red-brick universities. At least it was redder and brickier than was Nottingham.*

As with the town halls of a generation before, the new public libraries were designed to convince the passer-by of the greatness of the town or city. A wide variety of styles was followed but the most favoured were classic over-the-top, as in Cardiff (1896) LEFT (386), or Gothic, as in Nottingham (1890) BELOW (387).

free libraries in the British Isles. By the time of his death in 1919 there were 380 such libraries; today there are more than six hundred that owe their origin to his benevolence.

Most of the libraries in Great Britain were built by 1914; there was a further burst in the 1960s and 1970s, bringing the total up to some five thousand; but it was between the two World Wars that the public really acquired the habit of borrowing books. The total issued rose five-fold over those years. The growth was fostered by the establishment of mobile libraries, which trundled around the villages in the remoter parts of the country, bringing culture, or at least entertainment, to the inhabitants. The public library service today is starved of funds, it has in many cases been forced to truncate its services and reduce its purchases of books, but it is still among the finest in the world and brings pleasure and the possibility of self-improvement into the lives of many million citizens.

Camborne made do with something more mundane. It was built in 1894, and between that date, 1902 ABOVE (388) when Frith first photographed it, 1965 OPPOSITE ABOVE (389) and 1998 OPPOSITE BELOW (390), survived almost unscathed. The only serious change was the apparition of Richard Trevithick on a plinth in front of the main door.

Mining

1951 THORNLEY

THE INDUSTRIAL REVOLUTION, and Britain's status as the world's greatest power in the second half of the nineteenth century, was based on coal. Without an apparently limitless and easily accessible supply of that essential fuel, Britain's iron and steel production could never have risen to the level that it did, the manufactured goods that swamped the world would never have been produced. Exports of coal helped pay for the rising standard of living of the middle and working classes and fuelled the ships that took the goods to and fro: 'Oh, where are you going to, all you Big Steamers,' asked Rudyard Kipling,

'With England's own coal, up and down the salt seas?
'We are going to fetch you your bread and your butter,
Your beef, pork and mutton, eggs, apples and cheese.'

King Coal reigned unchallenged and in 1870 more than a million people worked in his service. The industry had its darker side. Conditions were appalling, the miners worked in damp, cramped tunnels, often in considerable danger, racked by a wide range of respiratory diseases. The collieries defaced some of Britain's most beautiful valleys, their workings covered the countryside with a film of polluting black dust, the waste tips loomed over the mining villages and sometimes – as recently as 1966 at Aberfan – descended catastrophically on the people that had erected them (plates 391-393).

But coal brought wealth, and some at least of that filtered down to the men who worked it. Coal created villages, and though the villages were often dispiriting to look at and bereft of any cultural embellishments, they were possessed by a strong sense of community, a loyalty and pride in their prowess which lent a touch of tragedy to what would otherwise have been their unlamented disappearance. Coal created ports: Seaton Sluice and Seaham in Durham would never have existed but for the demand for coal; the mess which such ports left behind them still bedevils a coastline of singular beauty, but they brought employment to a region sorely in need of it. Coal was part of national life. Only a bold man would have predicted in 1860 that it would ever cease to be so.

FINITE RESOURCES, BY DEFINITION, MUST HAVE AN END

Yet anyone who exploits a finite resource should be aware that, by definition, sooner or later he will have to look elsewhere for what he needs. Output from the mines was at its zenith just before the First World War, when 290 million tons a year were being extracted. The demands of a wartime

1998 THORNLEY

Thornley Colliery was
sunk in 1835. By 1951,
when the earlier photograph
was taken ABOVE (391),
it still employed a thousand
men, but it was largely
unmodernized and seemed
to cower in the shadow of
that monstrous tip.
It closed in 1971. Today
LEFT (392) tip and mine
buildings have disappeared,
so too have the miners'
cottages. The view is more
attractive, the environment
more salubrious, but a
community is dead.

Easington, in 1955 LEFT
*(393), had new buildings
and an altogether more
hopeful air. The 'NCB'—
National Coal Board — on
the railway truck marked its
new allegiance. But, with
all the other mines in
Durham, it had to close.*

*Wheel Edward at Botallack
(1960)* RIGHT *(394) and
the Levant Mine at St Just
(1950)* BELOW *(395) were
two of the Cornish tin
mines which have fallen into
disuse. When the ruined
buildings survive they often
possess an eerie beauty,
menace even.*

economy meant that this hectic pace was
sustained for several years and that the easier
seams were worked out while the deeper and
more technically tricky mines were neglected.
After the war, when it was hoped that exports
would take up the slack left by a dwindling
armaments industry, German reparations in the
form of coal began to flood the world's
markets and ensure that those export orders
were never secured. Reduced output per miner
in an industry that had signally fallen behind its
rivals in the mechanisation of its workings
meant that the cost of British coal became less
and less competitive.

Exports nevertheless did recover, and they
briefly reached their former peak in the mid-
1920s, but this proved to be a false rebirth.
Sales collapsed, and 100,000 miners lost their
jobs. It was the first of a series of blows that
was to afflict a stricken but still immensely
powerful giant.

'I saw a row of sharply conical little hills that
looked like a topographical freak until I came
close to them,' wrote J B Priestley in 1933, 'and
then realised that they were old slag-heaps now
almost entirely covered with grass.' The hills
were monuments to a vanished past. The pace
of change varied from region to region; 'New
England's shut down, so is Colwick Wood,'
remarked D H Lawrence's Mrs Bolton in *Lady
Chatterley's Lover*; 'yes, it's fair haunting to go
through that coppy and see Colwick Wood
standing there deserted among the trees, and
bushes growing up all over the pit-head, and
the lines of red-rusty. It's like death itself, a
dead colliery.' The problems were exacerbated
by a bloody-minded work-force and
intransigent employers; a century of bad
relationship between owner and miner had
created one of the most powerful and
unconciliatory unions in the entire country.
Two-thirds of all the days lost in strikes
between the two World Wars were suffered by
the mining industry.

DEATH OF AN INDUSTRY

As with other decaying industries, the Second
World War brought a brief reprieve. It also
brought an increase in open cast mining,
cheaper than orthodox deep mining and often
exploiting veins of high quality coal but
hideously destructive to the countryside in
which it took place. In the long term its
depredations could be patched up, but no one
who remembers the photographs of open cast
workings besieging the Yorkshire palace of
Wentworth Woodhouse can be left with any
illusions about the extent of the damage that

such mining wreaked on the landscape.

The stimulus given by the war soon wore off: mechanisation became the norm and productivity increased but the industry still could not compete with cheap and sometimes subsidized imports from Poland and other countries. Oil became a more economical and cleaner alternative to coal in some of its largest traditional markets. Off-shore gas began to be pumped ashore in increasing quantities. By the 1990s consumption in Britain was falling by seven percent each year and even that level was only maintained by a government prepared to protect coal producers on social rather than economic grounds.

Today there are still fifty or so deep mines in operation and ninety open cast sites but some of these are on the scale of cottage industry

It is not only in Cornwall that the mining of tin, lead and other metals has ceased to be viable. These lead mines at Loggerheads, Staffordshire ABOVE (396) *and abandoned copper mines at Penysarn in Gwynedd* ABOVE MIDDLE (397), *were by 1955 no more than ghosts haunting a countryside over which they once ruled.*

and for none does the future seem entirely secure. A million men underground has become a mere forty thousand. Visually the result is often a great improvement – some of the most cruelly scarred valleys of South Wales, for instance, have been transformed into green and tranquil open country – but in the process a society has been devastated and a way of life extinguished. Perhaps in a hundred years the end of coal mining will seem a wholly admirable phenomenon, but as of now there is still a high price to pay.

NOT ONLY COAL MINING DECLINED

It was not only coal mining which declined in the twentieth century; the proportion of the national income which derives from mining and quarrying – even though the term includes off-shore oil and gas – has dropped by nearly a third since 1985; the number of people employed in this sector has been almost halved. Outside the great coalfields it is Cornwall that has suffered most severely from this decline. Francis Kilvert visited the county in 1871. 'The first few miles looked bleak, barren and uninteresting,' he recorded, 'the most striking

feature being the innumerable mine works of lead, tin and copper crowning the hills with their tall chimney shafts and ugly white dreary buildings, or nestling in a deep narrow valley, defiling and poisoning the streams with the white tin washing.' No doubt his complaints were justified on environmental grounds but today the buildings possess an eerie beauty, romance even (plates 394, 395). Yet they survive only as derelict monuments. The great Cornish mining industry, which in its time was powerful enough to support a grandiose Mining School at Camborne, is now almost entirely a thing of the past.

Tin had been mined there for more than two thousand years and zealots from time to time still try to resuscitate some of the old workings. The industry was highly profitable when Kilvert went to Cornwall and new mines were still being opened as late as 1930. By that time, however, it was already obvious to all but the most fanatical that competition from such countries as Bolivia, Malaya or Indonesia was too strong for the local product. Lead was another mineral mined in Cornwall, though the leading producer, the London Lead Company,

worked more in Derbyshire or the hills of Wales. The industry followed the same course as that of tin: the most easily accessible lead — or, for that matter, silver or copper was extracted, the smaller and deeper deposits could only be reached at a price far greater than that charged by competing producers from other countries. The mines were one by one abandoned and left for future generations to wonder at and, occasionally, adventurous small boys to tumble down. All over Britain the story is much the same; the copper mines in Gwynedd or lead mines in Staffordshire, if they survive at all, do so only as ghosts haunting the landscape over which they once ruled (plates 396, 397).

QUARRYING IS ANOTHER MATTER

Quarrying is another matter. Mining involved burrowing in the ground, piling up the spoil round the hole, but leaving the rest of the surface more or less unscathed. Quarries were vast craters blasted in the earth's crust, creating a lunar landscape on an often awe-inspiring scale. The slate quarries are among the most dramatic man-made landscapes in Britain.

Slate quarries are some of the most dramatic and awe-inspiring of man-made landscapes. Quarrying by terraces was the norm. At Penrhyn Bay in 1890

ABOVE (398) *it looked as if some mad giant had hacked out shelves on which to store his toys, and had then tossed model houses at random here and there.*

The Clee Hill granite quarry in Shropshire in 1911 BELOW (399). *Most of the granite used to rebuild London in the nineteenth century came from Scotland, but there were rich workings in other parts of the British Isles.*

1903 ODIHAM

1910 ODIHAM

Quarrying by terraces was the usual method, as at Penrhyn in North Wales, but at some of the larger sites the slate had to be torn from deep caverns and mountains of spoil piled around the railhead. Penrhyn produced granite as well as slate; most of the granite that was used to rebuild London in the nineteenth century came from Scotland but it does crop up here and there in other areas – notably the Clee Hill quarry in Shropshire (plates 398, 399).

Extraction of chalk and gravel can make hideous scars on the landscape but at least the workings are relatively superficial and thus easily repaired. The demand for sand and gravel appears insatiable; more than three thousand acres are torn up each year in pursuit of the precious material, mostly in the valleys of the major rivers. The Thames Valley has suffered as much as any; the loss has not been total, however, since the demand for water seems as rapacious as that for gravel, and the exhausted pits make excellent reservoirs or centres for water sports. The landscape from which gravel is extracted is, anyway, unlikely to be of singular beauty; chalk, though, is taken from some of the most beautiful hills in Britain (plates 400-402).

It cannot be denied that there is a bleak splendour about monster chalk pits like that of Odiham, but how much one wishes that it was somewhere else. When there are chalk pits there are also often lime works, an industry which involves much noise as well as buildings on a monumental scale, and a fine white dust spread liberally over the surrounding countryside (plate 403).

The chalk pit at Odiham in Hampshire, photographed in 1903 ABOVE LEFT (400), 1910 ABOVE (401) and 1998 RIGHT (402), encroached on the town itself and seemed to have been considered a suitable playground for local children. Though there is little sign of activity here, excavation of chalk and flint continued until 1948.

1998 ODIHAM

CHINA CLAY AND STONE ARE STILL IN DEMAND

China clay, or kaolin, is one of the few areas of mining which still contributes substantially to Britain's export trade. The clay is used mainly for papermaking and it comes almost entirely from Cornwall. Britain is the second largest exporter of this material, in 1998 two million tonnes were sent abroad – it is curious, to think that so large a chunk of one of our loveliest counties should end up in paper mills all over the world. The china clay workings are huge, and the waste tips that go with them are particularly intractable; nobody could deny that they do possess a certain stark grandeur but, like the chalk pits, except for the foreign earnings that they generate for the nation, one could wish both workings and waste tips to be in Siberia or Tierra del Fuego or anywhere else far from British soil (plate 404).

And then there is stone. Seeing how much of it there is around, the layman might be forgiven for feeling surprise that so little seems to be actively sought after for building or otherwise. Of course, over the centuries huge quantities have been extracted; the Romans used local stone for all but their most prestigious undertakings, the Normans needed such vast amounts for their castles that they had to import extra supplies from the Continent. Most stone used today, however, is recycled from unwanted buildings, and fresh quarrying takes place only in limited areas and for stone of special quality. York stone, from quarries south of Leeds and Bradford, is particularly sought after for paving, Portland stone (plate 405) was used by Christopher Wren for his rebuilding of St Paul's Cathedral and it is still much favoured for construction work in those areas where dirt and pollution are most likely to take a toll of softer materials.

Such operations, however, are tiny compared to the great enterprises of the past. Except for china clay – and there too the supply is finite – and the more mundane chalk and gravel, the extraction of raw materials from Britain's mainland is effectively a thing of the past. One may regret the loss of much-needed earnings for the country, the once thriving communities that have been destroyed, the employment that is so sorely called for in present circumstances, but at least there is some compensation. Surely nobody could fail to feel a glimmer of satisfaction from the fact that the work has stopped while so much of the country's surface remains still unblemished.

The china clay workings at St Austell in 1955 LEFT *(404). In 1997 two million tonnes of china clay were exported, mainly for use in paper mills. Many of the old tips have now been disposed of.*

Quarrying for stone at Portland Bill in 1898 LEFT *(405). Portland stone is still sought after for use in areas where dirt and pollution might take toll of softer materials.*

Playing

THE CONCEPT OF ENTERTAINMENT – that people should engage in activities with the object of amusing themselves, or should pay other people to do things that will amuse them – assumes that those people have a certain amount of time and energy to spare, and probably some money too. In the mid-nineteenth century there was precious little time, energy or money to spare outside that small section of the population which comprised the upper and middle classes. It would be too much to say that there were no entertainments available to the poor. Cock-fighting, badger-baiting and other such bloodthirsty pursuits may have involved the audience in paying some entrance fee but the income that they generated came mainly from gambling and it cost little to be present. They were banned in the 1830s, however, as also were the more brutal forms of pugilism. But in the villages at least people were still perfectly capable of enjoying themselves at little or no cost. Dancing around the maypole and other such traditional rustic sports were already being viewed with some suspicion, as slightly precious pursuits which were kept going more to gratify the antiquarian than to give pleasure to the participants, but there were regular fairs offering more robust amusements, and travelling entertainers of various kinds would appear from time to time to bring a touch of urban sophistication. In the cities pigeon-flying was a pursuit which involved some expense for those who owned the birds but cost nothing to those who merely admired their prowess unless, if they happened to have the funds available, they wagered on their races. In Battersea, wrote Richard Church, it was 'a weekly sport, especially among the tattooed men in the poorer quarters of the parish'. Every Sunday morning, no doubt to the dismay of the parson, they would rattle off in their coster carts, each man furnished with a long wicker basket filled with pigeons.

The children, as always, made their own games. The children holding hoops (plate 407) could have been matched at any time in the nineteenth century, at any level of society and in any part of Britain. On the village green at Lark Rise the girls would dance and sing, playing games like Oranges and Lemons which were known throughout the kingdom, and others which were local or even devised spontaneously. There were marbles, peg-tops and skipping ropes. Boys would fight, kick around an old tin or anything else that would do in place of the expensive and rarely encountered football, fool around with a catapult, hunt for birds' nests. But organized sports as

such hardly existed. The idea that a village, a parish, a town, might assemble a team and play at some game or other against another similar unit of society had as yet hardly been conceived. Still less did many thousands of spectators flock to watch the champions of their city or country pit themselves against rival teams.

As the nineteenth century drew towards its end, so the number of diversions increased, in which an individual or a family could indulge without great cost or the need to purchase elaborate equipment. The idea of the 'outing' became established: to the Crystal Palace, to the Zoo, to the park, for a walk in the country. The train, the bicycle, the bus, finally

The idea of the family 'outing' became increasingly accepted towards the end of the nineteenth century. The Crystal Palace, built for the Great Exhibition of 1851 and moved to Sydenham five years later, was a favourite venue for Londoners. The visitors in this photograph of 1890 ABOVE (406) looked pretty well-to-do, but all classes felt it worth an expedition. Even the poor now had time and money for an occasional jaunt.

The children with hoops on the Promenade at Ramsgate in 1918 ABOVE (407) *could have been matched at any time in the previous century at any level of society and in any part of the British Isles. Some pleasures were classless and virtually free.*

the car came within the range of more and more people. Though it was the great growth of organized sport which caught the eye, one should never forget that the sixty years or so after Frith began to take his photographs witnessed an extraordinary enrichment of the life of all but the least fortunate members of society (plates 406, 408-413).

THE HORSES DRAW IN THE CROWDS

Except for prize-fighting, which was always viewed with some disdain by the more genteel (although not necessarily aristocratic) sections of society and not considered a spectacle suitable for women, horse racing was the first sport regularly to attract large crowds. Until the coming of the railway – and, indeed, in some cases well after it – racing was considered primarily a pursuit for the upper and middle classes. The presence of the general public was tolerated but not encouraged, no charge was normally made for admission except to some hallowed inner circles and betting on the course was informal if not illicit. At certain courses such as Newmarket and Goodwood the tradition of gentility lingered until well into the twentieth century. At Ascot in 1902 the course is clearly packed, but a reasonably high level of turn-out seems to have been maintained by all those present (plates 414-416). But already standards were crumbling. Thanks to the railway, what had been local race meetings open to all free of charge were now enclosed and run by private

The Lake District was still a distant myth for most Britons in 1887 when this couple admired Lake Windermere ABOVE (408). They had probably been rowed from their hotel to this vantage point by the man in the boat. But already the number of visitors was rising and it would not be long before a journey there would become a possibility for any except the poorest. Photographed a year later the girl LEFT (409) teetered nervously across the stepping stones over the water at Ambleside.

The pierrots in the Valley Gardens at Harrogate LEFT *(410), though playing to a thin house on this summer afternoon in 1907, were a regular attraction for those who found they had an hour or so to spare.*

To be photographed on one's day out, as here on Clapham Common in 1885 BELOW *(411), added an extra element to the pleasure. The photographer was pushing a glass slide into his mahogany and brass camera; Frith often used slides twice this size in a camera several times as large.*

The Zoological Society opened in Regent's Park in 1828 and at once proved a huge popular success. In 1913 the pelicans LEFT (412) were particular favourites while a ride on an elephant BELOW (413), then and now, was a thrill and a delight for children.

companies whose object was to make a profit out of the enterprise. Sandown and Newbury were early examples of courses run on this basis, and they proved immensely popular. By the 1920s many thousands flocked to the largest meetings: Derby Day at Epsom vied with the Cup Final at Wembley as the greatest day in the sporting calendar (plate 416).

SPORTS FOR THE GENTRY ONLY

The upper classes might not be able to keep the race-course as a privileged preserve but there were certain other sports where participation was effectively limited to a tiny part of the population. Hunting, whether of foxes or of stags, was a case in point (plates 417). To follow one of the grander hunts would have been far beyond the pocket of anyone who did not enjoy a considerable income, and unless he had certain social graces as well the newcomer would be made to feel thoroughly uncomfortable. Even a pack as undistinguished as Mr Jorrocks' East

Goodwood in 1904 ABOVE *(414) was a venue of some elegance. The general public was admitted but not much was done to encourage it, the crowd in front of the grandstand and the waiting carriages looked decidedly middle or even upper class.*

Much the same was true of Ascot in 1902 BELOW (415), though the fact that it was Gold Cup Day has meant that a slightly mixed attendance has been attracted. By 1925, at Epsom BOTTOM (416) for Derby Day, the mood was very different, however. There were, of course, enclaves for the privileged, but this was the people's day and the people turned out in force determined to make the most of it.

Hunting, ostensibly open to all, was in fact limited on social as well as financial grounds. Those following the hounds at Hunmanby in North Yorkshire in 1940 ABOVE **(417)** *did not feel themselves grand, but they knew how to make an intruder feel ill at ease.*

Shooting and stalking were also elitist pursuits. The tweedy character posed near Crieff, west of Perth LEFT **(418)**, *was either a gentleman or rich, and probably both.*

Surrey subscription foxhounds was not without its standards: 'It is all very well for old-established shopkeepers "to do a bit of pleasure" occasionally, but the apprentice or journeyman who understands his duties and the tricks of the trade, will never be found capering in the hunting field.' Shooting and stalking were similarly inaccessible to the great majority of the population; the sombre gentleman who posed on a moor near his shooting lodge at Crieff was either rich or a gentleman and probably both (plate 418).

Rowing, too, was a pursuit on the whole reserved for the upper and middle classes, though here the barriers began to crumble as the twentieth century wore on. The regatta at Henley-on-Thames of 1890 (plate 419) was in theory open to any participant and an

occasion when only athletic prowess was the password to glory but money or breeding provided the ticket that allowed one to compete at all. As for the languid figures punting at Oxford and Cambridge (plates 420, 422) they were not expected to show athletic skills beyond the minimum needed to avoid pitching their elegantly parasoled companions into the river. Messing about in boats was another matter. The rowing boats in plate 421 were occupied by passengers who, though eminently respectable, would have felt out of place at the Cambridge Eights Week. One might have said the same about the children at Skegness (plates 423, 424), but by the time the second photograph was taken in 1955 educational opportunities had opened so much more widely that it would not have been in the least surprising to find one of the small boys stroking his college crew ten or twelve years later. The yacht in the background in the earlier photograph was probably used for trips along the beach for half-a-crown a head; to have

At first rowing was a sport open only to the upper and middle classes. At the Regatta at Henley-on-Thames in 1890 BELOW *(419), the best athlete was the hero of the day but only those with money or breeding were likely to have the chance to compete at all.*

Punting on the Isis at Oxford in 1906 LEFT *(420) and on the Cam at Cambridge in 1914* OPPOSITE ABOVE *(422). Here no athletic skills were called for beyond a capacity not to pitch one's elegantly parasoled passengers into the usually murky water. Within a few weeks of the second photograph being taken an Archduke was assassinated at Sarajevo.*

owned a boat like that in 1910 would have involved a capital outlay and a continuing commitment far beyond the reach of most potential yachtsmen. Even today it would be a rarity. Sailing is now popular – many are the buildings like the Old Mill at Bosham which have been spruced up and renewed life as a sailing club (plates 425, 426) – but viewed in terms of the whole population sailing is still a sport that is watched and indulged in by only a tiny minority.

CRICKET BECOMES POPULAR

But minority sports reserved for the rich and privileged became increasingly the exception as the nineteenth century neared its end. Cricket, in a somewhat primitive form, had been in evidence since the end of the sixteenth century but for centuries it remained a pastime of the gentry. Then some of the more enlightened manufacturers, who happened also to be enthusiasts for the sport, felt that a factory cricket team would improve the morale of the workers as well as providing valuable fresh air and exercise (plate 427). Squires began to encourage cricket among their villagers, parsons

The family groups placidly rowing on the Thames near Kingston in 1896 BELOW (421) were eminently respectable but would have felt out of place at Cambridge Eights Week. They were within a few hundred yards of the spot where Jerome K Jerome's Three Men in a Boat began their pilgrimage seven years before this photograph was taken.

Messing about in boats wa
a national sport. The
children on the boating lake
at Skegness in 1955 LEFT
(423) were getting much th
same pleasure as their
grandparents on the beach
the same resort forty-five
years before BELOW (424,
The difference was that the
former group would have
had an outside chance of
carrying on with their
rowing and perhaps ending
up at Henley.

In 1903 the mill at Bosham
ABOVE (425) was shabby,
possibly disused, but
certainly still what it was
supposed to be. By 1960
RIGHT (426) it had been
spruced up, given some new
windows and a flagpole,
and had renewed life as
the headquarters of the
sailing club.

1960 BOSHAM

Cricket in the shadow of the
mine (1925) ABOVE
(427). Enlightened
employers, like those at New
Dalcoath colliery near
Camborne in Cornwall,
encouraged their workers to
field a cricket side and take
on neighbouring teams.

among their parishioners. In Marlborough in 1900 there were teams representing the Congregational Church, the Liberal Club and the Working Men's Club.

As cricket gained credence as a spectator sport and larger and larger crowds flocked to international or county matches, so the number of people who played themselves grew in proportion. By 1929 the London County Council could boast 350 cricket pitches, with more than a thousand teams vying to use them. Almost every village of standing had its own team. In *England Their England* A G MacDonell produced the classic account of the village cricket match, with the blacksmith, splendid in braces and bowler hat, unleashing his thunderbolts at a gallery of enthusiastic but for the most part unathletic literary figures. As the photograph of Hythe cricket ground in 1899 (plate 428) suggests, however, country cricket could be more formal. It also tended to take place on grounds of outstanding beauty. With the increasing mobility of would-be spectators

after the Second World War, village cricket matches became a feature of the tourists' country living, of a pattern with medieval churches, thatched cottages and the stocks on the village green. A village ground today may well be ringed by scores of cars and hundreds of spectators – more spectators, indeed, than can always be found at a county ground for the first dour morning of a match between two not particularly exciting teams.

BRITAIN'S GREAT SPECTATOR SPORT

Football has never enjoyed the same appeal for connoisseurs of the picturesque; the crowds that it attracts and the ferocity of its supporters are, however, immeasurably greater. It began as a dishevelled game played to sketchy rules in the streets of provincial towns; was codified and developed as a spectator sport in the mid-nineteenth century; and came of age in 1885 when the Football Association accepted professionalism. Here it diverged on class lines from its first cousin, Rugby football, which for far longer clung to the tenets of amateurism. Rugger maintained its pride of caste and had many followers but the numbers were nothing to the multitudes who flowed every Saturday to the football stadium. By the turn of the century 220 clubs entered for the Football Association Cup and 100,000 watched the final, between Sheffield United and Tottenham Hotspur at the Crystal Palace. In 1914 the ultimate accolade of respectability was conferred on Britain's greatest spectator sport when the King attended the Cup Final; Wembley Stadium staged its first Cup Final in 1923 and he was there again, 150,000 of his subjects tried to secure admission. But it was not just a spectator sport; there were more than a million people, of all ages, playing association football in Britain in 1914 and if one takes into account every variety of game which involves kicking or carrying a ball around a muddy field, it must be by far the most practised sport today.

HITTING LITTLE BALLS

'This morning Teddy set up the net and poles in the field just opposite the dining-room windows and we began to play "sphairistike" or lawn tennis, a capital game but rather too hot for a summer's day.' When he wrote this in 1874 Francis Kilvert was ahead of fashion; the great age of tennis was about to dawn. Three years later the first Wimbledon championships were held, within twenty years every country house or public school worth its salt had its own tennis court (plate 429). But it was not till the period between the two wars, with the popularisation of the hard 'all weather' court and the proliferation of tennis clubs in the outer suburbs, that tennis freed itself from the country house. It was the age of John Betjeman's Miss Joan Hunter Dunn, 'furnish'd and burnish'd by Aldershot sun', and tennis was one of the first games in which men and women could participate, if not as equals, then at least playing on the same ground and subject to the same rules.

So, too, was golf, though there the bastions of male superiority proved even harder to storm. Golf, in Scotland at least, has a history longer than that of any other game, and the Royal and Ancient Golf Club at St Andrews ruled the roost from the mid-eighteenth century. Nineteenth-century courses tended to be beside the sea and within easy reach of a

The cricket ground of Hythe in Kent in 1899 (BELOW 428). The pavilion, the sight-screen and the white flannels of the players suggest that this was a match of some consequence, at least socially.

Lawn tennis at Moffat in Dumfries in 1892 RIGHT (429) *in what was clearly a tournament of some significance. The first Wimbledon championships had been held in 1877 and were quickly followed by an enormous increase in the game's popularity.*

Nineteenth-century golf courses tended to be beside the sea and within easy reach of a railway. This course below Harlech Castle in Gwynedd (1908) LEFT (430) *must be one of the most picturesquely situated in the country.*

Bowls at Penzance in 1920 LEFT (431). *It was still something of a rarity for women to play the game at this date and mixed bowls were almost unheard of — at least they seemed ready to provide an appreciative audience, however.*

ilway (plate 430), with the availability of the otor car proliferation became inevitable. oday there are nearly two thousand courses in ritain, the majority of them private clubs, and ough the frantic growth of the 1970s and 980s seems to have slackened, the apparently satiable demand for more room to play reatens the parks and open spaces round ery urban centre in the country. Fortunately olf is unique in its territorial demands. mong the innumerable other sports indulged and often pioneered by the British some, like ckets or badminton, are confined to compact side courts; others, like bowls, require latively little space; yet others, like skating and allooning, can be practised wherever a suitable mporary site is available (plates 431-433). hough the golf course may be pock-marked ith greens and bunkers its very existence uarantees the preservation of an open space. golf loses its appeal, nature will resume its vay — the sooner, some may think, the better.

THEATRES AND MUSIC HALLS

The British at play are not necessarily the British playing games. Since the dawn of recorded history they have been entertained, in one form or another, by singers, dancers, actors. The theatre, in particular, is in the national bloodstream. Largely this is because of Shakespeare, probably the best known of all Englishmen and certainly the world's most famous dramatist. His supposed birthplace in Stratford-upon-Avon, enthusiastically 'restored' in the nineteenth century to what it was hoped was its former glory, is a shrine for tourists from every country; the Memorial Theatre, built and rebuilt with equal zest (plates 434-436) is a more potent tribute to his memory. In the mid-nineteenth century every respectable town had its theatre, most cities had several. The majority survived until the inter-war period. Some are still there, new ones have opened, but no longer can the existence of a theatre be assumed with any confidence.

The Crystal Palace was not just a pleasant centre for a family outing but provided opportunities which were not easily had in London. In the summer of 1890 it staged the launch of a giant balloon BELOW (432) and attracted a formidable crowd of spectators.

The same is true of the music hall. These reached their zenith at the end of the nineteenth century. In 1879 London had some thirty large music halls and a plethora of smaller ones, by 1905 there were twice as many. They varied in size from what was little more than a room tacked on to a pub, to West End palaces like the Alhambra or the Empire which played to audiences of thousands. Dan Leno, George Robey, Will Fyffe, Marie Lloyd: it is hard to believe that the stars of stage or screen today will seem such legendary giants in a hundred years.

Nor were they confined to London; in Manchester the Palace of Varieties which opened in 1891 had three thousand seats and the city could claim more than four hundred smaller halls and concert rooms as well.

The dance hall was one of the rivals that contributed to its weakening. The period between the two World Wars witnessed an explosive enthusiasm for dancing, fed by the invasion of jazz from the United States. The Hammersmith Palais de Danse, opened in 1919, was the first great temple of the new religion: it was warm, it was colourful, it was cheap, it was democratic, and it offered endless opportunities for boy and girl to get together in a propinquity that was pleasing yet still more or less proper.

Within a decade dance halls and big bands were to be found everywhere; even Rochdale, with only 100,000 inhabitants, had six dance halls open on a Saturday night. To the more censorious or old-fashioned among the populace, this seemed to mark the frivolity of modern youth. In *Lady Chatterley's Lover* Mrs Bolton grumbled about the colliery lads going off in evening clothes to the Palais de Danse in Sheffield. 'They don't give a serious thought to a thing,' she complained, 'save Doncaster Races and the Derby.'

Another advantage of the Crystal Palace was that in winter its lake made an excellent skating rink

ABOVE (433). *Several monsters like the one on the bank behind the lake were to be found in the grounds.*

1850 STRATFORD

In the late 1850s, when this unusually early Frith picture of Shakespeare's birthplace was taken RIGHT *(434), it had only recently stopped being a butcher's shop. Enough information was available to justify restoration to what was believed to have been its former appearance; by 1892* RIGHT BELOW *(435) it looked more or less as it does today.*

1892 STRATFORD

THE AGE OF THE MOVING PICTURE

Yet a far more serious threat to entertainment on the stage had been nurtured within the music hall itself. The demand for respectable family entertainment had led to the music hall diversifying into variety. A feature of such a programme was increasingly likely to be a bioscope display, usually consisting of a primitive film of notabilities – often Royal or sporting – jerking like clumsily controlled marionettes. In 1896 the Alhambra Music Hall commissioned a film of the Derby and soon longer and more sophisticated material was

being imported from the United States. Techniques improved, so did the quality of the performance; Charlie Chaplin did more than any other star to popularize the new medium. Suddenly cinemas were everywhere; many of them, like cuckoos in the nest of the music hall that had nurtured them, ejected the other fledglings and took over the theatre in its entirety, others nestled in any suitable or unsuitable building which happened to be available (plate 437). More and more, however, were built for the purpose. At first the ideas of the designer did not stretch far beyond an

mbellished version of a conventional theatre; en they entered the world of fantasy: neo-recian façades capped by a Babylonian ggurat; rocco detail imposed on a mock-udor front; the mad King Ludwig of Bavaria apted for the suburban housewife. Finally — ter still — came the austere but bulbous, a style articularly favoured by the Odeon chain of nemas and the more far-flung stations on the ondon underground railway (plate 438).

After the First World War the industry was eginning to wonder if it had reached aturation point; then came the age of echnicolor; then the talkies. Three thousand nemas in 1918 became five thousand in 939; in Liverpool the number was trebled, in irmingham doubled. This was the age of the ıper cinema; flamboyant baroque cathedrals esigned to convince their visitor that one went the cinema not just to see a film but to avour a new way of life. Twenty million tickets week were being sold.

And then, within the space of a few years, he bubble burst. It was television that killed Cock Robin. Today the average adult spends wenty-five hours a week transfixed in front of ne box, or at least sitting in front of the box. ight houses out of ten have got a video. Even f there were time to go to the cinema, people wondered what point there could be when any film one might wish to see would shortly be available for home viewing. Increasingly the generality of mankind went to the cinema only when the film shown was so spectacular that the big screen seemed essential, or so specialized in appeal that it would never be available on video. The cinema went into a decline that, without being terminal, has involved the closure of a majority of its outlets. Even today one cannot be sure that the industry has bottomed out.

The effect on the appearance of Britain's towns has been dramatic. Between 1910 and 1940 the cinema burst upon the squares and

The Odeon at Corby in Northamptonshire (c. 1955) ABOVE **(438)** *was built in a squat yet bulbous style much favoured by this chain of cinemas and – oddly enough – certain underground railway stations. Today* ABOVE RIGHT **(439)** *it is a store for cheap pine furniture and seems somewhat abashed by its transformation.*

high streets, usually in a prominent position, often flamboyant in style and dominating in appearance. Now some have been demolished to make way for flats or office blocks, others have been de-gutted and transformed into arcades of shops or amusement parks. The most common fate was to become a bingo hall; in the Byzantine or rococo splendours of the past elderly housewives pored over their cards and chirped delightedly at the cry of 'Legs eleven'. But this vogue too passed and many bingo halls in their turn were transformed for other uses (plates 438-441).

BRITAIN TAKES TO THE ROAD

In parallel with these developments, a new, healthier form of pleasure-seeking began to hold sway. With time to spare and money to burn, the British took to the road. It was the bicycle that first made it possible. 'I have almost forgotten there is such a pursuit as literature in the arduous study of – bicycling! – which my wife is making me learn to keep her company,' wrote Thomas Hardy in 1896. Soon all the youth and much of the middle age of Britain seemed to be keeping Mrs Hardy company, and though the mass popularity of the sport killed

it for those sensitive to the dictates of fashion for hundreds of thousands of bicyclists the companionship that they encountered on the road was half the pleasure.

The bicycle opened the eyes of city dwellers to the existence of the country. The Cyclists Touring Club had been set up in the 1880s; it was nearly fifty years before the creation of the Ramblers' Association formally acknowledged that it was possible to explore the countryside without the help of a machine. Between the two World Wars a new level of society discovered the pleasures of hills and moors, donned its stout shoes, shorts and rucksacks and strode out into the wilderness. The Youth Hostel, an idea borrowed from the Germans, spread rapidly across the British countryside and opened up new areas in an age when the lightweight tent and sleeping bag were still far in the future. For 1/- a night hikers could enjoy, certainly not luxury, barely even comfort, but at least a roof over their heads, drinkable water and basic facilities for cooking. But even by 1939 it was becoming harder to find the quiet and solitude that is so much a part of the pleasure for the true hiker. Today, as the frontiers of the undeveloped recede and the

1925 FARNBOROUGH

The Scala in Farnborough (1925) LEFT (440) was more exuberant in its appearance. Its adventures over recent years are typical of many cinemas. In the 1950s it became a bingo hall, then a 'Laser Shooting Gallery'. Today BELOW (441) it has just completed its refurbishment and is about to renew life for a third time as a church for Jehovah's Witnesses. May it rest in peace.

1998 FARNBOROUGH

umber of walkers relentlessly increases, the threat to the environment is becoming critical. At beauty spots scars are gouged across the hillside by the feet of the would-be nature worshippers; in August in the Lake District certain favoured paths look more like Oxford Street at rush hour than the secluded haven beloved of poets.

The caravan added to the exodus from town to country. Even in 1998, with all the lures of 'abroad', nearly forty percent of British holiday-makers headed for the seaside or open spaces and of these an ever-increasing proportion took their homes with them in the shape of a caravan. One man's traveller is another man's tourist. The climber of high mountains has always felt that his experiences were subtly superior to those of the lesser mortals who remained on the plains to visit medieval churches or provincial art galleries (plate 442); the connoisseur of churches in his

turn despised the sun worshippers of the Riviera or the Costa Brava. It has always been so; in the 1870s Francis Kilvert exploded in, for a clergyman — a singularly un-Christian tirade: 'Of all noxious animals the most noxious is a tourist. And of all tourists the most vulgar, ill-bred, offensive and loathsome is the British tourist. No wonder dogs fly at them and consider them vermin to be exterminated.' There is no sure scale by which one can adjudge the rival merits of those who seek their differing pleasures in the open air. The good thing is that many millions who previously knew only town and city now find new pleasures in the countryside; the bad that in so doing they pollute and ravage the source of their new delights. Somehow, a balance must be maintained.

THE BUTLIN FORMULA FOR ORGANIZED COLLECTIVE JOLLITY

What Kilvert would have made of a holiday camp defies imagination. The movement began when a few enlightened bodies conceived the idea of providing centres where their staff could enjoy cheap holidays in each other's company. The Civil Service Clerical Association led the way in 1924; by the time Billy Butlin opened his first commercial holiday camp at Skegness in 1937, there were already more than a hundred semi-private camps in existence. The Butlin formula of organized jollity and wall-to-wall entertainment was an instant success; Nicholas Blake made it the back drop to his detective story *The Summer Camp Mystery*, and had his sociologist, Paul Perry, gaze with approval on the 'massive fun factory' of Wonderland, with its 'vast dining halls ... ballroom, whose sprung maple floor positively incited you to the light fantastic; to say nothing of bars, an indoor swimming pool equipped with aerofilter and coloured

fountains, a concert hall, a gymnasium, and innumerable playrooms'. During the Second World War, Wonderland probably served as a barracks or internment camp, but soon it was back in business again. Most of the visitors came from the lower middle classes, and their increasing wealth and sophistication meant that the holiday camps first modified to meet the new demands and then largely went out of favour. Today the massive and self-contained entertainment centre is more likely to cater for day visitors. There were always a few institutions of this kind – but the new pleasure palaces like Alton Towers offer far greater variety. The holiday-makers who huddled dispiritedly around the pool at Southport or made merry on curious tricycles at Caister-on-Sea (plates 443, 444), would today demand blue lagoons, water-chutes, stomach-churning helter-skelters and all the traditional fun of the fair dressed in more fashionable clothing. Whether the sum total of their happiness is notably the greater is another matter.

One could forgive this little group on Striding Edge, Helvellyn, in 1912 OPPOSITE ABOVE (442), *if they felt themselves on top of the world, not merely physically but spiritually as well.*

The pleasures of the traditional British holiday would seem drear indeed to today's pleasure-seekers. The great-grandchildren of the dispirited revellers beside the bathing pool at Southport in 1914 OPPOSITE BELOW (443), *or the grandchildren of the cheery tricyclists at Caister-on-Sea holiday camp in 1955* ABOVE (444), *would expect very much more today.*

Praying

I<small>T WAS IN</small> 1867 that Matthew Arnold compared the 'melancholy, long, withdrawing roar' of the pebbles on Dover beach to the retreat of the Sea of Faith as the tide remorselessly drew it back 'down the vast edges drear and naked shingles of the world'. The image was a striking one; today it seems curiously inept, however, for the Victorian world was at that time swept by something near to a gale of religious fervour. Church going was as prevalent as it had ever been, except perhaps in certain rural parishes where the despotic rule of squire or parson in the past had ensured that only the boldest neglected their duty on a Sunday morning. New churches or dissenting chapels seemed to open every week; those that already existed were often extensively enlarged; the idle and self-indulgent clergyman who ignored his pastoral duties or left them to a poorly paid curate was still to be encountered but far more common were young and energetic evangelicals ceaselessly preoccupied by the spiritual and physical needs of their flock.

Corners of Wales and Scotland were consistently devout but England had never been a particularly religious nation. Parsons spoke of a golden age when everybody went to church, but it had only existed in their imagination. The census in 1851 showed that less than half the adult population had been to church or chapel the previous Sunday. In Flora Thompson's Lark Hill practically all the villagers were christened, married and buried in the church a mile and a half away at Fordlow and went there regularly as children, but only a dozen or so regularly attended when grown up. The Catholic inn-keeper was the most assiduous churchgoer; even the Methodists, who held their services in one of the cottages, were more attentive in their worship than the Anglicans.

But in spite of Arnold's melancholy, things were getting better. The number of Anglican baptisms and confirmations rose year by year, not just in overall numbers but in the proportion of eligible children whose parents took the trouble to present them at church. So did the number of Easter communicants; the new industrial cities and towns fell far below the national average but in the country as a whole congregations were growing, and were to continue to grow until well into the twentieth century. Even in cities like Leeds or Manchester — godless, the more censorious might say — the new churches were hard to ignore. In the smaller towns and villages the church was still a part of daily life. The harvesters at Netherbury (plate 446)

In towns like Largs (1897)
ABOVE **(445)**, *where the*
sea was all-important, the
church (in this case, the

churches) came down into
the harbour and joined in;
their towers were land-
marks not to be ignored.

Harvesting at Netherbury, Dorset, in 1912 RIGHT (446). *The farm labourers might not have been inside the church for a year or more but their children went there, they knew the parson, the parson knew them, it was a part of their lives.*

At Cromer too (1890) RIGHT (447) *the church towered over the port. It was a landmark for many miles out to sea and, indeed, for many years served as a supernumerary lighthouse.*

might rarely have ventured inside the church but their work took them within a few hundred feet of it, they knew the parson and the parson knew them, their children would have been christened there and attended Sunday School. In ports, where the sea was all-important in the lives of the inhabitants, the church came down to the quayside (plate 445), its tower was a landmark for sailors, it could not be ignored; even where it kept its distance, it often still dominated the town, as at Cromer (plate 447) where it was set a little way back from the sea.

DISSENT: STRONG ON FERVOUR, WEAK ON ARCHITECTURE

Far more than was the case with the Church of England, the dissenting chapels were centres of social life and education. The Methodists, Congregationalists, Baptists, Presbyterians, Quakers, Unitarians, were all perpetually conscious of the fact that they were a minority, not oppressed perhaps but certainly under-privileged compared with the establishment Anglicans installed in their usually far grander church. Probably the Methodists at Lark Hill were able to move into some sort of building of their own before the end of the nineteenth century but it would have been on a simple scale (plate 448). Where something more imposing proved possible, the dissenters turned out to have an almost infallible instinct for the brash and the tasteless. Richard Jefferies in 1872 stormed against the new chapel which plain beyond plainness, stood beside a fir copse … nothing could have been designed

Sometimes dissenters were forced to worship in the house of one of their number; where they did have a building of their own it was usually small, simple and curiously charmless — the Baptist Chapel at Llwynhendy, Dyfed (1936) BELOW **(448)**.

The Wesleyan church at Brighton in 1898 LEFT **(449)**, *on the other hand, was assertive in the extreme. Unfortunately, when dissenters did have the money to build something grand, their taste often lagged behind their religious fervour.*

1893 LOOE

Between 1893 LEFT (450) and 1906 LEFT BELOW (451), the church at Looe was divested of the building which obtruded on it. Aesthetically the gain was questionable, but the church certainly looked more imposing as a result.

1906 LOOE

more utterly opposite to the graceful curve of the fir tree than this red-bricked crass building'. No doubt the consciousness that they were looked down on by the worshippers at the established church induced a certain assertiveness in the dissenters' building projects; the Wesleyan church at Brighton (plate 449) must in part have been inspired by a wish to affront the Anglican majority. In aesthetic terms the mellow and ancient Anglican church almost always scored over its architecturally upstart rival. The Roman Catholics had still more reason to feel aggrieved since the worshippers down the road were occupying *their* building, filched at the Reformation. Possibly it was shortage of money; possibly a sublime assurance of their own superiority made display unnecessary; whatever the cause, nineteenth- and twentieth-century Roman Catholic churches were rarely beautiful but lacked the swagger which marked the creations of the more affluent among the dissenters.

The Anglicans had been at it too
The Anglicans had been hard at it too. Between 1840 and 1876 more than seventeen hundred new churches were built in Britain. Some were

magnificent; George Gilbert Scott's tower and spire at St Mary Abbots in Kensington stands comparison with its noble progenitor at St Mary Redcliffe in Bristol. Many were more humdrum, some downright ugly, but on the whole Victorian church building commands respect. It is when they indulged in radical renovation that criticism is called for. Repairs were often urgently necessary; extensions could from time to time be justified (plates 450-457); but the seemingly gleeful degutting of medieval interiors and the reconstruction of towers and spires so as to produce results which were deemed to be more in keeping with the shibboleths of contemporary fashion can never be condoned. 'If all the medieval buildings in England had been left as they stood ...' wrote Thomas Hardy indignantly in 1906, 'to incur whatever dilapidations might have befallen them at the hands of time, weather and general neglect, this county [Dorset] would have been

Truro in 1890 ABOVE *(452), from the Viaduct, showed the somewhat truncated roofline of the cathedral; by 1912* LEFT *(453), in memory of Queen Victoria, it had sprouted a grand new tower and spire, 250 feet high, one foot for every mile it was from London.*

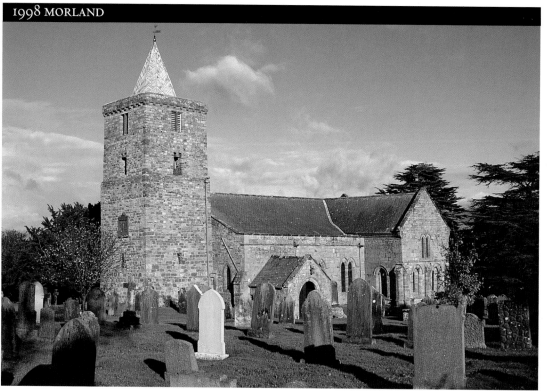

The church of Morland in Cumbria in 1893 ABOVE (454). The Victorian urge to rebuild or renovate did not generally extend to removing the vegetation from romantically ivied walls. If this tower had been left in the state it was in for much longer, it might have been in a sorry plight today. For all that, in 1998 LEFT (455), it still looks rather like a shorn poodle.

The wooden chapel of Sedbergh School, Cumbria, in 1890 LEFT (456), was not monumental enough to satisfy the school's administrators; by 1901 BELOW (457), it had been replaced by a more imposing stone structure.

Church Causeway, Billingshurst, in Kent LEFT (458). It is typical of a thousand similar views in Britain in that, between 1912 and 1928 BELOW (459), nothing much changed except for the apparition of a war memorial. By 1998 BOTTOM (460), typically too, the memorial had weathered, bushes had grown up, and it had slipped unobtrusively into the background. Meanwhile, the rough road in the foreground had graduated into the busy A29 running from London to Bognor, caught at an unusually tranquil moment.

1928 BILLINGSHURST

1998 BILLINGSHURST

richer in specimens today than it finds itself to be after the expenditure of millions in a nominal preservation.'

THE TIDE OF FAITH RECEDES

By then, however, Arnold's gloomy vision had indeed been realized; the tide of faith had reached high water and was beginning to recede. The middle class stands for England, wrote Charles Masterman in *The Condition of England*. 'It is the middle class which is losing its religion; which is slowly or suddenly discovering that it no longer believes in the existence of the God of its fathers ... Among the middle classes – the centre and historical support of England's Protestant creed, the drift away is acknowledged by all to be conspicuous.' The combined membership of the Roman Catholic and Protestant churches in 1914 was about eight million. Thirty years later it was formally much the same, but the statistics masked a catastrophic decline. Especially in the towns the church ceased to be a focal point: the football club commanded the loyalties of the new generations, the cinema and dance hall provided all that was needed by way of glamour

The church of St Peter's on Market Hill at Sudbury, Suffolk, in 1900 ABOVE **(461)**. *Except for a statue of Gainsborough that now stands outside it looks much the same today, but it has been declared redundant and is now used only for concerts and such events.*

The shops clustered around the church at Richmond in 1929 BELOW (463) *suggested that God and Mammon could co-exist at every epoch. But co-existence has not always proved possible; the name of the auctioneers, Phillips, blazoned across the face of the clock of St Mary's, Gateshead* RIGHT (462), *shows that here at least Mammon has triumphed and the church become an auction house.*

Dryburgh Abbey, a twelfth-century abbey sacked by the English, was in 1897 BELOW (465) a splendid ruin, with various notabilities buried in its grounds, but otherwise no more than a museum-piece.

and excitement. In York, to take one example, church attendance dropped from 17,000 in 1901 to 12,770 in 1935 and 10,220 in 1948. Over the same period, the number of engaged couples who eschewed church for their wedding and opted for a registry office, almost doubled. On the whole, the Non-Conformists held their share of congregations better than the Anglicans, and the Roman Catholics better than either, but overall the trend continued steadily downwards.

Though Wales and Scotland stuck with greater determination to accepted standards, the rigorous rules of the English Sabbath crumbled year by year between the wars. Pubs and cinemas began to open – at first for limited periods only, but once the gap was made the pressure to widen it proved irresistible. The Sunday afternoon spin in the car around the neighbouring countryside became part of the ritual of family life and garages and cafés were only too happy to provide the new market with the services it demanded. It was still a long way to the Sunday of the 1990s, almost

On the other hand, some of the picturesque ruins in which the Christian churches of Britain are so rich have survived as lively places of pilgrimage. Iona, photographed in 1903 RIGHT (466) and even then much visited, is pre-eminent among them.

indistinguishable from other days except in those urban areas where offices and factories are concentrated, but the way ahead was clear.

THE WORLD WARS BRING A RESPITE

The two World Wars brought a temporary reprieve to the churches: when things became really black, there did not seem to be anything to do but pray; it could do no harm and might do a certain amount of good. Remembrance Sunday, the Cenotaph, war memorials in every town and village in the land, meant that the impetus was not wholly lost (plates 459, 460). The solemn procession of veterans to church on every 11 November reunited church, state and people in unwonted harmony. But the effects of such a ceremony were as transitory as a Coronation or royal wedding, and as the veterans died off attendance dwindled. The new generations could not really see what the fuss had all been about.

The abandonment of organized religion did not necessarily mean that people no longer believed in God. A Mass Observation survey in

The church at Grantchester near Cambridge BELOW (467) is a museum-piece for another reason. Each year thousands of visitors crane their necks to see whether, as in Rupert Brooke's celebrated poem, the clock stands at ten to three. Disconcertingly, this photograph, taken in 1914, shows it at ten to two.

1947 showed that only one in ten of the population regularly attended church, two thirds never entered its doors, but only one in twenty was a committed atheist; four out of five women and two out of three men believed in the existence of a deity. A quarter of a century later, a similar questionnaire suggested that three-quarters of the population were still believers. For every three 'believers' who gave their religion unthinkingly as Church of England, only one bothered to ensure that their child was confirmed. It may be felt that a religion so diffuse and undemanding is worth little. Such figures, however, do imply that at least a propensity to worship still exists. The otherwise inexplicable enthusiasm which can be generated by dynamic priests working in the context of an evangelical crusade supports such a view. And though the actual attendance figures may have slumped, society's support for the structure of organized religion has remained remarkably constant. A survey of holiday camps after the Second World War showed that nearly all of them offered a chapel

St Paul's in 1880 reared triumphantly above the surrounding roofs. Many of the views that could then be gained of it have been blocked off by new developments. The view from Southwark Bridge LEFT (468), *however, can still be brought up to date. Both the riverfront and the skyline have altered drastically, but the little inlet which can be seen just to the right of the dome is Queenhithe Stairs and still exists in 1998* BELOW (469) *as a barge dock.*

1998 ST PAUL'S CATHEDRAL

among their facilities; often they were little patronized and secreted in obscure corners, in one case between the beer-store and the bicycle shed, but they were there if wanted. The numbers of pilgrims visiting shrines like Walsingham continued to grow; it seems that the human instinct to believe and worship will not easily be eradicated, even in this most materialistic of ages.

THE STRUCTURE SURVIVES, BUT HAS BEEN SADLY BATTERED

But though the structure of the church has survived it has taken quite a battering. In the Church of England the number of theological colleges and of ordinands has been more than halved in the last thirty years. That the handsome Georgian rectory is now the 'Old Rectory' and lived in by a retired businessman, while the rector has moved to a nearby bungalow, is no doubt entirely proper, but when the church itself is found to be surplus to requirements it is harder to feel that all is well (plates 461, 462). More than a thousand churches have been declared redundant, some pulled down, some turned into flats or concert halls, a few made over to other faiths. In some cases the German bombers lent a hand (plate 464). The Methodists, in a hectic rationalisation, closed nearly five hundred chapels between 1971 and 1974. Roman Catholics managed better, but the number of infant baptisms in Catholic churches, the surest indication of the future, fell by almost a half during the 1960s and 1970s. Picturesque ruins have long been a speciality of the church in Britain; sometimes, as at Iona, retaining a role as a place of pilgrimage, more often kept up for tourists or suffered to decay (plates 465, 466). Faced with the ever-increasing cost of maintenance, some of the greatest churches have been forced to charge admittance.

Westminster Abbey plays two roles, those of the nation's parish church and a museum of Britain's history. St Paul's once reared in splendid isolation above the dwarf city at its feet; today it is hemmed in by the temples of Mammon and admission will cost most of us £4.00 (plates 468, 469).

RELIGION IS VERY FAR FROM DEAD

There have, of course, been gains as well as losses. Basil Spence's Coventry Cathedral is one of the noblest examples of post-Second World War architecture; the Roman Catholic Cathedral at Liverpool, Guildford Cathedral and many lesser buildings show that the Christian faith does not intend to go gentle into that good night (plate 470).

And religion in the British Isles is by no means confined to the Christian faiths. In 1945 there were some 300,000 practising Jews in Britain, at that time the largest of the non-Christian communities. Soon they were overtaken by new waves of immigration. Today there are nearly 300,000 Hindus, well over a million Muslims. As is so often the way with minorities, they are more ardent in pursuit of their faith than the better established worshippers who were there before them. Every city, and nearly every large town, is likely to have at least one synagogue, one Sikh gurdwara, one Hindu temple, one mosque, and all these are eagerly frequented (plate 471).

Britain today is a multi-faith society and the status of the Church of England as the national church is increasingly open to question. With their well-known skill at avoiding contentious issues, the British will probably contrive to avoid posing themselves that question, let alone answering it, for many years yet, but the Coronation of the next sovereign is going to make inevitable some awkward facing of the facts.

The Hindu Temple at Neasden in North London RIGHT (**471**). *When it wa. built the temple seemed extravagantly out of place ir a London suburb; already it is beginning to look surprisingly much at home.*

The church is not in retreat everywhere. Basil Spence's Coventry Cathedral (1960) ABOVE **(470)** *was one of the finest examples of post-war architecture, and is as well frequented as its predecessor before the Second World War.*

Shopping

'SHOPPING' IS REALLY A MISNOMER. The word suggests a degree of pleasure; what Thackeray described in *Vanity Fair* as: 'The delightful round of visits and shopping which forms the amusement ... of the rich London lady.' No rich London lady would have wasted her time on the acquisition of meat, bread or other staples of life — that was marketing and was left to the servants. Nor did shopping necessarily even take place in shops. Until the last decades of the nineteenth century most food was bought from market stalls and a wide range of other goods from itinerant pedlars (plates 472-474). Some of the more go-ahead towns had covered markets (plate 475), precursors of the shopping mall, but no village would have boasted such a facility. There might be a baker's shop, attached to the bakery; a butcher needed a cool place in which to store his stock, but the greengrocers operated in the open. Even today they exhibit their wares on the street in front of their shop in a way which few other shopkeepers emulate, except for ironmongers who also like to colonize the pavement.

Until the end of the nineteenth century a great deal of household buying was done from open-air stalls or more-or-less itinerant pedlars. This ginger-cake seller in London RIGHT (473) was an example; the man behind him has obviously had his attention caught by the still unfamiliar camera.

The small boys selling onions in Plymouth in 1907 LEFT (472), were part of the same family. The one on the right was keen to cultivate the Breton look, though both boys and onions were probably local.

The ice-cream vendor, with what was called a 'Hokey Pokey' stall, in Greenwich in 1884 LEFT (474) was another popular part of the street scene — father or grandfather of the stop-me-and-buy-one bicyclist.

John Doyle's spectacular Market Hall, photographed in 1897 RIGHT **(475)**, *was built for Accrington thirty years before at a time when the town was at its economic zenith and was eager to demonstrate its wealth.*

THE EVOLUTION OF THE MODERN SHOP

The evolution of something resembling the modern shop began in the 1830s, when gas-lit fronts with large window panes began to appear. Dickens thought it a development to be regretted: 'Quiet, dusty old shops … were pulled down; spacious premises with stuccoed fronts and gold letters were erected instead … doors were knocked into windows; a dozen squares of glass into one.' The draper succumbed, then the chemists, then the win merchants. But the phenomenon was at firs mainly confined to London, it was not till afte the excise duty on sheet glass was abolished in 1845 that the fashion for large plate-glas windows spread outside the capital to th provinces. The architect, George Gilbert Scott was outraged. 'The very idea of its being

The cult of 'Ye Olde' was rife in 1899. 'Ye Olde Woode House' in Beckenham LEFT **(476)** *included not only 'Ye Old Curio Shoppe' but also 'Ye Olde Laundry' where shirts could be washed for 4d and waistcoats for 5d (olde pence). The building was demolished in 1920.*

1911 KNARESBOROUGH

necessary to the satisfaction of the eye to see how a building is supported is utterly ignored,' he stormed, 'and fronts of towering altitude are erected with no apparent super-structure but plate glass! Surely no age but our own would have endured such barbaric building?' Both the shopkeeper and the public, however, were delighted to sacrifice aesthetics for convenience and glamour; the cramped old windows were swept away, till by 1914 they were only to be found in torpid backwaters or where the owner decided to make a selling point out of picturesquely anachronistic premises (plates 477, 478). Other shops tried to have it both ways, converting their windows into something more up-to-date but pronouncing themselves 'Ye Olde' with what they felt to be suitably Gothic letters (plate 476). If the premises were too cramped for modernisation and lacked the clientele or the resources to get by on antique charm, then the demolition men moved in.

'Shutters for shop windows were going out,' wrote George Orwell of the market town of Lower Binfield, 'most of the shops in the High Street didn't have them.' Both Godalming and Christchurch (plates 479-484) were prosperous little towns which prided themselves on being

1998 KNARESBOROUGH

up-to-date; there would have been no shutters in their high streets. Yet both towns showed remarkable continuity over the next sixty or seventy years, the most noticeable trend being towards more prominent advertising and larger and, on the whole, uglier fascia above the shops.

The discreet reticence of the mid-nineteenth century was now being left behind (plates 485, 486). Window dressing was not yet taken

1895 GODALMING

The High Street of Godalming in 1895 ABOVE **(479)**, *1907* OPPOSITE ABOVE **(480)** *and 1955*

OPPOSITE MIDDLE **(481)** *showed remarkably few changes, though there had been a drift towards more*

assertive advertising and prominent fascia above the shops. By 1998 OPPOSITE BELOW **(482)** *this had*

commendably been checked and the street had been more or less pedestrianized. Things were clearly better.

1907 GODALMING

1955 GODALMING

1998 GODALMING

1900 CHRISTCHURCH

Christchurch, in Dorset, was similarly unchanged in essentials between 1900 LEFT (483) and 1998 BELOW (484), though Mr Smeed for one would not have contemplated announcing his wine business so brazenly at the earlier date and some attractive iron-work had been lost from the nearest shop on the right. The buildings in 1998 were not that different, though the shoppers looked as if they lived in another world. So, indeed, they did.

seriously as an art; the shopkeeper aimed to crowd as much of his stock into the window as he could possibly contrive; and in certain cases even to overflow on to the pavement (plates 487-490) thus colonizing it to attract buyers while possibly impeding passage.

By 1921 it was becoming clear how much the up-to-date grocer relied on branded and pre-packed goods, compared with the boxes of tea, sacks of sugar and flour, barrels of butter, jars of syrup, which were still to be met with in older-fashioned establishments and from which the proprietor would blend mixtures to suit the tastes of his clientele. Bookshops, like chemists, were allowed to affect a certain air of antiquity, but even they could not stand completely aside and were being forced to edge a little reluctantly towards the modern world (plates 491, 492).

1998 CHRISTCHURCH

In 1894 in Church Street, Ormskirk LEFT (485), the discreet reticence of the nineteenth century was already disappearing. Mr Stoner was determined that everyone should know, not only that he was the People's Hatter, but that he was Mr Stoner and that this was his shop. In Parliament Street, Harrogate, in 1907 BELOW (486), rival chemists shouted defiantly at each other across the street. A drug store was first so-called in the United States in 1845, but Mr Taylor was in the vanguard of British fashion.

Window dressing was not an art taken seriously by the shopkeeper in the early twentieth century. The proprietor of Burton's Cash Stores in Romford in 1908 ABOVE (487) *was concerned to cram as much of his stock into his window as he could possibly contrive though he seems to have lost the attention of the be-hatted lady in the foreground. His handsome gas lamps were clearly and rightly a source of much pride.*

THE DAWN OF THE DEPARTMENT STORE

It was Thomas Lipton who, more than any other one man, pioneered the concept of mass marketing; that there was more to be made out of selling large quantities of goods at a small profit than smaller quantities at a larger mark-up. He opened his first grocery store in Glasgow in 1872; installed bigger windows, better lighting, brasher fascia; cut prices; advertised in ways which his competitors found vulgar and disquieting; and before the end of the century had 250 branches across the country. The multiple store had arrived. The other great revolution had its genesis in the draper. Mr Baines, the leading draper of Bursley in Arnold Bennett's *Old Wives Tale*, deplored 'puffing' to the extent that he would

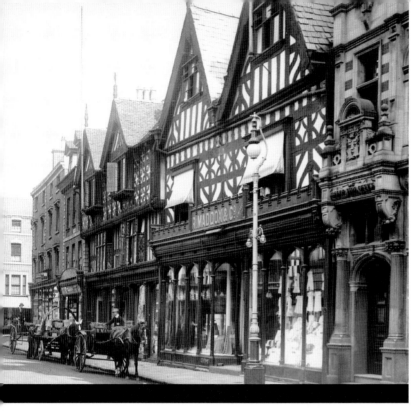

Between 1911 LEFT (488) and 1931 LEFT BELOW (489) Mr Maddox shed his initial and his 'Co' but seems, if anything, to have regressed in the art of presenting his stock to best advantage. For nastiness, there is little to choose between the two lamp-posts. Today BELOW (490) the shop is for sale, but the authorities of Shrewsbury have at least removed the offending lamp-post.

1998 SHREWSBURY

1909 BRIDPORT

not even replace his sign-board when it blew down in a gale. When his future son-in-law took over, however, all was changed; new styles were imported, placards read 'Very dainty', 'Unsurpassable', 'Exquisite 1/11ᵈ'. He and his wife 'without knowing or guessing it, were making history – the history of commerce. They had no suspicion that they were the forces of the future insidiously at work to destroy what the forces of the past had created.' In Candleford the 'plain draper's shop with rolls of calico and red flannel in the window' had been ripped apart, plate-glass windows put in, dress-making and millinery departments established and the shop renamed 'The Stores'.

The expanded draper, though it seems unlikely Candleford provided the necessary market, was on the way to becoming a fully

W Frost of Bridport, while in 1909 ABOVE (491) presenting a decently traditional appearance, had come to terms with the need to be able to display a wide range of stock.

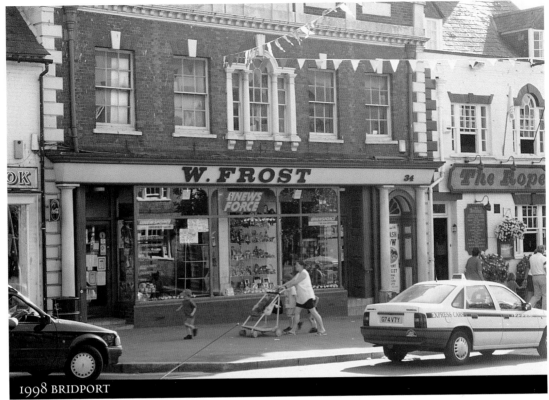

1998 BRIDPORT

In 1998 ABOVE RIGHT
(492) *the firm still trades
as W Frost, but seems to
have lost its printing side, as
well as some of the attractive
trimmings considered most
fitting nine decades earlier.*

fledged department store. The idea had first taken root in France and had been cautiously tried out in the north of England, but it was not till William Whiteley opened his first 'universal provider' in Westbourne Grove that London was able to see the full splendours of the future. Whiteley boasted that he could supply anything from a pin to an elephant. 'Depot, emporium, bazaar, warehouse – none of these seem to possess the slightest descriptive power,' reported an awe-struck *Modern London* in 1887. 'Whiteleys is an immense symposium of the arts and industries of the nation and of the world; a grand review of everything that goes to make life worth living passing in seemingly endless array before critical but bewildered humanity' (it would have been less surprising if the humanity had passed before the array, but the general sense is clear). The fashion spread: soon Lewis's of Liverpool, Kendal Milne's of Manchester, John Anderson's of Glasgow; Debenham's, Swan and Edgar's,

Derry and Toms of London; were doing roaring trade. In the 1880s Charles Digby Harrod's grocery shop on the Brompton Road branched out into carpets and furniture. A few years later drapery and fashion goods were added to the repertoire.

But it was Gordon Selfridge who carried the department store to its majestic zenith. He learned his trade in America and opened his store in Oxford Street with £100,000 worth of goods, a staff of eighteen hundred and a phenomenal £36,000 to spend on advertising. Selfridge's set new standards in the size of its windows, the brilliance of its lighting, the spaciousness of its lifts; even more significant, its portentous Ionic columns and vast façade proclaimed that it was no mere store but a temple in which Mammon could be worshipped as well as a good time had by all. Selfridge felt that his store must be a place in which people – women in particular – could realize their dreams. They flocked there not just

By 1914 the multiple stores were beginning their take-over of British high streets. On Station Road in Harrow ABOVE (493) one could already see a Home and Colonial Stores, a Boots and a Sainsbury's.

to buy a skirt or a packet of pins but as an experience. 'They come here as guests,' he declared, 'not customers to be bullied into buying. This is not a shop, it is a social centre.'

THE MULTIPLE STORE TAKES THE LEAD

Though neither Selfridge nor his customer-guests could have believed it, the department store like the dinosaur had reached the peak of

than the department store and were unafraid to offer lines cheaper than anything with which the more supercilious Harrod's or Selfridge's would wish to be associated. Lipton had not invented the multiple store – the Aerated Bread Company (ABC) was selling its products all over London before he had opened his first shop, while W H Smith had cornered the market for railway bookstalls twenty years earlier still – but he dramatically popularized the idea. Soon it was all the rage. Jesse Boot ventured beyond his redoubt in Nottingham and began to extend to other towns during the 1890s; Michael Marks made a success with a market-stall in Leeds, took Thomas Spencer into partnership ten years later, and was busily opening branches around the British Isles by 1900; W H Smith's for many years contented themselves with their monopoly of railway passengers, but as the twentieth century wore on they too moved out on to the high streets. The first Woolworths crossed the Atlantic in 1909. At first the 3^d and 6^d bazaar seemed the acme of vulgarity to the middle classes, but there were many good bargains among the rubbish and by the 1930s they had achieved some of the *réclame* which was to be enjoyed by Marks and Spencer's in the 1970s and 1980s. By the Second World War almost any town of any size had its Boots and its Woolworths, its Lipton's and its Sainsbury's. More and more the casual browser at shop windows would see little to tell him what part of the country he was visiting, still less what town it might be (plates 493-497).

The multi-store wreaked fearful damage on the sort of high street shop which Francis Frith would have known and photographed. 'Tastes and ideas were changing,' wrote Flora Thompson in the early 1890s. 'Quality was less in demand than it had been. The old, solid, hand-made productions, into which good

its development and could go nowhere but downwards. No new stores of any significance were added after the First World War. Instead, the movement which Lipton had pioneered in groceries, multiplied in different fields and in so doing cut inexorably into the market of the traditional department stores. Multiple stores, specializing in clothes, or furniture, or stationery and books, could carry a larger stock

Stamford market place in 1922 ABOVE (494) was still mainly populated by local shops, but a large branch of Freeman, Hardy & Willis — the boot and shoes chain — dominated the far side. In 1998 LEFT (495) the appearance of the square was decidedly improved — though it is hard not to deplore the grisly metamorphosis of Mr J Pepper's shop on the left of the picture.

1925 CLEVEDON

materials and many hours of patient skilled craftsmanship had been put, were comparatively costly. The new machine-made goods cost less and had the further attraction of a meretricious smartness.' Tastes and fashions have always changed and always will, but the pace was quickening. Small specialist craftsmen fared somewhat better than the more general merchant but even they were under pressure and if they were still in existence by the 1960s or 1970s, still more at the present day, their survival verged on the miraculous. Even rarer was the craftsman grocer, lovingly compounding from a row of boxes the blend of tea to suit his customer.

1998 CLEVEDON

EVERY CLOUD HAS A SILVER LINING

The process was not to be entirely deplored; many of the traditional shops whose demise so grieved the sentimentalist were squalid and inefficient. The butcher's shop in plate 498 may have been picturesque enough but would one not do better to buy one's meat at a rather more hygienic Dewhurst's? The 'old, solid, hand-made productions,' whose disappearance Flora Thompson lamented, were often heavy, cumbersome, expensive; the vegetables were encrusted with dirt, the tea stale and dusty. The mass-produced products which now dominated

the high street windows were not necessarily shoddy or meretricious, the consumer durables which were the fastest area of growth – electric irons, refrigerators, hoovers – were to save the housewife many hours of unnecessary labour and raise dramatically the standard of living of all but the very poorest.

THE WAR CHECKS THE REVOLUTION

The next revolution would no doubt have come more quickly if the Second World War had not checked all development; in some cases reversed it, indeed, since moribund and inefficient

W H Smith's were relatively late in escaping from the railway stations where they had been ensconced for so many years, but by 1925 TOP (496) they were already prominent on the high street. They were still in Clevedon in 1998 ABOVE (497), but could no longer boast of a circulating library.

SHOPPING 353

enterprises which should have perished in the early 1940s were given a new lease of life. The quota system meant that their share of the market could not be lost; the black market provided for the less scrupulous a source of business that was probably illegal, or close to being so, but was far more profitable than their licit trade. It was the 1960s before the pace of change once more began to quicken. By then one in five shops in the British Isles was part of a chain; some small, with only a dozen or so shops in a particular area; others nation-wide, with hundreds or even thousands of outlets under the same management if not always under the same name. One in five may not sound much, but they accounted for half the total trade; the remaining eighty percent of British shops scrambled for what was left. It was the golden age of the co-operative – the Co-op – non-profit-making stores run by co-operative societies. They had established

A butcher in Godalming High Street in 1895 ABOVE (498). *No doubt the scene was picturesque enough, but most people were glad to transfer their allegiance to a shop which belonged to a larger and, with luck, more hygienic chain. Even the pony seems to have had its doubts.*

themselves in the north in the late nineteenth century, had never achieved great success in the major cities, but by 1960 were firmly settled on the high streets of most towns of consequence (plates 499, 500). Their hour was brief, soon they were to be pilloried – even by Labour ministers who owed them loyalty on doctrinal grounds – as models of antiquated inefficiency. In the brave new world of the supermarket that was about to dawn there was as little room for them as for the old-fashioned butchers, bakers and candlestick makers who had preceded them in the nineteenth century.

The brave new world of the supermarket

There was even less room perhaps. What the small shop could and still can offer as a defence against the incursions of the supermarket was personal service. There will always be a demand for convenience shopping at the corner shop which stays open till all hours and which can supply a pint of milk or a packet of cigarettes to the housewife who has unexpectedly run short. There will always be a satisfaction in being recognized, in answering enquiries about the state of one's children's health or the progress of one's garden. Whether such attractions, though, will generate enough turnover to sustain the small shopkeeper in competition with the vastly greater range and lower prices of the supermarket must be uncertain. At one time the readiness of the small shopkeeper to deliver goods to customers who found it difficult to attend in person was a strong argument for their preservation, but refrigeration at home has diminished the need for such a service. One visit to a supermarket will stock up the average housekeeper for a week or more, why then resort to deliveries from the more expensive local grocer? The village shop, or corner shop in a town, may

The Northamptonshire Co-operative Society in Abington Street, Northampton, in 1922 below left *(499). This imposing institution was non-profit making and offered a range of special savings schemes to loyal patrons. By 1965* below *(500) most co-operative stores had become part of the nation-wide 'Co-op', one of whose stores was in Allport Lane in Bromborough, to the south of Liverpool.*

The Tesco store in Wantage in 1955 RIGHT **(501)** *had little in common with the great cathedrals of commerce that would be commonplace in 1999; nor did the Supermarket at Rockley Sands in Poole, Dorset* BELOW **(502)**.

hold on to some trade by staying open at hours when the supermarkets closed; but this can impose intolerable burdens on the staff and the advantage has anyway been whittled away as the supermarkets extend their hours. Shop numbers have declined everywhere; over a long period five thousand a year have closed: because trade dropped to an uneconomic level, because the old owner died and nobody could be found ready to take on the worry and hard work, because the reluctance of wholesalers to provide small quantities of goods made problems of supply increasingly difficult. In the remoter areas of Scotland the number of village stores and sub-post offices has halved over twenty years; in the high streets of provincial towns greengrocers, fishmongers, ironmongers, have given way to bookmakers, estate agents, unisex hairdressers.

Many of the greatest names of the supermarket era were familiar long before the

950s. They did not explode instantly into anything resembling their present glory: the diminutive Tesco in Wantage in 1955, the so-called supermarket at Rockley Sands near Poole, have little in common with the great cathedrals of today. But they were signposts to the future; by the 1980s it was impossible to find any town which did not have a Tesco or a Safeways, a Sainsbury's or a Waitrose – often two or more of them. The multiple stores, too, got bigger and more comprehensive – becoming something close to supermarkets in their own right. Even more destructive to the traditional high street shop was the new vogue for giant out-of-town shopping centres (plate 503). Such centres may contain a plethora of shops, including all the major multiple stores, as well as cafés and restaurants, petrol stations and acres of car park, possibly cinemas and a swimming pool as well. Shoppers can buy everything they need – and much that they do not need – without venturing into the centre of town at all. At least when the supermarket was in or near the high street customers had the chance to compare prices and quality with their smaller rivals, now they need not even be aware of their existence. Theoretically, of course, the high street greengrocer could move out to the shopping centre, but the rents are high, competition fierce. In practice he stays where he is and watches his trade wither to nothing.

AND THERE IS STILL WORSE TO COME

A still more stark threat lies ahead. Increasingly it is going to be possible for customers to do their ordering from home, to call up on the screen catalogues of all that is available, to punch in a series of numbers, and to loll back with the satisfaction of a good job well done. Before the twenty-first century has progressed too far there may be no need for shops at all, except a few eccentric outlets selling antique furniture or cats and dogs, where personal inspection will still be desirable. The best hope for the shopkeeper in an electronic world is that people value the human contact of shopping and like to be able to shuffle around the shelves, viewing what is on offer and making impulsive snatches at products which they had never previously known existed. Shopping is not just a way of acquiring goods, it is, or can be, a pleasure and a pastime in its own right. In all probability it will remain so; but the traditional shopkeeper is likely to have quite a lot more unpleasant shocks awaiting him or her along the way.

The shopping centre at Winsford, Cheshire, in the mid-1960s BELOW *(503). Then it seemed gigantic; today this structure is dwarfed by the vast complexes of shops, petrol-stations and apparently boundless car parks.*

Travelling by Rail

B Y 1860 THE BASIC RAIL NETWORK of the British Isles was in place. 'Network' is perhaps the wrong word; it was still a pretty ramshackle affair. Passengers wishing to travel from the north of Scotland to the depths of Cornwall would have had a bewildering range of possibilities open to them; a dozen companies or more would have vied for their custom on different sections of the route; finding out how the different lines meshed together and how the journey could be performed most rapidly and economically was a task that taxed even the experienced traveller. But the trains were there, the competition of the canal had been brushed aside, the service was far faster and less arduous than horse-drawn traffic on the roads could offer. Consolidation and refinements were obviously still called for but it seemed that the railway would reign supreme for the foreseeable future if not beyond.

As befitted a reigning monarch, the railways cloaked themselves in splendour. Victorian railway architects thought on the grandest scale and welcomed problems as a reason for displaying their boldness and technical virtuosity. Some of their bridges and viaducts were among the most noble monuments of industrial architecture (plates 504-509). Sometimes to suit the taste of the landowner through whose land the line was passing, more often to please themselves, they were

The Forth Railway Bridge, opened in 1890 and photographed seven years later ABOVE (505), was daringly innovative in technical terms but also a majestic spectacle; the Monsale Dale Viaduct, in 1914 LEFT (504), was a fine example of how man's intervention could sometimes embellish an already beautiful landscape.

preoccupied with the appearance of their creation as well as its ability to carry whatever loads were laid upon it. Stephenson's bridge over the Menai Straits was sternly functional in its essentials, but grandiose in its decoration; it could have been built more cheaply but economy was rarely at the forefront of their minds. The Forth Bridge, built nearly forty years later, was daringly innovative as a feat of engineering but also immensely satisfying as a spectacle. When one considers the extent to which the architects of these gigantic edifices, and all the other great bridges and viaducts which adorn the countryside, were dependent on manual labour to translate their visions into reality, one realizes that their's was an achievement to rank with the pyramids or the medieval cathedrals.

THE STATIONS WERE OFTEN RESPLENDENT, SOMETIMES POMPOUS, RARELY DULL

The stations were no less resplendent (plates 510-517), though function dictated form to a less marked extent and thus left more scope for pomposity, flamboyance or sheer bad taste. The railway station was the first thing which new arrivals in a town or city would be likely to see, and the

The builders of Britain's railways in the nineteenth century thought on the grandest scale and had no time for austerely utilitarian considerations. Stephenson's Britannia Bridge over the Menai Straits, photographed in 1890 ABOVE (506), was a fine piece of engineering and equally grandiose in decoration.

The splendidly dramatic Runcorn Railway Bridge (1905) LEFT (507), the sweep of the railway coming into Perth (1901) ABOVE RIGHT (508) and the Chirk viaduct with an aqueduct running by its side RIGHT (509), all illustrate the Victorian gift for executing grand engineering works in a way that was both effective and handsome.

councillors of that town were as determined as the railway proprietors that they should be suitably impressed. The main London termini were in place by the time Francis Frith could have wanted to make use of them: the noblest, Euston, was vandalized almost out of existence in the 1960s but most of the others have survived substantially intact. King's Cross, formerly the terminus of the Great Northern Railway was one of the least extravagant. To Margaret Schlegel, of *Howard's End*, it suggested infinity: 'Those two great arches, colourless, indifferent, shouldering between them an unlovely clock, were fit portals for some eternal

adventure.' There was nothing colourless or indifferent about the stations at Shrewsbury or at Stone, which were resounding statements on the part of the architect and had nothing whatever to do with the trains within. Other stations were less pretentious though no less quirky, but the true cathedral of the railway age must be York, whose noble and spacious curve lends an element of excitement to an anyway grand interior.

Though they got their passengers from A to B with considerable success, Victorian trains were not luxurious. Francis Kilvert travelled from Hay to Bath in 1871. 'In the Box tunnel,

The railway station at Chingford, Essex BELOW *(510), was unsurprisingly built on a modest scale, but when Queen Victoria visited Epping Forest towards the end of her reign, the station was the public face of the town and resolved to look the part for the occasion.*

King's Cross, in 1886 ABOVE (511) the terminus of the Great Northern Railway, was one of the more austere of London termini, possibly because its creator, Lewis Cubitt, was more of a builder and an engineer than an architect. To Margaret Schlegel in Howard's End it suggested infinity. Today RIGHT (512) the Euston Road has encroached on its forecourt and it has sprouted a roof to shelter passengers, but essentially it is little altered since she knew it.

as there was no lamp, the people began to strike foul brimstone matches … All the time we were in the tunnel these lighted matches were travelling from hand to hand in the darkness … The carriage was chock full of brimstone fumes, the windows both nearly shut, and by the time we got out of the tunnel I was almost suffocated.' If the windows had been open, Kilvert would have complained about the smoke and smuts from outside; if he had been travelling third class he would not even have enjoyed upholstered seating for another five years or more; even in the first-class carriages corridors and lavatories were a rarity; food and drink could be procured at the stations but the idea of providing refreshments on the train itself had hardly yet occurred to the men who ran the lines. The railway authorities could take assurance in the certainty that, however far

from perfect the service they offered, travel by road would always be quite as uncomfortable and far less convenient. Only with the coming of the car and bus and the dramatic developments on the roads in the early part of the twentieth century was that superiority seriously challenged.

Evolution to meet competition from the road

By then the railways were a major industry and an employer on the grandest scale. Whole towns had sprung up to service their needs (plates 518, 519). The operation was enormously expensive. If it was to maintain its status in the face of increasing competition from the roads it was clear that it would have to rationalize its operations so as to achieve economies and suit the convenience of its

1904 SHREWSBURY

Victorian railway stations were often extravagant stylistic statements on the part of their architect, but had little to do with trains. The Colonial Dutch station at Stone in Staffordshire (1900) LEFT **(513)**, *with some adjustments, would have made a fine country house for a nouveau riche industrialist. Shrewsbury in 1904* ABOVE **(514)** *and 1998* RIGHT **(515)** *could have served as a town hall.*

passengers. It was 1923 before any effective steps were taken, but then the evolution was rapid. With a certain amount of persuasion and bullying by the government, who had finally realized during the First World War that the railways were too important to the nation to leave entirely to their directors and had set up a Ministry of Transport, the 120 companies which one way or another were responsible for virtually all Britain's main and branch lines amalgamated into four major units. A bevy of idiosyncratic organisations, some of them comically small, with their own uniforms and their own uniquely decorated rolling stock, renewed life as the Great Western,

1998 SHREWSBURY

Godalming in 1906 LEFT
ABOVE (516) *provided a
good example of the rustic
style of station building; it
would have done nicely as a
home for a senior game-
keeper or junior land-agent.*

*York was the railway
capital of the North and its
station, built in 1877 and
photographed in 1909* LEFT
(517), *was appropriately
majestic. The most notable
difference the contemporary
passenger would notice is the
number of porters awaiting
the arriving train.*

The railways were labour intensive. The station at Farncombe, Surrey LEFT (518), was one of little importance, but in 1906 nearly a dozen employees were grouped in front of it, with the station master proudly to the fore.

Some towns were created by the railway or grew to accommodate its needs.

Before the railway came to Clapham it was no more than a tiny hamlet; by 1899

ABOVE (519) it had become one of the largest and busiest junctions in the world.

the London, Midland and Scottish, the London and North Eastern and the Southern. This was as far as they were prepared to go, it was to take the nationalisation of the railways after the Second World War to complete the process, and even that has proved to be no more than a temporary solution.

But no amount of reorganisation was going to remove the growing competition from the roads. Between the two World Wars the coach — cheaper, more flexible, able to pick up and drop its customers at a variety of stopping places — began to draw passengers away from the train, while the lorry, which enjoyed the

inestimable advantage of being able to carry goods from door-to-door, challenged the primacy of both rail and canal for the carriage of freight. As the demand for their services fell year by year, the railway companies found it more and more difficult to make economic sense of their widely stretched commitments.

The solution was painfully obvious. Increasingly, the companies tried to save money by closing railway lines that ran at a loss. As a result of this harsh but necessary pruning, between 1923 and nationalisation of the railways in 1947 more than twelve hundred miles of track were closed.

The underground stations in London's suburbs developed a style of their own — unfussy, strong, yet not over-assertive. Oakwood ABOVE (521) *and Cockfosters* OPPOSITE (522), *on the outer reaches of the Piccadilly line, are good examples.*

ELECTRIFICATION AND THE CITY RAILWAYS

Electrification seemed to be the best hope of the railways. It was expected that it would reduce the need for manpower and lead to increased speed and reliability. Gradually it was introduced into certain areas, particularly the Southern Railways on the lines running into London. Electrification, too, was the essential element in London's underground railways. The first 'tube' railway was in fact cable-operated and opened between Tower Hill and Bermondsey in 1870. It closed, however, after only a few months, and it was not till 1890 that the concept of trains powered by electricity and running far below the surface became a reality. In that year the Prince of Wales opened the world's first electric tube railway — the City and South London, from King William Street to Stockwell. After that, development was mainly towards the north and west; the area south of the river progressively felt itself more neglected, though the Bakerloo line, which opened in 1906 and carried 37,000 passengers on its first day, ventured some way beyond the Thames. The Piccadilly and Northern Lines completed the first phase and in 1913 the routes were fused into a single network. This by no means ended the operation — the Victoria and Jubilee lines have been added since the Second World War and further expansion towards the east is now taking place — but effectively it can be said that

London has enjoyed an integrated underground railway system for more than eighty years. Other cities followed its example, Glasgow got its first subway in 1897, though it did not adopt electrification for almost another forty years. Liverpool took another course, chose to go above ground and opened its Overhead Railway in 1893 (plate 34) – the first electric urban railway in the world.

In central London the entrances to the new tubes were often little more than a hole in the ground with a sign above it to indicate the existence of a station. In the suburbs a distinctive form of architecture evolved: clean lines, sound proportions, a taste of *art nouveau* without flamboyance or exaggeration. The examples that Frith photographed (plates 521, 522) are not among the most distinguished – Charles Holden's Arnos Grove is probably the best known and generally liked – but they are admirably unfussy and strong while managing not to be too assertive.

British Rail and the Beeching axe

On the first of January, 1948, the railways were nationalized and the four surviving companies renewed life as British Rail. As in 1923, picturesque diversity was sacrificed in the interests of – supposedly – great efficiency. Many people deplored the development but in the straitened post-war times it seems unlikely that private investors, left to themselves, would have been able to raise the capital needed to repair wartime damage and make up for a decade of neglect. With this new impetus, modernisation proceeded apace. The replacement of steam locomotives by diesel or electric models was a first priority. Huge sums of money were spent on new rolling stock, many stations were rebuilt almost from scratch. And yet competition from the roads, and now too the air, grew more fierce every year. By 1956 the railways were losing the nation £17 million a year, by 1961 the figure had risen to £87 million. Either the maintenance of

1908 CALSTOCK

1998 CALSTOCK

Nearly all wayside halts, manned by a staff of one or two and serving only a handful of passengers, were victims of railway closures. Calstock, on the Tamar Valley line in Cornwall, had only been operating for a few years when photographed in 1908 LEFT *(523). It was closed by Beeching but the line survived and today* LEFT BELOW *(524) provides a regular service to Plymouth. Where the line has disappeared resurrection becomes almost impossible. Another Cornish station, Callington, also recorded in 1908* BELOW *(525), is beyond redemption.*

the present railway network had to be accepted as a responsibility of the government, to be paid for like the National Health Service out of taxes, or drastic steps would have to be taken to curb the losses.

In fact steps which to some people seemed too drastic had already been taken. Nearly three thousand miles of passenger track were closed between nationalisation and 1959. But it was not enough. The decision was taken that British Rail had to make a profit, or at least run without subsidy, and in 1961 Richard Beeching was imported from I.C.I. to put the decision into practice. His reports revealed the startling fact that half the passenger stations together produced only two percent of the total passenger revenue and half the freight stations three percent. If economic issues only were considered, the best way to straighten out British Rail's accounts would be to close at least half the stations and, if practical, the connecting lines. The government realized that

economics could not be the only factor; certain loss-making rural lines served communities that would be devastated if they were abruptly closed. In the 1960s, the motor car was becoming common, but many people still did not have access to one. Country buses were few and far between, the railway offered an indispensable lifeline. But any line under threat had to justify itself on the most pressing grounds. The Beeching Axe duly fell. He recommended the immediate closure of two thousand stations and five thousand miles of track; by 1966 his target for stations had been met and 4,500 miles of track had been abandoned. All over Britain railside halts, even quite substantial town stations, were closed and either demolished or converted (plates 523-527). Beeching's final target had been a network reduced to eight thousand miles; the Labour government concluded that eleven thousand was the least that must be retained on social grounds. But the effects were still devastating;

1921 WOLFERTON

1998 WOLFERTON

As the station for Sandringham, Wolferton in Norfolk (1921) ABOVE (526) might have hoped to merit a royal dispensation from closure. It enjoyed no such good fortune, however. By 1998 LEFT (527) the buildings on the right — formerly the Royal Waiting Room — had been converted into two bijou residences but they still flaunt their gilded wind vane.

in the course of the 1970s Norfolk lost nearly three-quarters of its original mileage. The picturesque branch lines that had meandered along the valleys and ventured daringly across the hills were almost entirely obliterated; often, it must be said, to the benefit of the valleys and hills, whose appearance was much enhanced and which were no longer cut in half by a barrier impassable to horses and cattle.

The picturesque steam trains that chugged along those lines were vanishing too. As *Thomas the Tank Engine* and *Murder on the Orient Express*

attest, the British have always had a soft spot for steam engines — whether those noble monsters which thundered up the main line or the more domesticated creatures that pottered from rural halt to rural halt. Their supremacy had been absolute for more than a century, now they were displaced and much romance vanished with them (plate 528). The last commercial steam train ran in 1968. All that remain today are a few lines of particular scenic beauty which have been rescued by enthusiastic antiquarians and run for the delectation of similar zealots, the passing tourist or even the genuine passenger trying to get from A to B. Travelling by steam train has joined visits to Madame Tussaud's as part of the great nostalgic theme-park experience which Britain offers its visitors today (plates 529-531).

The railways and an — alas — disintegrated transport policy

What remains of the network has in some ways been improved. High speed trains now run at up to 125 miles an hour on most of the main lines. But British Rail — or the fragmented replacements which have now emerged as de-nationalisation takes effect — seems always to falter when on the point of taking a lead technologically. The tilting train tilted too far and was shunted off into obscurity; British rail tracks will not support the level of speed which is now a commonplace in France or Japan; even the effort of getting a train from Dover to London at something approaching the speed the same train achieves between Calais and Paris seems to be posing insuperable problems (though

The picturesque steam trains that had thundered along the main lines or chugged amiably from rural halt to rural halt, have now disappeared. The engine about to venture into the countryside outside Dolgellau in Dyfed (1960) ABOVE (528) *will grace the track no more.*

none which much money and an authoritarian government could not solve — whether it is worthwhile to spend hundreds of millions of pounds and blight the lives of thousands of residents along the way so as to cut twenty minutes off the train time which is taken to get from London to Paris, is another matter).

Successive parliamentary oppositions have proclaimed — and no doubt always will proclaim — that the country needs an integrated transport policy, and that when they are in office they propose to supply it. So far they have conspicuously failed to do so. Every year more freight transfers from rail to road, every year more putative passengers acquire a car, the result is congestion, pollution, the exhaustion of a finite supply of oil. Where the French spend £31 a head each year on maintaining and improving the railways, the Germans £20, the Swiss £50, the British figure is £5. Railtrack, the body now responsible, still operates on a grand scale. The rail network covers more than ten thousand miles, there are forty thousand bridges, tunnels and viaducts, 2,500 stations. But it is only a shadow of what it once was and it is hard to see that it can ever be restored.

The cost and social problems of rebuilding those deserted lines, of buying back and refurbishing those stations, would be far beyond any government even if the will to do so was present. It is probably true that the existing lines could be used more fruitfully, greater efficiency and lower costs could tempt back some passengers and freight, but though the railways may one day play an important part in a truly integrated transport system, it will still be peripheral compared with the starring role they once enjoyed.

All that survives of the mighty empire of the steam railway are a few lines that the enthusiasts have kept going to serve tourists and provide an enjoyable outing along scenic routes. The Snowdon Mountain Railway (1897) FAR LEFT (529); or the Ffestiniog Railway, originally opened for the carriage of slate in 1873 but made available for passengers two years later (1955) LEFT (530); were never fully part of the national railway network but still carried passengers on a regular basis. Even the narrow-gauge Ravenglass and Eskdale railway in Cumbria (1950) LEFT BELOW (531) was once more than the toy it now appears, having been built to carry iron ore and granite.

Travelling by Road

I F YOU HAD A GREAT WAY TO TRAVEL in the 1860s you would probably have done the larger part of it by rail. Unless both your starting point and your destination were very close to a station it would have been necessary to cover some distance on the road, but the railway grid was by then so well developed that unless you lived in an extremely remote area not more than a few miles would be involved. Once on the train you could travel at modest cost and at a speed which does not seem absurdly slow by the standards of today. For heavy freight the canal offered a reasonable alternative, though even more than in the case of the railway, you would be lucky if the journey started and ended at the spot you wanted to be. For points which the canal and the railway did not reach, for any journey by road, there were effectively only two possibilities: you walked, or you used a horse. Theoretically other animals could be used – the goat, for instance, could be called into service for light work in towns (plate 534), though it could do nothing that a man or strong boy could not achieve. But the horse ruled the road.

It was infinitely flexible. A stage coach, expertly driven and drawn by relays of horses bred and trained for the work, could complete the journey from Edinburgh to London in two and half days; today both the delay and the discomfort would seem intolerable, but speed and comfort are relative, in 1860 travellers felt that they were enjoying the best that modern technology could provide in luxurious and rapid transport (plates 532, 533). The train or barge could obviously manage heavier burdens than even the most powerful horse, but it was possible to carry the most astonishing amounts by road without apparent damage to the horse (plate 535). Keeping the roads open and in a relatively good condition was an expensive and laborious business, but no worse than the maintenance of railways or canals (plate 536). The horse-bus seemed a leisurely means of transport even then but it was probably not that much more dilatory than a modern London bus at rush hour; the bus that took H G Wells's Mr Kipps from New Romney to Folkestone was 'painted a British red, and inscribed on either side with the words "Tip-top" in gold amidst voluptuous scrolls. It is a slow and portly bus; even as a young bus it must have been slow and portly. Below it swings a sort of hold, hung by chains between the wheels, and in the summertime the top has garden seats. The front over those two dauntless unhurrying horses rises in tiers like a theatre …' Two equally dauntless horses pulled the horse-drawn tram (plates 537, 538). Their task was eased by the rails but the enterprise depended on their strength and resolution. It is unsurprising that for many years the standard by which a motor car's engine was evaluated was not by cubic centimetres but by horse-power.

The coach in Fore Street, Sidmouth could well have covered fifty miles or more that day (1904) ABOVE (532); the elegant carriage in Coney Street, York, in 1909 LEFT (533), might have already been left behind by the dashing motor car on the other side of the street but most people would still have felt it a more reliable and decorous form of transport.

Regent Road, Great Yarmouth, in 1896 ABOVE (534). *The goat was occasionally used to pull a light cart though it could do* nothing that a man, or even a strong boy, could not achieve and was usually both cantankerous and evil-smelling.

The oppressively laden wagon in the square of Kirriemuir, north of Dundee, in 1890 LEFT *(535), showed vividly that, though heavy loads could best be carried by rail or canal, a horse could still pull an extraordinary amount of miscellaneous goods.*

Clearing snow from the road at Cairnwell, Braemar, in the winter of 1879 BELOW *(536). Road maintenance by hand was a laborious business but the horse could make do with a far worse surface than the early motor car. The road now leads to the ski slopes.*

Horse-drawn trams were never a rapid means of transport but they were reliable and not uncomfortable. Here they are to be seen at work in Manchester, *outside the Royal Entrance to the Exhibition of 1889* TOP (537), *and a year later in a tranquil Oxford High Street* ABOVE (538).

BLOWS TO THE HEGEMONY OF THE HORSE Liverpool was the first British city to experiment with electric trams and, in so doing, strike the first blow at the hegemony of the horse. By 1891 all horse-drawn trams in Leeds had been replaced by this new device, which had been pioneered in the United States. At first London was more cautious and rejected them as inflexible, expensive, and a peril to other users of the road, but in the rest of the country they caught on; by the turn of the century they were carrying five million passengers a year (plates 539, 540). It was the superior manoeuvrability of the motor bus that

The electric-powered tram was established in the provincial towns before it caught on in London. In Chingford, in 1906 LEFT (539) it defiantly proclaimed the virtue of Everett's tea against the Whitbread's stout advertised by the nearby pub. They 'lumber and grind like a sick elephant' wrote J B Priestley, and there was something a little elephantine about their progress through the main street of Poole, Dorset, two years before BELOW (540).

finally overcame them; in 1931 a Royal Commission recommended that no new tramways be constructed and that the existing network should gradually be replaced.

The electric tram could operate only in towns and cities; outside those areas it was the bicycle, or in the early days, tricycle, which seemed to offer the most serious opposition to the horse. Some of the earliest machines seem comically cumbersome to the contemporary eye; the tricycles (plates 541, 542) were lumbering but at least secure — one could imagine the stateliest dowager afloat on one — while the pennyfarthing, with vast wheel in

front and tiny one behind, seemed acutely perilous as well. The bicycle, as it is known today, took some time to evolve. The real breakthrough came when John Boyd-Dunlop, a vet from Belfast, tried pneumatic tyres on his small son's tricycle and found the result immeasurably smoother in the driving. The chain-drawn bicycle with pneumatic tyres was developed in the 1880s. At first it was a toy for the rich; gilded youths attending a week-end house party at the end of the nineteenth century were as likely to arrive with a bicycle as

The bicycle was not only faster and more convenient than a tricycle, it was infinitely more adaptable. In Capel, Surrey, in 1906 LEFT (543), it towed behind it a chaise for a child (a seat belt might have been a desirable addition). Two years later in Stoke D'Abernon BELOW (544) it pushed a chair in front of it, like the bicycle rickshaw so often seen in Asia.

with golf clubs or tennis rackets. Soon, however, mass-production brought prices down, cycling clubs popularized the idea of exploring the countryside on this exciting new machine; it became a working-class tool, by which the factory labourer or the farmhand could get to and from his place of work quickly and cheaply.

It was the demands of the bicyclist, not of the motor-driver, that led to the first great improvements in road surfaces and sign-posting. For a decade at least they were the fastest machines on the road, whirling contemptuously past the primitive motor car which still had a man carrying a red flag walking deferentially in front of it. Orwell's George Bowling was given his first bicycle in 1908. It was 'a fixed-wheel — free-wheel bikes were very expensive then. When you went downhill you put your feet up on the front rests and let the pedals go whizzing round.' The bicycle was infinitely adaptable, it could be used to tow a pram or child's chaise or to push

a chair in front of it as in the bicycle rickshaw still so often seen in Asian countries (plates 543, 544). It throve throughout the 1920s and 1930s, became indispensable when petrol shortages drove the private car off the road in the Second World War, is now back in fashion

By 1904, when this photograph was taken in East Grinstead High Street BELOW (545), *the motor car was no longer a freakish novelty but was still not often seen — the speed limit had been raised to twenty miles an hour the previous year.*

again as the most environmentally correct, if often decidedly hazardous, method of getting oneself from A to B and back again.

THE COMING OF THE CAR

But its reign as king of the road was quickly over. At first, except to a few fanatics, the motor car was a joke in doubtful taste; it was not till the Red Flag Act was abolished and the speed limit raised to twelve miles per hour that people began to take it seriously. It was in 1895 that Arnold Bennett's Derry Machin bought one of the earliest motor cars to be seen in the Five Towns and on his first outing reached his destination without mishap: 'This was in the days when automobilists made their wills and took food supplies when setting forth. Thus Derry was pleased.' Eustace Forsyte got his first car before Machin but it shook him about horribly and broke one of his eye teeth. The Forsytes as a clan decided to wait a little, but they could see which way the wind was blowing and knew the wait would not be long. On 17 August 1896 Mrs Bridget Driscoll, a forty-

four year old Irishwoman, was knocked down by a private car and killed. The motor car had come of age. In 1900 young Jolyon Forsyte counted the new motor cars and cabs as he drove through central London and calculated there was one for every twenty horse-drawn vehicles. 'They were one in thirty about a year ago,' he thought, 'they've come to stay.'

Some time the same year, if he had been near Hyde Park Corner, he would have seen sixty-five cars of different models assembled to take part in a thousand mile test over various types of country. Not many passed with flying colours but every year the motor car grew in speed and reliability. Soames Forsyte, taking one of the 'new-fangled motor cabs' out to Putney, was amazed to find it bowling along at

fifteen miles an hour. It was exceeding the speed limit, which was not raised to twenty miles per hour until 1903, but by that time there were already 23,000 cars registered in Britain (plate 545). Rolls and Royce went into partnership in 1907; another three years and Herbert Austin was employing a thousand people at his works at Longbridge; three more again, and Henry Ford was setting up his first European factory in Trafford Park, Manchester. Mr Wilcox's chauffeur sped up the Great North Road towards Howard's End, his employer protesting that the Easter traffic made progress intolerably slow. Both the children and the chickens would be in peril, protested Margaret Schlegel. "'They're all right," said Mr Wilcox. "They'll learn – like the swallows and the telegraph poles." "Yes, but while they're learning …" "The motor's come to stay," he answered. "One must get about.'"

NOTHING COULD CHECK THE ADVANCE OF THE MOTOR CAR

For a time car and horse co-existed uneasily. In 1910 in central London one could see horse and motor buses, hansom cabs and taxis, carriages and private cars (plate 546). But every year showed a further decline in horse-drawn traffic. By 1913 only six percent of passenger vehicles in London were not motor-powered, the last horse-bus was withdrawn the following year. In the countryside the superior speed of the motor-bus meant that its victory came still more quickly (plates 547, 548). For the

Whitehall, 1910 ABOVE (546). *Motor cars and horse-drawn vehicles co-existed uneasily, but every year the pendulum swung further in favour of the former. Here it seems to have been about fifty-fifty.*

Motor buses at Hindhead, Surrey. The roofless 1906 model BELOW *(547) could only be boarded by means of a ladder that looked slightly precarious.*

By 1909 BELOW RIGHT *(548) the bus outside the Royal Huts Hotel was more sophisticated and its passengers were not so far off the ground.*

carriage of goods the process took longer, before the First World War the lorry had not become large or reliable enough to replace the horse, but the needs of the army in France gave a powerful stimulus to its development, and when in 1920 the Ministry of Munitions released twenty thousand surplus vehicles at bargain prices a fatal blow was struck at the horse's most important remaining function. The lorry and the tractor between them

reduced the horse to the decorative and sporting purposes that it serves today. The blacksmith's forge was translated into garage and petrol station (plates 549, 550).

Nothing could check the advance of the motor car. At the end of the First World War it was still a luxury reserved for the rich and the professional classes. In the average village the squire would probably have one, perhaps the doctor, but there it would end. Then, between the early 1920s and the early 1930s, the cost was halved. The first mass-market car, the Austin 7, was produced in 1921; Morris and Ford soon followed suit. Fifteen years later a new small car could be bought for a little over £100, still quite a lot in a period when £500 a year seemed a reasonable salary for all but the affluent yet within the reach of the lower middle classes. With second-hand cars now entering the market the number of drivers

1919 MERROW

In 1919 the forge at Merrow LEFT (549) was still what its name implied; by 1927 BELOW (550) it had succumbed to the irresistible tide and transferred its loyalties to the motor car.

1927 MERROW

swelled irresistibly. In 1914 there had been 140,000 vehicles of all kinds in Britain; by 1939 the figure was three million. Not everyone was pleased. Country people at first resented the noise and dust and smell, were outraged that the roads where their children had safely played and their cattle strayed had suddenly become death traps from which they felt themselves excluded. In some villages children were encouraged to pelt passing cars with stones or to strew nails in their path. But soon the country dwellers found the car first a convenience, then a necessity. By the outbreak of the Second World War it was a fact of life.

AT FIRST THERE WERE MORE CARS THAN THERE WERE FACILITIES

The proliferation of motor cars far outstripped the facilities available. By 1918 relatively few roads had been tarred, there were no car parks,

no lights, virtually no signs (plate 551). Any sort of control of the flow of traffic was a rarity. At a few crucial points, like Hyde Park Corner, policemen posted at every entrance would try valiantly to co-ordinate their efforts and achieve a regular progress. They did not always succeed; jams were horrendous. In country towns people parked as the mood took them (plates 552, 555). Usually there were so few other cars that little harm was done but on market days chaos could quickly be contrived. Gradually order began to rule: driving tests were imposed in 1935; traffic lights, roundabouts and pedestrian crossings were introduced. Leslie Hore-Belisha, the energetic Minister of Transport, insisted on a thirty miles per hour limit in built-up areas and gave his name to the yellow beacons at street crossings. A programme of road-building was undertaken; the Great West Road and the

Lynchford Road in Farnborough, Hampshire ABOVE (**551**). *In 1913 the injunction to drive slowly was rarely seen; there was no special speed limit for built-up areas and not much was done to enforce any sort of driving restriction at all.*

Kingston by-pass were opened in the mid-1920s and many more by-passes came into existence over the next fifteen years. Inevitably traffic grew more rapidly than the roads on which it was supposed to travel, but the chaotic free-for-all which had temporarily threatened was gradually averted.

Motor bicycles had become popular well before the First World War (plate 556) and by 1920 there were more of them than there were motor cars. Many young fathers – and not so young – who could not afford even the smallest car would load the wife and baby into a sidecar and set off for the seaside. It was cheap to buy, cheap to run and infinitely manoeuvrable but it was also dangerous and left room for little luggage (plate 554). The motor-cycle was never to lose its charm for the young who relished speed and wanted to show off to their friends but increasingly it lost its appeal for the family man. By the mid-1930s a second-hand Baby

1998 BANBURY

In Banbury market place in 1921 LEFT *(552) people parked as the mood took them and no one really minded; in 1998* ABOVE *(553) the photographer has caught the town at a quiet moment, but clearly the disorder of an earlier age would not be tolerated.*

In East Grinstead in 1923
RIGHT (555) *things were a*
little more orderly than in
Banbury two years before
but the mood was still the
same – almost as relaxed,
indeed, as shown twenty
years earlier in plate 545.

A motor-cycle with sidecar attached at Cobham, Surrey, in 1919 LEFT (554). For young fathers who could not afford a car this was a cheap and convenient means of taking the family for a spin in the country. The traffic here did not seem unduly concerned with keeping to its side of the road.

An early motor-cycle parked outside an antique shop in Farnham, Surrey, in 1913 RIGHT (556). Motor-cycles were already popular before the First World War, though an even more dangerous means of progress than they are today.

Austin or Morris Minor would cost little more than a motorcycle with a sidecar and had become the favoured solution for the middle and lower middle classes. For those who could not run to such a luxury there was always the charabanc. The long-distance coach became popular in the 1920s and 1930s; it was cheaper than the train, could get nearer the final destination and offered the bonus of a guaranteed seat. At first it was open to the elements and short on comfort (plate 557) but very quickly it became more sophisticated. 'There seems to be a motor coach going anywhere in this island,' wrote J B Priestley in 1934. 'They are voluptuous, sybaritic, of doubtful morality. This is how the ancient Persian monarchs would have travelled, had they known the trick of it.'

The roads along which they ventured were ribbon-developed to distraction and became ever more congested (plate 558). Planning controls scarcely existed and the opening of a

Charabancs outside the entrance to the pier at Eastbourne in 1925 ABOVE (557). *Soon they were to acquire protection against the elements and graduate into motor coaches.*

Heavy traffic on Reigate Hill in 1935 RIGHT (558). *Every year the number of vehicles was growing dramatically, congestion increased and accidents became more common.*

new arterial highway was an invitation to every predator to spatter its borders with residential suburbs, light industry or advertising hoardings.

Most representative of the age were the road-houses, built usually in mock-Tudor or bastard Georgian, and equipped with dance floors, restaurants and swimming pools. Such oases served not only the traveller but became destinations in themselves – an evening in the road-house was a favoured delight of every young blood who could afford it and lay his hands on some sort of vehicle.

THE POST-WAR WORLD CONTEMPLATES THE IMPOSSIBLE

The traditional methods of traffic control could no longer cope and police manpower was anyway not available to enforce it (plate 559). Garages in the centre of towns became a source

of intolerable encumbrance to the through traffic and were driven out to make new homes in vast caravanserais situated on the outskirts (plates 560, 561).

The strikingly vicious circle of increasing demand for cars, leading to the construction of more and better roads, leading to a yet greater demand for cars, seemed to be ever more unbreakable as the twentieth century neared its end. There were just over two million cars on the road in 1938, by the end of 1996 the total was more than ten times as great. Motor traffic over all was still rising by an average of three percent a year.

Everybody knows that it cannot go on, that we will run out of oil, that the pollution is unacceptable, that too much of Britain's limited land-space is being lost to roads and car parks, that many towns and villages are

In 1957 in Redcar ABOVE (**559**), *the traditional method of controlling traffic by a policeman on a platform was still employed, but already it was becoming obvious that such methods were inadequate and that, anyway, the necessary manpower was simply not available.*

The garage and filling-station, often the former blacksmith's forge, was at first usually to be found in the centre of the town or village — as at Histon, Cambridgeshire, in 1965 LEFT (560). Here it co-habited with a shop selling toys and hardware, more often it shared premises with the post office. But pressure of traffic gradually forced them out to caravanserais on the edge of town. By 1998 LEFT BELOW (561) in Histon, litter baskets had replaced the petrol pumps.

being rendered almost uninhabitable by the weight of traffic. Nobody seems to know what to do about it. The car conveys the citizen to the coastal resort or beauty spot of his choice — good for the car. It then destroys the amenity that it has made accessible — woe to the car (plate 562). Everyone wants to see less vehicles on the road — provided it is understood that

their own essential travel should be allowed to continue. The first eight miles of motorway were opened around Preston in 1958. At the time it was to believed that the motorway system would clear the clogged arteries of the existing network and provide safe and rapid long distance travel. Today it is painfully obvious that great lengths of the motorways

are as badly clogged as the roads they were intended to relieve, while the old roads are often as full as ever.

Pricing the car out of the market has been the solution most often favoured by the government of the day. It does not and will not work. In 1973 an explosive rise in the price of oil precipitated galloping inflation but in the long or even medium term did nothing to reduce the mileage covered by the British motorist. If a five-fold increase in the price of petrol in a single year was not enough to deter the driver, why should the far smaller tax increases which governments cautiously impose year after year have any more success?

Most branch railway lines have been closed, country bus services have been severely reduced, the village shop has been killed by competition from the supermarket in the nearest town, the rural motorist has nothing to resort to but his car. In the cities the authorities try to encourage greater use of the bicycle; there should be 6,500 miles of designated bicycle track in place by the year 2005. Even if there are, however,

this will be no more than a palliative. The fundamental problem will remain unabated.

It is still possible to travel with pleasure on Britain's roads. There are many thousand miles of country lane down which one can bumble in peaceful enjoyment of the scenery. If one picks one's time with care it is even possible to drive hundreds of miles along a motorway with little stress or pressure from other traffic. But no one could view the approaches to any of Britain's great cities at rush hour or visit a popular coastal resort or the Lake District in the holiday period, without realizing that travel by road can be the direst of experiences. It is to the credit of the public and the police that this has not been translated into the sort of murderous mayhem encountered on the roads of certain other countries. It is a remarkable and cheering statistic that in 1996 3,598 people died on Britain's roads. This was the lowest figure since 1926. And yet, over the same period the number of licensed drivers rose by no less than 35 million. Something, at least, must be going right.

Black Rock Sands, Morfa Bychan, Gwynedd, already in 1960 ABOVE (562) *demonstrated what was to become ever more apparent over the next decades — that a beauty spot could rapidly be destroyed by the attentions of those who sought only to admire and enjoy it.*

Travelling by Water

1896 BOWNESS

FOR THOSE WHO WANTED TO TRAVEL or to transport goods around the British Isles before the coming of the railways, water was likely to be an essential element; indeed the importance of the waterways and coastal waters survived the railways by many years and is by no means wholly lost today. At the most basic level, bridges were expensive to build, sometimes they fell down, to maintain them was a constant pre-occupation. A ferry was cheap to run; with the addition of a primitive steam engine it could handle substantial loads. Some were powerful enough to carry a coach and four with all its passengers and still have room for a few more people, others were only equipped to carry two or three at a time (plates 563-565, 567), all played an important part in Britain's transport system.

The coastal sailing and steam boats were no less essential. Before the railways, if coal from Newcastle was to arrive in London it had to travel by water; even in the later nineteenth century the boat might well have been more economical than the train. The steamboats at Fleetwood, Rothesay and Aberdour were carrying passengers, possibly on a joyride, more probably on a journey to a nearby seaport or an off-shore island, but they were no less essential to the nation's economy (plates 566, 568-570). If John Masefield's 'Dirty British coaster with a salt-caked smokestack' had not butted through the Channel in the mad March days, then its cargo of Tyne-coal, road-rail, pig-lead and the rest of it would never have reached its destination and Britain's factories would have ceased to work.

THE NETWORK OF CANALS MADE THE INDUSTRIAL REVOLUTION POSSIBLE

Ferries and coasters served a vital purpose, rivers linked many of the largest towns and could carry their produce to the seas, but without a network of canals the Industrial Revolution could never fully have taken off. The Duke of Bridgewater had set the pattern in the mid-eighteenth century, within twenty years canals were being gouged through every part of Britain's industrial heartland. New towns grew to service them – Stourport, as the name implies, would have been no more than a hamlet if it had not been fortunately placed at a junction of canal and river. In the process some of Britain's noblest architectural extravaganzas were created: the beauty was incidental, the canals did what they had to do and their appearance was dictated by this need; the extravagance was no more gratuitous but the work of an engineer soberly calculating how best to achieve the improbable if not impossible without worrying too much about the cost.

1998 BOWNESS

The Bowness steam ferry boat carrying passengers across Lake Windermere in 1896 ABOVE (563). But for the ferry the coach and four would have had to make a fifteen-mile journey over rough roads to reach the other side. The ferry still runs today LEFT (564). It could manage four coaches and have space left over, but the modern chain ferry lacks the charm of its predecessor.

A sailing ferry at Fleetwood at the mouth of the Wyre ABOVE (565). *In 1901 travellers would have had to travel even further than their contemporaries on Lake Windermere if they wanted to cross the river.*

Rothesay, the principal town on the Isle of Bute, was inaccessible except by boat in 1897 RIGHT (566). *Probably most of the people crowding aboard the steamers in this photograph were holiday-makers from the mainland, but it was the only link for those who had business to do as well.*

On an even humbler scale
the ferry at Shrewsbury in
1911 ABOVE (567) *saved
the building of an expensive
and unnecessary bridge or
much inconvenience to the
riverine inhabitants.*

*The Barrow Boat at
Fleetwood in 1908* ABOVE
(568). *Paddle steamers of
this kind would carry
passengers across Morecambe
Bay to Barrow in Furness.*

1897 ABERDOUR

1900 ABERDOUR

A steamer at the stone pier in Aberdour. In the photograph of 1897 RIGHT ABOVE (569) it seems to have been taking passengers aboard and in 1900 RIGHT (570) letting them off — in both cases the boat had probably been crossing the Firth of Forth.

The Canal Basin in Sheffield in 1870 RIGHT *(571) and the Latchford Locks and Manchester Ship Canal in 1894* BELOW *(572). These were the main roads of British industry, having little in common with the tranquil backwaters which the word 'canal' usually evokes today.*

To look at photographs of the Canal Basin at Sheffield or the Manchester Ship Canal (plates 571, 572) is to enter a different world to the tranquil back-waters and amiably gliding long-boats which is the image that the word canal conjures up today. These were motorways compared with country lanes; the M25 indeed, clamorous, congested, sometimes dangerous, resolutely unseductive. But even when they stumbled accidentally into the picturesque, the nineteenth-century canal was hard at work: the sailing boats on the canals at Bude or Exeter may look as if they had no destiny in life beyond a little gentle fishing, but they were part of the chain that kept the commerce of the nation moving (plates 573, 574, 576, 577).

The barges were the work-horses of the canals — literally at first in that the traditional means of propulsion was a horse on the tow-path. A horse could without difficulty pull a load many times heavier than anything it could

*The canal at Bude in 1890
LEFT (573) and 1998
BELOW (574). The boats in
the earlier photograph might
seem unbusinesslike but they
were used for transporting
sand to other parts of
Somerset. The canal was
deserted when the later
photograph was taken, but it
still provides a similar
service today.*

manage on land (plate 578); they needed
feeding and attention but they broke down less
frequently than the engines that replaced them
and they were friends as well. They survived
long after their economic justification had
strictly passed. Mr Toad was living in 1908,
well into in the age of the motor car, let alone
the railway, when, 'Round the bend in the canal
came plodding a solitary horse, stooping
forward as if in anxious thought. From rope
traces attached to his collar stretched a long
line, taut, but dipping with his stride, the
further part of it dripping pearly drops.'

THE RAILWAYS STEAL THE BREAD FROM
THE BARGEE'S MOUTH

Pickford's, a firm whose name was to become
almost a synonym for the pantechnicon, was
already carrying freight by canal in the 1770s.
By 1820 it owned a fleet of eighty boats, yet
was by no means the largest company doing

work of the kind. Many industries kept their own fleets of barges and would have viewed with some dismay any suggestion that they should put the transportation of their raw materials or manufactured products into the hands of an independent carrier. But they soon had cause to review their arrangements. Pickford's armada of barges peaked in the 1820s and, though the firm continued to expand, the canals did not have the benefit of its custom. The railways were so much quicker, and so much more flexible, in that rails could run into the heart of a factory and link it with the main line a mile or more away. Increasingly their competition grew; Pickford's gave up use of the canal altogether in 1848. But the defeat

was never total and the battle was often hard-fought. A business which needed to transport bulky goods and was installed on the side of a canal could still find barge traffic extremely useful at a time when even the all-conquering railway was receding in face of the heavy lorries (plates 579, 580). Malt was being sent from Ware to London by way of the River Lea, and cargoes of timber, coal and fertilisers brought back, until well after the Second World War.

The railways did not merely compete with the canals, they actively interfered to sabotage their facilities. In the mid-nineteenth century the railways invested in canals which at that time they presumably considered to be a useful complement to their work. They were always a

Two sprit-sail barges unloaded opposite Messenger's Boat House at Surbiton in 1896 BELOW *(575). The foremost of the two barges was registered in Glasgow and its cargo seem. to have been pig-iron.*

1896 EXETER

1998 EXETER

The canal leading into the port of Exeter in 1896 TOP (576). This was the first ship canal in England; it was opened in 1564 and put Exeter on the map as a serious port. In 1998 ABOVE (577) it was still very much open for business though the scene was considerably less busy than a century before.

side-show, however; essential repairs were not undertaken or were done half-heartedly, revenue dwindled, the case for keeping them open grew ever more tenuous. But one could not shut down one canal without having a disastrous effect on its neighbours. Canals that still belonged to owners who wished to tend them properly found their access to major waterways cut off, their usefulness diminished or totally destroyed. By 1918 there were still many canals doing valuable trade, but by the standards of what it had been in its heyday, Britain's canal system was in a mess.

For lovers of the picturesque or the bird watcher and botanist this was no bad thing. The sluggish trickle of a disused canal, beset

The canal at Carnforth, Lancashire, in 1918 BELOW (578). A horse working on the tow path of a canal could manage a load many times heavier than anything it could pull behind it on dry land.

Many canals were still in active commercial use long after the Second World War. The Grand Union Canal at Uxbridge in 1955 BELOW (579) showed that a business handling bulky goods — in this case timber — could find the barge of value even in the age of the lorry.

The same was true all over the British Isles: the canal at King's Lynn BOTTOM (580) was flourishing five years later.

with reeds and lilies, with crumbling banks and overhanging bushes, provided a rich habitat for a variety of flora and fauna which had found it hard to secure a foothold when the waterways were in trim good order (plates 581-583). It was in fact possible to make some sort of progress along the apparently most cluttered passages, but no one could have supposed that such canals in the mid-twentieth century were fit for anything except the most amateurish pottering around in boats. Or, of course, for fishing: canals had always offered a promising venue for the fisherman, or the fisherboy for that matter; now it seemed that one of their principle purposes was to offer him entertainment (plates 584, 585).

PLEASURE AT THE HELM

But this was not the only entertainment that they could offer. Water and pleasure had been associated since time immemorial, wherever there was a river and a primitive society some sort of festival would be held at some time of year. To embark on a boat – any sort of boat –

The canal at Kinver, Staffordshire in 1955 BELOW *(581), and the Basingstoke Canal at Odiham c. 1960* RIGHT *(582). Improbable though it might seem it was usually possible to make sluggish progress down these encumbered waterways. In 1998 the Basingstoke Canal* OPPOSITE BELOW *(583) had been cleared and was open for heavy duty.*

C. 1960 ODIHAM

1998 ODIHAM

It might seem to the modern eye that these tranquil backwaters could serve little purpose except to offer a fishing ground for small boys, but in fact the canal near Lancaster was in working order in 1918 BELOW *(584), while the canal at Market Harborough in 1922* RIGHT *(585) still offered access, if somewhat precarious access, to the Grand Junction Canal a few miles away.*

and take off on an expedition was among the most popular diversions which the Victorian employer could offer his workers as an annual outing or a Victorian paterfamilias could treat his family to on their summer holiday (plates 586, 587). Certain canals, also, had always been associated with pleasure boating. The Regent's Canal in London was opened to small pleasure boats as early as 1883. The mere mention of Boulter's Lock at Maidenhead conjures up images of summer afternoons, parasols, strawberries and cream, a hand dangling in the water – though at the risk of having it crushed against the next boat in the turmoil of an August bank holiday week-end (plates 588-591). The boat edging peacefully along the canal at Llangollen (plate 595) can never have done anything so utilitarian as carry coals from Newcastle or malt from Ware.

But the rehabilitation of the canals for pleasure boating was not seriously undertaken before the 1960s. By then much had already been lost for ever; if the rescue operation had

been delayed much longer there would have been little left to rehabilitate. When the Docks and Inland Waterways Executive was set up in 1948 the importance of the canals for the purpose of recreation was for the first time officially recognized but precious little was done about it. A few of the largest waterways were designated as being relevant to the needs of contemporary commerce, the rest were more or less left to moulder. The Kennet and Avon Canal, to take one conspicuous example, had gone to rack and ruin by the 1950s (plates 592, 593); the British Transport Commission tried to close it in 1958; a group of enthusiasts

The pleasure steamer Teal at Bowness in 1896 RIGHT *(586) and the Sir Walter Scott steaming up Lake Katrine in central Scotland three years later* BELOW *(587). Excursion boats like these were immensely popular in the later nineteenth century and were much favoured for both factory outings and for family expeditions.*

protested passionately, funds were raised and
the work of salvage undertaken; now one can
go by water from Bristol to Reading. Nearby,
within a mile or so of central Bath, a notice
reads proudly: 'The Somerset Coal Canal,
opened 1801, closed 1904, restored 1985.'

THE LONG-BOATS MADE THE RENAISSANCE
OF THE CANALS A POSSIBILITY

'Towards the bridge from the north,' wrote
Arnold Bennett in *Clayhanger*, 'came a long
narrow canal-boat roofed with tarpaulin, and

towards the bridge from the south came a
similar boat, sluggishly creeping.' Those long
narrow boats were to make the renaissance of
the canals a possibility. In the nineteenth
century they had become the most convenient
means of transport – able to slip along the
narrowest canal yet confront the perils of the
greatest rivers – while at the same time
providing homes for the boatmen and their
families. A curious, nomadic, riverine society
developed, policed with only limited success by
a canal inspectorate who tried to ensure that

1893 MAIDENHEAD

minimal standards of hygiene were observed and that the children were given some basic education. Most of the long-boats belonged to canal companies which encouraged their employees to paint their boats in uniform patterns; the boatmen made some concessions to standardisation but had their own ideas; a rich variety of decoration in which roses and castles were the predominant motifs became a feature of canal life.

A few of those working long-boats survive today, refurbished, repainted, fitted out with refrigerators and television sets and all the other appurtenances of good living required by the contemporary holiday-maker. Many more have been built subsequently, specifically for the pleasure-seeker. Basically the design is the same, however. There are many other craft to be found on the canals and rivers today but none has surpassed the long-boat in its economy and practicality. By the 1950s they were becoming popular; as more canals opened and the idea of a family holiday on the water became common currency, their numbers have increased. The lavish gin-palaces of the opulent may make more of a splash, both literally and

1913 MAIDENHEAD

metaphorically; the long-boat is the vehicle for those happy warriors who really know and love their canals (plate 594).

When the British Waterways Board was set up in 1963 waterways were divided into three categories: 'commercial', which meant that they could still be used for the transport of goods or raw materials; 'cruise-ways', which were maintained only for pleasure traffic but for which the Board accepted responsibility; and the rest, which private enterprise was welcome to keep in order if it wished to, but at its own expense. Of the two thousand miles of waterway under the British Waterways Board's aegis, only 385 have passed the test as being properly 'commercial'.

The rest are for pleasure, for the quarter of a million or so holiday-makers who each year hire a boat of some description and take to the canals and rivers. Add in a million or so anglers and an unquantifiable number who merely take pleasure in living or walking on the banks and there can be little doubt that, though today British Waterways have ceased to make a serious contribution to national trade, they have instead become part of the ever-growing and all pervasive leisure industry.

1925 MAIDENHEAD

1998 MAIDENHEAD

The Kennet and Avon
Canal and Dunn Mill near
Hungerford in 1955 RIGHT
(592). At that time the
canal was in something close
to total dereliction and
within a few years the
British Transport
Commission was to try
formally to close it. Only a
group of passionate
enthusiasts rescued it for the
pleasure of future
generations; their success can
be seen in the photograph of
the same spot in 1998
BELOW (593).

1955 HUNGERFORD

1998 HUNGERFORD

A long-boat on the canal near Great Haywood, Staffordshire, in 1955 LEFT (594). Both the boat and the boatman's dress would today probably be more garish, but this early holiday-maker was the progenitor of many thousands of others.

A boat with attendant horse peacefully slid along the canal at Llangollen in Clwyd in 1913 RIGHT (595). Such boats were built for passengers and had nothing to do with the serious business of the working canal.

The Francis Frith Collection Plate Numbers

All the period photographs in this book are from The Francis Frith Collection and may be ordered as framed or mounted prints at half our normal mail-order prices. Simply contact The Francis Frith Collection at the address below, quoting the Frith Reference Numbers of the plates in which you are interested. The cost and method of ordering will be confirmed.

The Francis Frith Collection, Ref BTN, Frith's Barn, Teffont, Salisbury, Wilts SP3 5QP. Tel: +44 (0) 1722 716 376; Fax: +44 (0) 1722 716 881; E-mail: thenandnow@francisfrith.com

Half title page: Plate 162/Frith Ref. No.: 62868
Title page: Plate 408/Frith Ref. No.: 20461
Contents pages:
Page 4, above: Plate 474/Frith Ref. No.: L130110
Page 4, below left: Plate 97/Frith Ref. No.: 53847
Page 4, below right: Plate 445/Frith Ref. No.: 39852
Page 5, above: Plate 108/Frith Ref. No.: 82112
Page 5, below: Plate 120/Frith Ref. No.: 61633A

Plate Reference	Frith Reference	Plate Reference	Frith Reference	Plate Reference	Frith Reference	Plate Reference	Frith Reference	Plate Reference	Frith Reference	Plate Reference	Frith Reference
1	Francis Egypt	42	39050	91	21428	138	W44094	187	33721	234	55623
		43	22159	93	R42029	139	L53004	189	61180	235	61650
2	Francis camp	44	N16018	94	32357	140	82733	190	85605	236	87551
		45	N16020	96	59762	141	67330	192	39400	237	P317019
3	647E	47	37359	97	53847	142	74561	193	71518	238	P317042
4	5010	48	22808	98	57007	143	29160	194	A14382	239	M109084
5	6984	49	L60002	99	63997	144	R334004	195	45165	240	M109104
6	Francis family	50	B303002	101	45932	145	R334178	196	28076	241	L1305214
		52	P188085	102	40511	146	8755	197	62865	242	C151089
7	Francis UK	53	37243	103	42442	147	H21039	198	S134150	245	48127
		54	W107026	104	56261	148	31812	199	29151	246	56407
8	68605	56	39103	105	63994	149	79989	200	W76196	247	58145
9	L130013	58	39121	106	57011	150	L13119	201	20067	248	56532
10	L130037	59	51938	107	82040	152	B82039	202	68533	249	56186
11	L130026	60	33271	108	82112	154	64983	203	53015	250	76299
12	L130108	61	45756	109	31388	155	76533	205	52613	251	46002A
13	L130107	62	S137035	110	60104	157	25326	207	49072	252	66206
14	L130109	64	32280	111	86279	158	44793	208	60647	253	24178
15	L130079	65	R32071	112	L123032	159	60393	210	49993	254	54530X
16	L130050	66	63338	114	45779	160	76042	211	115003	255	63226
17	L1305138	67	73791	115	79060	161	D50145	212	80163	256	L130055A
18	L130120	68	60795	116	G46073	162	62868	213	38545	257	27649
19	L130277	69	75755	117	64292	163	C208002	214	31800	258	28163
21	L130330	70	85040	118	6982	164	L130047	215	23214	259	69579
22	L130169	72	33257	120	61633A	165	L130118	216	L75071	260	36250X
23	L130151	73	G43032	121	23356	168	L130285	217	65731	261	50080
24	L130221	74	53747	122	83188	170	L130055	218	77778	262	54133A
25	44033	75	46190	123	A1735008	171	S108002A	219	76401	263	18716
26	62085	76	36791	124	44117	172	22886	220	22871	264	C14701
27	41570	77	48560	125	28103	173	22881	221	38839	265	72715X
28	L130064	78	49887	126	54907	174	80825	222	53857	266	68114
29	L1305226	79	30397	127	43199	175	43514	223	44482	267	73955
30	L130056	80	39816	128	34531	176	59580A	225	P43148	269	87888
31	L130139	81	63551	129	115002	177	61542	226	B100001X	270	18659
32	20001	82	64395	130	A001007	178	B437007	227	39088	271	81266
34	36658	83	43327	131	L123013	179	63147X	228	36990	272	78781
35	B100001	84	50869	132	61686	180	63123	229	52659	273	53543
36	39759	85	73381	133	L406043	181	78635	230	60689	274	H89033X
38	A90009	86	G65381	134	E185009	183	L310009	231	H412005	275	67383
40	34765	88	81374	135	L294009	184	L130186	232	L509010	276	76839
41	39136	89	88927	137	20438	185	L1305194	233	61432	277	69128

Plate Reference	Frith Reference	Plate Reference	Frith Reference	Plate Reference	Frith Reference	Plate Reference	Frith Reference	Plate Reference	Frith Reference	Plate Reference	Frith Reference
278	56524	335	39137	387	24706	436	31055	494	72298	546	L130014
279	B6100	336	56879	388	49116	437	L102039	496	77665	547	55506
281	82900	337	C376016	389	C13034	438	C337001	498	36153	548	61434
282	64923	338	27557	391	T123008	440	78118A	499	72171	549	65231
283	R35069	340	36170	393	E71027	442	64343	500	B445034	550	79918
285	06302	341	23472	394	P273003	443	67465	501	W251011	551	65201
286	S79068	342	S249001	395	S255008	444	C450025	502	P72188	552	70572
287	51153	343	22474	396	L432088	445	39852	503	W561053	554	68859
288	D45205	344	33273	397	P275010	446	65068	504	67588	555	73352
289	27423A	345	55749	398	23133	447	49059	505	39141	556	65929
290	41708	346	F63002	399	63207	448	87750	506	23200	557	77946
291	L130029	347	61074A	400	49208	449	41899	507	45434	558	R20303
293	L130210	348	43203	401	63017	450	32371	508	47430	559	K16031
294	L130095	350	A93001	403	L260050	451	56400	509	C366144	560	H442003
295	82248	351	72651	404	S6050	452	23919	510	C95301	562	M96141
297	64884	352	65658	405	41149	453	64729	511	L130067	563	38800
298	74918	354	56293	406	C207020	454	32967	513	46175	565	47069
299	B94032	355	G44009	407	68463	456	30450	514	51362	566	39836
301	27091	356	23552	408	20461	457	46923	516	54682	567	63218
303	71017	357	R31004	409	20484	458	64881	517	61850	568	59940
304	M109036	358	A210016	410	58645	459	81440	518	53238	569	39147
305	47503	360	30538	411	C327217	461	45067	519	44026	570	45912
306	51700	361	46186	412	65252	463	82555	520	S254607	571	S108001
307	75164	362	56326	413	65249	464	W132016	52	O105004	572	33697
308	75754	363	58749	414	52290	465	39201	522	C579027	573	23782
309	40986	364	43385	415	48276	466	50891	523	59704	575	38336
310	78064	365	31106	416	E37307	467	66907	525	59722	576	38034
311	75708	366	22850	417	H143301	468	L130126	526	71064	578	68306
312	34497	367	52641	418	45957	470	C169076	528	D39251	579	U52006
313	G188029	368	44554	419	27200	472	59208	529	40059	580	L122026
314	L202015	369	47270	420	53704	473	L130111	530	P31053	581	K37055
316	Z100001	370	65107	421	38333	474	L130110	531	E194071	582	O8066
317	84558	371	66815	422	66906	475	40117	532	52071	584	68332
318	S210047	372	75615	423	S134045	476	43376	533	61723	585	72272
320	52709	373	B280050	424	62867	477	63543	534	37959	586	38795
321	71401	374	A310001	425	50921	479	36154	535	K50002	587	44590
322	A001008	376	B233051	426	B152028	480	57513A	536	B266003	588	31753
323	33595A	377	55040	427	78622	481	G23039	537	21901	589	65542
324	59424	378	C13045	428	44788	483	45043A	538	45181	590	77624
325	C376034	379	70772	429	M113003	485	34138	539	55341	592	H134018
326	C567031	380	47416	430	60251	486	58649	540	52811	594	G303010
327	24806	381	62213	431	69739	487	59808	541	18131	595	65830
329	24792	382	50812	432	L130021	488	63228	542	55595		
331	67019	383	39785	433	L130059	489	83877	543	53526		
332	75109	384	81574	434	S21601	491	61645X	544	51789		
334	28091	386	38710	435	31059	493	66820	545	52900		

Photographs by John Cleare

Following are the plate numbers of the photographs that are copyright © John Cleare:

20, 32, 37, 39, 46, 51, 55, 57, 63, 71, 87, 90, 92, 95, 100, 113, 119, 136, 151, 153, 156, 166, 167, 169, 182, 186, 188, 191, 204, 206, 209, 224, 243, 244, 268, 280, 284, 292, 296, 300, 302, 315, 319, 328, 330, 333, 339, 349, 353, 359, 375, 385, 390, 392, 402, 439, 441, 455, 460, 462, 469, 471, 478, 482, 484, 490, 492, 495, 497, 512, 515, 524, 527, 553, 561, 564, 574, 577, 583, 591, 593.

Table of Comparative Values

The pound sterling was decimalised in 1971; previously it had been divided into 20 shillings (20s) and 240 pence (240d). A shilling, which comprised 12 pence, was written 1/-; one and a half shillings would have appeared as 1/6d. The main units in the old currency, with their equivalents in new pence, were:

I farthing (1/4d) - just over 0.1 of a new penny.
I halfpenny (1/2d) - just over 0.2 of a new penny.
I penny (1d) - just over 0.4 of a new penny.
Sixpence (6d) - 2 1/2 new pence.
I shilling (1/-) - 5 new pence.
Half a crown (2/6d) - 12 1/2 new pence.

Comparisons between prices at different periods conceal a large number of factors which are in fact incomparable and should therefore be taken with a pinch or, better still, a peck of salt, but the formula which follows is not entirely misleading. If we take the pound sterling as purchasing £1's worth of goods or services in 1860, then, with minor fluctuations, it remained pretty constant in value until 1914. Inflation during the First World War was such that, by 1919, one would have had to multiply by two to attain the same results. Between the wars prices fell back, so that, by 1939, the factor had fallen to 1.5. Inflation then resumed, but only moderately, so that it was 1948 before the pound had reached its level of 1919. By 1960 it would have taken £3 to buy what £1 would have procured in 1860, and by 1970 £5. Oil price linked inflation then exploded; by 1980 the factor was 17 and by 1990 32. In 1999 the 1860 pound is worth £42.

I am indebted to my friend Sir Peter Petrie, Adviser to the Governors of the Bank of England, for taking expert opinion and assuring me that this over-simplified summary more or less makes sense.

Notes for Further Reading

THE WRITER OF A BOOK OF THIS KIND — or, at any rate, *this* writer of a book of this kind — is dependent on the labours of those who know far more than he does about the various subjects on which he touches. To try to list every writer who has in some way contributed would be both pretentious on my part and intolerably cumbersome; all I propose to do is to mention some of the books which I have found exceptionally useful. I include a handful of general memoirs from which I find that I have quoted with particular frequency. I am disconcerted by the number of books which contain the word 'England' or 'English' in their titles. I have done my best not to be unduly anglo-centric and apologize in advance for any instance in which Scottish or Welsh readers may feel that they have not had justice done to them.

Ashley, Maurice. *The People of England*. London, 1982.
Best, Robin and Coppock, J P. *The Changing Use of Land in Britain*. London, 1962.
Bracey, H E. *English Rural Life*. London, 1959.
Bonham-Carter, Victor. *The Survival of the English Countryside*. London, 1971.
Brooke, Iris. *A History of English Costume*. London, 1937.
Brown, Jonathan. *The English Market Town*. London, 1986.
Brown, Jonathan and Ward, Sadie. *Village Life in England 1860-1940*. London, 1985.
Brown, Jonathan and Ward, Sadie. *The Village Shop*. Salisbury, 1990.
Bryson, Bill. *Notes From a Small Island*. London, 1995.
Burton, Anthony. *The Great Days of the Canals*. London, 1989.
Cecil, Robert. *Life in Edwardian England*.

London, 1969.

Chadwick, Owen. *The Victorian Church. Part I,* London, 1966. *Part II,* London, 1970.

Church, Richard, *Over the Bridge.* London, 1955.

Church, Richard, *The Golden Sovereign.* London, 1957.

Clunn, Harold. *London Rebuilt. 1827-1927.* London, 1927.

Daunton, M J. *Royal Mail. The Post Office Since 1840.* London, 1985.

Davis, Dorothy. *A History of Shopping.* London, 1966.

Driver, Christopher. *The British at Table.* London, 1983.

Drummond, J C. *The Englishman's Food.* London, 1957.

Ernle, R E P. *English Farming.* Fourth Edition, London, 1927.

Evans, Keith. *The Development and Structure of the English Educational System.* London, 1975.

Fraser, W Hamish. *The Coming of the Mass Market. 1850-1914.* London, 1981.

Furth, Charles. *Life Since 1900.* London, 1927.

Girouard, Mark. *The English Town.* London, 1990.

Goldsmith, Edward (ed). *Can Britain Survive?* London, 1971.

Hall, Peter. *London 2001.* London, 1989.

Hardy, Dennis and Ward, Colin. *Arcadia For All.* London, 1984.

Harvey, Nigel. *A History of Farm Building in England and Wales.* London, 1984.

Hastings, Adrian. *A History of English Christianity 1920-1985.* London, 1986.

H H P and N L C (ed). *The Face of the Land. The Year Book of the Design and Industries Association.* London, 1930.

Humphries, Steve and Taylor, John. *The Making of Modern London.* London, 1986.

Jenkins, Simon. *A City at Risk.* London, 1971.

Johnson, Paul (ed). *Twentieth Century Britain. Economic, Social and Cultural Change.* London, 1974.

Johnstone, James. *British Fisheries.* London, 1905.

Lawson, John and Silver, Harold. *A Social History of Education in England.* London, 1973.

Mansfield, Alan and Cummington, Phillis. *Handbook of English Costume in the Twentieth Century.* London, 1975.

Nevett, T R. *Advertising in Britain.* London, 1982.

Office for National Statistics. *Britain 1998. An Official Handbook.* London, 1995.

Oliver, Basil. *The Renaissance of the English Public House.* London, 1947.

Phillips, David and Williams, Alan. *Rural Britain. A Social Geography.* Oxford, 1984.

Plomer, William (ed). *Kilvert's Diary.1870-1871.* London, 1938. *1871-1874.* London, 1939. *1877-1879.* London, 1940.

Priestley, J B. *English Journey.* London, 1934.

Ryder, Judith and Silver, Harold. *Modern British Society.* London, 1970.

Samuel, Raphael (ed). *Village Life and Labour.* London, 1975.

Seaman, L C B. *Life in Britain Between the Wars.* London, 1970.

Short, Brian (ed). *The English Rural Community.* Cambridge, 1992.

Simmons, Jack. *The Railways of Britain.* London, 1986.

Smith, Anthony. *Beside the Seaside.* London, 1972.

Stamp, Gavin. *The Changing Metropolis.* London, 1984.

Stamp, Gavin. *The English House. 1860-1914.* London, 1986.

Stevenson, John. *British Society. 1914-1945.* London, 1984.

Thompson, Flora. *Lark Rise to Candleford.* London, 1939-1944.

Trench, Richard. *London Before the Blitz.* London, 1989.

Walvin, James. *Beside the Seaside.* London, 1978.

Williams, Gwylmor, and Brake, George. *Drink in Great Britain. 1900-1975.* London, 1980.

Wood, Eric S. *Historical Britain.* London, 1995.

Index